# HIGH WIRE ANGEL
## THE ANGEL WALLENDA STORY

PAUL W. HEIMEL

PICCADILLY BOOKS
COLORADO SPRINGS, COLORADO

Cover Design by Robin Axtell

Copyright © 1992 by Paul W. Heimel
All rights reserved. No part of this book may be reproduced in any form, except for brief reviews, without written permission from the publisher.

Piccadilly Books
P.O. Box 25203
Colorado Springs, CO 80936


Library of Congress Cataloging-in-Publication Data

Heimel, Paul.
    High wire Angel: the Angel Wallenda story/Paul W. Heimel.
        p.    cm.
    ISBN 0-941599-15-9
    1. Wallenda, Angel.  2. Aerialists--Biography.  3. Cancer-Patients--
Biography.  I. Wallenda, Angel.  II. Title.
GV550.2.W35H45  1992
791.3'4' 092--dc20                                    92-32467
[B]                                                   CIP

## ACKNOWLEDGMENTS

I am deeply indebted to many individuals for their support, advice, assistance and encouragement in the completion of this book. Special appreciation is extended to my loving wife, Lugene, who held my life together while I became immersed in this project. Others deserving of special mention for their contributions include John F. Domaleski, B. Mark Schmerling, Douglas H. Graves, Frank Pintye Jr., Francis X. Sculley, Joseph A Majot, and Thomas R. Shaffer. In addition, Angel and Steve Wallenda wish to express their thanks to the following: Bruce E. Colfin, Steven Owlett, Dave and Diane Muffley, Jim Hopkins, and Henry Hurt. As is often the case with a project such as this, there are dozens of other people who provided assistance in one way or another. The fact that their names are not mentioned here does not diminish their contributions.

Paul W. Heimel

To Karl Wallenda, who has no equal.

## FOOTPRINTS IN THE SAND

One night, a man dreamed he was walking along the beach with the Lord.

Across the sky flashed scenes from his life. For each scene he noticed two sets of footprints in the sand; one set belonged to him, the other to the Lord.

When the last scene flashed before him, he looked back at the footprints in the sand. He noticed that many times along the path of his life there was only one set of footprints. He also noticed this happened at the very lowest and saddest times of his life.

This really bothered him and he questioned the Lord about it. "Lord, you said that once I decided to follow you, you would walk with me all the way. But, I have noticed that during the most troublesome times in my life, there is only one set of footprints. I do not understand why in the times I needed you most, you would leave me."

The Lord replied, "My precious, precious child. I love you and would never leave you. During the times of trial and suffering, when you saw only one set of footprints, it was then that I carried you."

—Author unknown

# CONTENTS

| | | |
|---|---|---|
| 1 | Crossing Over | 9 |
| 2 | What's A Wallenda? | 12 |
| 3 | Come To Jamaica | 21 |
| 4 | 'He Doesn't Know You' | 28 |
| 5 | Worlds Apart | 34 |
| 6 | Meant To Be | 42 |
| 7 | Back Home Again | 46 |
| 8 | We're Different | 51 |
| 9 | A Bad Girl | 55 |
| 10 | Born To Be Wild | 62 |
| 11 | On My Own | 67 |
| 12 | Stabbed In The Back | 72 |
| 13 | You're My Angel | 81 |
| 14 | Something's Not Right | 90 |
| 15 | I Can't Do It | 95 |
| 16 | Sombody Do Something! | 100 |
| 17 | You've Got Cancer | 108 |
| 18 | Fighting Back | 114 |
| 19 | Back On The Wire | 122 |
| 20 | Surgery Revisited | 126 |
| 21 | Meant To Be | 133 |
| 22 | Push To The Limit | 139 |
| 23 | An Incredible Sunday | 145 |
| 24 | Help Wanted | 150 |
| 25 | A Place In Pennsylvania | 156 |
| 26 | A Fond Farewell | 162 |
| 27 | Change Of Plans | 170 |
| 28 | Coping | 176 |
| 29 | Angel Wallenda Speaks | 183 |
| | Appendix | 186 |

Chapter 1

# CROSSING OVER

The lights nearly blinded her. Squinting, she cautiously slid her left foot forward to test the slender cable that stretched far into the distance. Tonight, this was Angel Wallenda's lifeline—sixteen strands of twisted steel pulled taut between two anchoring towers.

Angel trembled uncontrollably as she peered out to zero-in on her destination, a small platform that was barely visible at the other end of the high wire. Weeks of intense practice leading up to this moment had left her with two large blisters. They throbbed every time the stump of her right leg jarred against the inside of the plastic prosthesis that now supported her just below the knee. A simple step, even a casual weight shift, would send a wave of pain gushing through her.

Yet Angel was determined to hide her suffering, part of a lifelong desire to convey a natural sense of security about whatever she was doing. This performance was too important to her for a minor inconvenience such as pain to stand in the way.

A hush came over the crowd, followed by the thumping of loudspeakers carrying the song, "Angel of the Morning." That was the cue to begin her walk. Angel's time had come.

The spotlight zoomed in closer as she paused to savor the moment. Never again after this night would she step out onto the narrow wire that, for so many decades, has separated so many members of the Wallenda family from their destiny. In keeping with family tradition, Angel refused to allow a life net to be assembled below her prior to the performance. If she lost her footing, only the hard wooden floor would brace her fall.

Angel had already come face-to-face with quite another life-threatening challenge: cancer. For several months the doctors had told her to abandon any notion of being a professional aerialist and to prepare for a life of limitations and pain. A third, and possibly a fourth, lung operation just three short weeks away would surely ground her forever.

Angel Wallenda ascends the sloping wire to the mounting platform. (Photo by Paul W. Heimel.)

# HIGH WIRE ANGEL

But Angel could not simply walk away from it all without a curtain call—her "Farewell Performance," as it was being officially billed. This was one final chance to send the message that was central to her career: that people have within themselves the ability to overcome many of the obstacles that are placed in their way. Angel saw herself as a living example of that belief.

No one with an artificial leg had ever walked on a high wire before. She had established that as her goal and had worked tirelessly to develop the necessary strength and ability. It was that important to her. She wanted people to look beyond the glitter of her sequined costume and the drama of the Wallenda tradition on the high wire. She wouldn't have to say a word to get her special message across.

The glaring lights made it difficult for Angel to see the crowd, but she could sense the warm presence of many caring people. It was a sellout—three thousand men, women, and children, jammed shoulder-to-shoulder into the performance hall and millions more watching through the eyes of television cameras.

"Steady now," said her husband, Steve Wallenda, who stood behind, awaiting his turn on the wire. "Just take one step at a time and, remember, it doesn't matter how fast you go."

"It does to me," Angel whispered over her shoulder. "I *have* to look good!"

Tightening her grip on the long, white balancing pole that she held waist-high, Angel took a deep breath and released the air in a steady stream as she brought her lips together. Small beads of perspiration began to form on her forehead. The dark blue silk costume stuck to her back. Each beat of her heart sent a stabbing pain through the blisters at the end of her leg. She felt as if the whole world was watching her struggle. There was no turning back now.

"I love you, Angel," Steve said softly as Angel cleared her throat, steadied the pole, and gracefully began her ascent. "You're looking great, honey, really great," he assured her.

Angel's mind flashed back to the first time she had seen Steve gliding so effortlessly across the high wire. She had become enamored by this mysterious performer and his special talent.

Only a few years had passed. It seemed like an eternity.

Chapter 2

# WHAT'S A WALLENDA?

"What's a Wallenda?"

These words from Elizabeth Eve Pintye—the bright-eyed teenager who was soon to become Angel Wallenda—raised some eyebrows among the crowd. Several dozen people had gathered near the fountain at the center of the Westchester Mall in Mohegan Lake, New York. They were frozen in their tracks, drawn away from their shopping by the circus-like atmosphere that filled the thoroughfare. All eyes were fixed upon a man who, at first glance, appeared to be walking on air.

A pair of large stereo speakers sent the rocking beat of "Eye of the Tiger" echoing back and forth between the walls. Lizzie wedged her way deeper into the mass of spectators to get a closer view. The man was supported by a narrow wire strung from the floor to a platform located well above the heads of the suburban New Yorkers who had gathered there. The wire stretched straight across to another platform about forty feet away. He carried a long, white pole, held waist-high, parallel to the ground, and extending out for several feet on both sides.

"What is that guy doing?" Lizzie asked nobody in particular as she squeezed closer.

"He's a Wallenda," somebody answered.

"A what?"

"A Wallenda!" was the impatient response.

"What's a Wallenda?"

Like many others of her generation, Lizzie had never heard of The Great Wallendas, The Flying Wallendas, or any other kind of Wallenda. She didn't even know it was a proper name.

There was nothing below this wire-walker except the linoleum; nobody standing on guard, ready to catch him, or at least help to break his fall if he lost his balance and plunged toward the floor.

"This is far out," Lizzie said as the aerialist progressed across the wire, twirled his body around on one foot to face the crowd, and started walking forward, the white pole swaying ever so slightly with each step. Suddenly, she recognized that the performer was Steve, the strange visitor who had spent the better part of that day as a customer at Dipper Dan's, the mall's ice cream and coffee shop Lizzie had recently been hired to manage.

"Wait a minute—I know that guy!" she told the woman next to her who, until then, had been politely tolerating her annoying display of ignorance. Now, she was a bit more interested.

"I just met him today and he's really neat," Lizzie continued.

"Oh yeah?" the woman said, looking at Lizzie and then back up at the high wire. "Well, he's one of the great ones. All of those Wallendas are just incredible. You know, they never use a net. I think they're crazy."

As Steve moved closer, Lizzie noticed that even though his eyes were focused straight ahead, a slight smile suggested he was very content to be doing what he was doing—and very confident.

Three times earlier that day he had come into her shop to have some coffee and a snack, and never once did he mention that he was a professional performer. On the first visit, he had found a quiet corner and plunked himself down in the booth, all by himself. While others were talking and laughing, he sat alone, seemingly deep in thought. Lizzie had broken his concentration when she approached to take his order. He gave her a pleasant smile and asked for coffee. She was instantly intrigued by a look in his eyes that suggested he was special.

Lizzie recognized something magnetic, even mystical, about the man. Although he was a stranger, she immediately felt at ease in his presence as she began to make small talk. Steve said he was just passing through the area with a couple of co-workers.

He returned to the shop later that afternoon and once again, just before closing time. Despite his outward friendliness, Lizzie never suspected that he was more interested in her than in anything Dipper Dan's had to offer. She couldn't help noticing his tendency to spend an extra second or two looking into her eyes each time they spoke. And now, here was this same mysterious visitor thrilling the crowd as he walked effortlessly across the high wire.

"Who wants to join me later on tonight for a walk across the wire?" Steve yelled down, his straight expression blossoming into a devilish grin as he cast his gaze around the crowd. "I'm serious. If anyone wants to come up on the wire, I'll take you across. Do what I tell you and you won't get hurt. Does anybody dare?"

A murmur swept through the crowd, but no one came forward—nobody, that is, except a young ice cream shop manager who was never one to turn down a chance for adventure.

"I'll do it!" Lizzie shouted.

Her comment hushed the crowd as all eyes turned toward her. Steve stopped on the wire and peered down. Lizzie's face brightened.

"Are you sure you're up to it?" he asked, looking directly at her.

"If you'll tell me what to do, I'll do it."

The crowd erupted in applause and Lizzie realized that she was now committed to follow through. That was okay with her. She saw the high wire act as an opportunity to show off for some of the other mall "regulars" she had befriended since she began working at Dipper Dan's.

Not too many other seventeen-year-olds were living on their own and managing a store besides. But Lizzie was a street-smart survivor. She had packed a lifetime of experiences into those seventeen years. She carried herself well, and she knew how to get what she wanted. Nobody at the ice cream parlor batted an eye when she claimed to be twenty-one.

Steve was greeted with loud clapping from an appreciative crowd as he completed his descent and stepped to the floor, the bright floodlights reflecting off his moist forehead. He told everyone to be certain to attend the evening performance when he would take to the high wire again with a special guest. Lizzie waded through the autograph-hounds and other curiosity seekers who stuck around after the show.

"You again!" Steve said as he spotted her approaching. "What are you doing out of your shop?"

"How come you didn't tell me you were a big circus star?" she shot back. "I didn't know you did anything like this."

"You never asked me. Besides, I'm not the type to go around bragging. I'm just a regular guy who has the kind of job that puts me in the spotlight. It's nothing special. This job just happens to be a bit more glamorous than most."

There was something different about this man, Lizzie thought. He didn't put on airs or go out of his way to impress people. He was down-to-earth.

After the last of the autograph hounds departed, Lizzie and Steve situated themselves on a bench next to the fountain as Steve began to explain what she would have to do in order to follow him up the wire and across to the opposite platform. As long as she held on to his shoulders and kept her feet on the wire, Steve could keep them both balanced by shifting his own weight and adjusting the angle of the long, white pole. Lizzie was fascinated by the idea that a person could maintain his footing and walk so confidently across something that wasn't any wider than one of her fingers.

Steve reached into his pants pocket and pulled out a couple of half-dollars, giving one to Lizzie and holding on to the other. "Make a wish and throw it in the fountain," he said, tossing a coin over his shoulder. It disappeared into the shower of misty water that reflected the brilliant, multi-colored lights.

Lizzie paused to think for a few seconds. "I want to learn to walk on the high wire," she whispered underneath her breath as she flipped the half-dollar with her thumb. It soared through the cascading water and plunked into the pool below.

"Do you really believe in that stuff—making a wish and having it come true?" she asked.

# HIGH WIRE ANGEL

"Naw, not really. I think we make our own wishes come true. But I also believe that God has a plan for us. It's hard for me to explain. I'll tell you more about it sometime—if you're really interested."

"What did you wish for?" Lizzie demanded.

"Nothing," Steve insisted. "I didn't make a wish. How 'bout you?"

"Oh, I can't tell you that. It won't come true if I do."

He smiled at her for the longest time, then looked away as if he had caught himself staring and was embarrassed.

"It wouldn't hurt to practice," Steve said, abruptly changing the subject. "Do you know anywhere that's less crowded where I could show you a little more about what you're going to have to do tonight?"

Lizzie suggested the top of the mall and Steve nodded in agreement. "You lead the way," he said.

A series of narrow water pipes crossed the roof, just a few inches above the flat surface, giving them a perfect setting to begin practicing. If Lizzie felt uncomfortable, she could simply step off the pipe down onto the roof. Steve said she should imagine there was nothing but a wire beneath her feet, with the ground far below.

"If you're going to learn from me, you can forget about using a net," he warned. "I don't believe in them. Never have."

He first showed Lizzie how to walk along behind him, letting his wide, muscular shoulders support her weight as she clung to him and carefully slipped one foot in front of the other. Steve assured her that as long as she held on and didn't try to fight his balancing movements, she would have no problem. He then taught her how to climb aboard his shoulders and sit on them, positioning her body precisely so they could cross the high wire together.

"You're really going to have to trust me if you want to go across like this," he said, telling Lizzie to stretch out her arms so that they were parallel to the balancing pole. "I've done this hundreds of times, and I've only dropped three or four people so far."

"Maybe you'd better let me down," she said, nervously lifting her right leg to hoist herself from his shoulders and step back down to the roof.

Steve started laughing. "Hey, I'm just pulling your leg. I've never dropped anybody." Lizzie forced a nervous smile to cover up her gullibility.

A light drizzle began falling as they spoke, bringing an early end to Lizzie's training session.

"How did I do?" she asked Steve as they walked back down the stairs to the floor of the mall.

"I'm not sure I want to tell you," Steve replied. "It might sound like I'm trying to feed you a line of bull."

They passed by Dipper Dan's and Lizzie sneaked a scoop full of chocolate ice cream, cramming the oversized bite into her mouth, as if she was getting away with something. "Come on. Tell me how I did," she begged him.

Steve finally responded. "Okay, I'll be honest with you. You really do have the coordination and the physique to be a good aerialist. What can I say? You're a natural. Now all you need is someone to teach you how. If you want me to, I can be that someone. See, I told you it would sound like a line."

Lizzie was suddenly struck by the notion that something wasn't right. She had just met a rather peculiar man, practically a celebrity; she barely knew the guy, and already he was offering to be her personal trainer.

"Wow!" she responded, hoping to buy some time to sort out her thoughts. "I'll have to think it over."

"No problem," said Steve. "Just so you know that I'm very serious. A prospect like you doesn't come along every day, you know." Lizzie was thankful that he didn't press the issue any further.

It turned out that Steve was appearing at the mall to do a promotional appearance, complete with a mobile "Wallenda Museum." It was a stripped-down mobile home filled with old equipment, family heirlooms, circus posters, framed photographs of prominent family members performing daring acts, and other souvenirs dating back more than a century.

Steve was traveling with a former Barnum & Bailey clown named Jelly Belly, along with her long-time boyfriend and manager, Richard Bollinger. Because Steve didn't like to be bothered with the paperwork—he said he was a performer, not an administrator—all of the business responsibilities fell to Richard.

A devout Wallenda fan since his childhood, Richard had become Steve's booking agent after actively recruiting him because he admired the family. He began telling people that he was Steve's cousin, just so he could be thought of as part of the family. He even adopted "Wallenda" as his middle name.

After the mall booking, the trio would be leaving for Kingston, Jamaica, where Steve was scheduled to appear before the House of Parliament and other high government officials for an exclusive skywalk on a 1,000-foot-long cable extending across the top of Kingston Stadium.

Lizzie gasped when she heard the details. It seemed so much more dangerous than the 40-foot walk at the mall. Perhaps Steve was out of his mind.

"Do you think you're ready to give it a try tonight?" Steve asked as he walked Lizzie out to meet the bus that would take her home.

"Sure," she said. "It seems easy enough to me, as long as an expert like you calls the shots. I can't wait to tell my friends."

The bus pulled up to the curb and Lizzie stepped aboard. "I'll be looking for you tonight," Steve said, pointing his finger toward her as the door began to close. Lizzie laughed. "Don't worry," she said. "I'll be there. I promise."

Lizzie was living with the family of a middle-aged woman, Mary Ellen Mihalchik, who provided room and board in return for some help with housework and a modest amount in rent. Mary Ellen had witnessed the gradual transformation of Elizabeth Eve Pintye from a homeless teenage drifter to a blossoming young woman who was determined to make something out of her life.

# HIGH WIRE ANGEL

"You're not going to believe this," Lizzie said as she kicked open the door and took a seat in Mary Ellen's kitchen. "Pour us some coffee and sit down. I've got quite a story to tell you." She went on to detail her encounter with Steve and the plans for that evening.

"This I've got to see!" said Mary Ellen. "I remember the Flying Wallendas from when I was just a kid. They were the big hit of the circus. To tell you the truth, I didn't even know they were still at it."

"I don't know about the rest of 'em" Lizzie interjected, "but I can tell you that Steve Wallenda is still at it. He's really good, too."

Gulping down her coffee, she rose to leave. "I'm gonna change my clothes and get ready so I can catch the bus back to the mall. I want to look my best."

Mary Ellen grabbed the back of Lizzie's blouse, stopping her in her tracks. "You don't have to take the bus. I'll drive you down. I have to see this guy. You're not making this whole thing up, are you?"

"No way!" Lizzie said. "You'll see. Let me get ready and let's hurry. I don't want to be late for something like this."

As Mary Ellen drove, Lizzie gazed out the car window at the utility lines and imagined herself walking on them, high above the early evening traffic.

"I just remembered something," Mary Ellen said, drawing Lizzie back to reality. She went on to relate how she had looked on in horror as the television news showed the great Karl Wallenda falling to his death during a wire walk in Puerto Rico several years earlier.

"There have been other accidents, too," she continued. "In fact, there's a joke about the Wallendas, but it's kind of sick. It goes like this: What do the Wallendas and Maxwell House coffee have in common?"

Lizzie gave her a blank stare.

"Give up?" she teased. "It's easy. They're both good to the last drop!"

Lizzie squirmed in her seat. "What have I gotten myself into?" she thought, squeezing the car door handle.

Steve had said he would meet her a few minutes before the show. However, when she and Mary Ellen arrived, he was nowhere to be found. Nervous anticipation overcame Lizzie as she eyed the wire—that fine line between death and glory—wondering what would happen if she fell. Recognizing that a drop from that height would not be fatal, she started thinking of ways to land without breaking every bone in her body.

Lizzie's concentration was broken by the driving beat of "Eye of the Tiger," ushering Steve down a walkway toward the wire. Grinning as he waved to the crowd, he jogged past Lizzie like a boxer about to enter the ring. Wasting no time, he picked up his balancing pole, stepped from the floor to the sloping wire, let out a deep breath, and began his ascent.

The thumping loudspeakers seemed to shake the whole building. Mary Ellen looked at Lizzie and shrugged her shoulders. "I guess I'm supposed to come on later in the show," Lizzie shouted, trying to be heard above the music. Mary Ellen cast a skeptical eye on her young friend.

Steve progressed up and across the wire with incredible ease, reaching the platform on the other side in a matter of seconds, reversing his feet on the wire, and returning to the nearest platform as the music died down. Then he walked back down the sloping wire to ground level and was greeted by thunderous applause.

"Ladies and gentlemen, we have a special guest," he announced over a wireless microphone. Lizzie's heartbeat quickened. "Here's a man who needs no introduction."

"A man?" she whispered to Mary Ellen. "What about me?"

"He's going to come over here and show the world how easy it is to walk on the high wire," Steve continued. "From TV 10 Action News, put your hands together for Chuck Emerson!"

A camera crew followed Steve's every move as he greeted the man with a handshake, then turned around, stepped onto the wire, and told the reporter to do the same. Away they went, the man following Steve's every step. They obviously had rehearsed the act before.

The reporter was a large, lumpish man who seemed to approach the whole thing as a joke, smiling for the camera and hamming it up. He removed one hand from Steve's shoulders, grinning to the crowd.

Steve's expression changed from concentration to irritation. As they passed the midway point on their return trip from the far platform, the newsman recklessly started to lean to his left. A silence fell over the crowd, followed by several gasps. Steve stopped walking so they could regain their balance. He said something to the reporter, who now had a sober look on his face. This close call brought an end to the high wire high jinks. After that, they managed to complete the walk without any further incidents.

Lizzie stood dumbfounded, disappointed that Steve had decided to walk the wire with some character from the TV news, after promising he'd take her across. She had assumed that Steve appreciated her sincere desire to learn. Instead, he had chosen some joker who just wanted to have some fun and show off.

After the applause died down from the first walk and the newspaper photographers and TV crew finished their work, Steve picked up the microphone and asked the crowd to be quiet. "I have one more performer to introduce—a beautiful young blonde gal who spends most of her time scooping ice cream right over there at Dipper Dan's."

Lizzie could feel herself blushing as he called her forward. Steve's reassuring look—that half-smile that she had already become accustomed to—gave Lizzie a sense of security as she approached him.

"Just don't shake too much," Steve implored her. "Hold on and I'll do the hard part. Whatever you do, don't let go!" He also told her to forget what the TV man had done on the wire. "That damned fool could have killed himself," Steve said. "When he started screwing around, he just about lost his balance. He could have caused a lot of problems for both of us. I fixed him, though."

"What did you do?" Lizzie inquired.

"Oh, I just told him that if he didn't cut it out, I'd leave him alone right where he was." Steve paused. "Okay, let's go. Just remember what we did on the roof."

He turned to face the wire, and Lizzie took her position behind him. Steve stepped up onto the sloping wire, just a couple of inches from the mall floor. Lizzie remained at ease as she placed her left foot up onto the wire, but when she hoisted the rest of her body up and stepped down with her right foot, she began to shake uncontrollably.

"It's okay. That's normal," Steve said calmly. "Just hold on to me."

Lizzie's eyes were glued to her feet for every step she took. In contrast, Steve never once looked down at his feet. He focused straight ahead, trusting his instincts and more than thirty years of experience.

"Are you all right?" Steve whispered out of the corner of his mouth, loud enough for only Lizzie to hear.

"I'm fine," she answered, as her shaking intensified and her stomach twisted into knots.

Lizzie realized that if things got too bad, she could leap on him, wrap her arms around his neck, and let him carry her piggyback the rest of the way to the anchoring tower so she could climb down the ladder.

Only a minute or two passed before they finished climbing and reached the platform, pausing to rest. Sweat poured from Lizzie's forehead. She looked out over the flat wire.

"Are you ready to go across?" Steve asked. The audience started chanting, "Go! Go! Go!" For a moment, Lizzie was torn between giving in to the crowd or surrendering to her fear.

"You go on by yourself," she told Steve. "I think I've had enough." He nodded in agreement. Red-faced, Lizzie slowly climbed down the narrow pegs that extended down the base of the platform. She wanted to dig a hole in the floor of the mall and crawl into it.

As soon as she got to the ground, she peered back up at the wire in awe. It really had been a thrilling experience, she thought. While she and Steve were climbing, she had felt a burning desire to test herself and see if she could maintain her balance on the wire alone, but she hadn't dared to take her hands off Steve's shoulders.

Even as she made her way through the crowd to where Mary Ellen was standing, Lizzie felt as if she were walking on air.

"You're a hell of a lot braver than I'd ever be," Mary Ellen said reassuringly.

"Oh, yeah. It was really different," Lizzie responded, turning away to look toward Steve. He had already walked to the far platform and returned to the floor of the mall.

He put down his balancing pole and straightened up with a deep sigh of satisfaction. Then he began signing autographs and chatting with the fans. Many of them carried old photographs and scrapbooks with tattered yellow newspaper clippings. Lizzie could make out the words "Great Wallendas" in one of the headlines.

Chapter 3

# COME TO JAMAICA

Lizzie's brief wire walk had been almost as exhausting as it was exciting. Her leg muscles ached as she stood, keeping her eye on Steve, who continued to mingle. She feared their relationship would be over nearly as quickly as it started. Surely, he would go on to travel from city to city, entertaining thousands of people with his special talents, while she would continue to dip ice cream cones and refill coffee cups.

Young and impressionable, Lizzie remained wholly fascinated by Steve and his special talent. She felt herself being drawn by the excitement of walking the high wire, and realized she would do practically anything to persuade him to let her go up with him again.

Much to Lizzie's delight, Steve sought her out and asked her to join him for a late dinner at a Chinese restaurant near the mall. "You won't have to wait for us," he said rather rudely to Mary Ellen. "I have a car here. I can take her home later."

Mary Ellen had serious reservations about leaving her young friend with an older man who, she speculated, had grown up in the moral decadence of a circus environment. However, she had learned from the outset of her relationship with Lizzie that any maternal instincts she might feel toward this young woman should best be left unexpressed. Elizabeth Pintye was not one to take orders from anyone.

"I'll be fine, " Lizzie said, sensing her landlady's uneasiness. "I'll be home in a while."

The air conditioning of the restaurant was a welcome relief to Lizzie, who was still tense from her recent experience. She considered herself fortunate to be in Steve's company and to have his undivided attention. Broodingly quiet and intense, he stirred something inside her; she yearned to find out what he was really all about.

Despite long periods of silence as they ate, she felt a natural comfort that only intensified as Steve drove her home in his agent's car. They pulled into the driveway of Mary Ellen's house and Steve turned off the engine.

"Can we talk for a while?" he asked.

"Sure," Lizzie said. "I don't have anywhere to go. Tell me those ideas you have about God's plans and all that. You said you would."

Steve grimaced ever so slightly. "Are you sure you want to hear it?" he said. "I don't want to come off like I'm preaching to you. It's an awfully long story."

"Like I said," Lizzie replied. "I don't have anywhere to go."

With that, Steve motioned for her to move closer to him in the front seat. He put his arm around her and proceeded to speak at great lengths about his spiritual beliefs. Faith in God and a deep understanding of Christ's teachings had saved him from a path of self-destruction, he told her.

"I'm only alive today because I was able to understand all this," Steve said. "Well, not everything. I'm learning more every day. I don't have any important people in my life anymore; nobody who cares about me. That's why my faith means that much more to me."

Lizzie tried to mask her own ignorance as she listened intently. She found it so easy to learn from Steve.

"I know there's a reason our paths have crossed," Steve said, reaching to take her hand. Lizzie's hand met his and she gently slipped her fingers between Steve's. It was a gesture of friendship and affection, not one of romance, and each of them recognized the difference.

"It's not just a coincidence that I came into the ice cream shop and sought you out," Steve said. "This is something that is very serious to me. That's all I'm going to say right now."

"Do you really believe in that stuff—fate and all that?" Lizzie asked.

"It's not that simple," Steve replied. "Please don't ask me anything more about it. I'm going to have to sort things out in my own mind before I can share my feelings or tell you anything else. I don't want to say anything I might regret later."

The morning sun was just starting to shine over the horizon when Steve finally drove away. Lizzie paused to listen to the lonesome coo of a mourning dove on the rooftop of a neighbor's home, then walked into the house, too excited and confused to even think about going to bed.

Mary Ellen was grinding the beans for her morning coffee. "Don't tell me—you're in love," she said as Lizzie entered the kitchen.

"That's not it at all," Lizzie answered, pouring herself a glass of orange juice and taking a seat at the kitchen table. "I've never met anybody like Steve in my life, but it's not love. It's more like fascination. I really don't know what it is."

"That's usually the way it starts," Mary Ellen teased. "First comes a little crush on a guy and, the next thing you know, you're falling all over him."

"Oh, cut it out, Mary Ellen. If you knew Steve at all, you'd understand that it's not like that. It's just really weird."

# HIGH WIRE ANGEL

That day at the mall, Lizzie's friends tried to convince her she was foolish to be spending time with someone as strange—even frightening—as Steve. She shrugged off their concerns, suspecting that they were motivated more by jealousy than out of any true concern for her own well-being.

Steve came into Dipper Dan's early that afternoon, accompanied by his agent. Business was slow, so Lizzie had a chance to sit down and chat for a couple of minutes between customers. She told them how captivated she was by the high wire and how much she would like to learn all about it and maybe even become a performer herself someday.

"Come on down to Jamaica with us and you can start your real high wire education right there," Steve said.

"Yeah, right," Lizzie laughed, assuming that he was teasing.

"What are you, nuts?" Richard interjected, giving Steve a nudge with his elbow.

"I'm dead serious," Steve insisted. "We've got room for you, and it's the only way you're going to learn. What are you waiting for?"

Lizzie was stunned, scared, and a bit excited. She absorbed his words like a sponge. "Well, uh, let me think about it," she said, fumbling for words. By then, several customers had lined up and were patiently waiting at the ice cream counter. One of them cleared his throat, finally getting Lizzie's attention.

"Oh my God! Sorry about that," she said, hurrying over to begin serving them. By the time she was done scooping ice cream, Steve and Richard had left the shop. Next to their empty cups was a five-dollar bill to cover the cost of their coffee, plus a healthy tip. A napkin with writing on it was wrapped around the money. Lizzie unfolded it and read the scribbled message: "Please come to Jamaica. You won't regret it." It was signed with the initials "S.W."

Not surprisingly, her mall acquaintances thought the idea was ridiculous.

"Those guys are spaced-out," said John, a security guard and part-time fashion model. "Don't you know that they sell blonde-haired girls in Jamaica? If you go down there, you'll never be heard from again."

Lizzie didn't put much stock in his opinion. For several months, he had been trying unsuccessfully to land a date with her. Opportunities for dating were frequent for an attractive young woman who was in the public eye as an ice cream shop clerk, but Lizzie had grown too career-oriented and fun-loving, possibly too self-centered, to become emotionally involved with anyone.

"There's something awfully wrong here," added Roger, the middle-aged shoe store manager who stopped at her shop every day on his coffee break. "What does he want with a girl like you? He's rich and famous, and who are you? No offense, Liz, but you better watch out. He's got to have something up his sleeve."

Steve's antisocial behavior practically invited such suspicions. He didn't care what people thought of him. He had been taken advantage of so often by people who were greedy and materialistic that he had become a loner, a free spirit who often acted on impulse. Steve had only one real friend on earth, a man named Gene who had been a stunt man for actor Clarence Williams III on "The Mod Squad."

"Gene understands me," he said during one of his stops at Lizzie's shop. "He's not out to take advantage of me. He's about the only person in the world I can trust—except for you, maybe."

The Wallenda exhibit was still booked for a few more days at the mall. Lizzie saw Steve every day and the two talked for hours at a time. Regardless of her friends' admonitions, she felt a sense of security that drew her toward him.

Lizzie's own religious background had consisted of childhood Sunday School lessons and the rituals she was forced to observe in a Catholic elementary school. As she listened to Steve, it dawned on her that, for the first time in her life, she was beginning to confront some of the questions that had been repressed in the turmoil of her troubled adolescence.

"What you need is a Holy Bible, along with someone who is willing to help you learn," Steve emphasized during one of their conversations. The implication, though unspoken, was clear to Lizzie: Steve was willing to be that someone.

Nothing had ever weighed more heavily on her mind than the decision she now had to confront. "Should I risk everything I have built and go to Jamaica, or should I stay behind to test Steve's commitment to our relationship?" she asked herself. "If destiny has truly brought us together, he's not going to just walk out of my life and never return."

Richard, Steve's agent, wanted to make the decision for her. He had done everything within his power to encourage a romance between his daughter and Steve, even though Steve had consistently rebuffed her. Richard still hadn't given up, and he saw Lizzie as a direct threat to his hopes of becoming a father-in-law to an honest-to-goodness Wallenda.

The first couple of nights, Richard had allowed Steve to borrow his car to drive Lizzie home. Once he became worried that the relationship was blossoming, Richard's generosity ended in a most abrupt fashion. Steve and Lizzie had been sitting in the car outside of the mall having one of their serious discussions when Richard appeared at the passenger's side door and hopped in, sandwiching Lizzie in the middle.

Reeking of whiskey, he gradually slid his hand to the inside of Lizzie's thigh and began to massage it as he made small talk. Frightened and nauseated, she leaned over and huddled up against Steve. Each of them had been politely tolerating Richard's rudeness up until that point. Steve insisted on trading places with Lizzie. Then he reached over and started to paw away at Richard's chest and thighs.

"How do you like it, Richard?" Steve asked with a half-joking, half-angry laugh. "She's not that kind of a girl, so leave her alone."

Richard charged out of the car, grabbing his keys out of the ignition and vowing that Steve would never be allowed to borrow the car again. "There's no

# HIGH WIRE ANGEL

way she's going to Jamaica with us!" he shouted as he staggered across the parking lot.

Steve and Lizzie looked at each other and erupted in laughter at the same instant. "What a lunatic," Steve said. "He gets that way when he drinks. You never know what he's going to do. He thinks he's some kind of ladies' man or something. What he really is, is a jerk."

"Why do you stay with him?" Lizzie inquired.

"Because he knows the business. I just put up with the fact that he's a pain in the ass."

They decided to take a walk and enjoy the evening air. "He's right you know," Lizzie said. "I don't have anything to offer you guys on the trip. I'd just be a burden."

"That's not true," Steve said. "I'd like you to start learning how to walk the wire right away. With the right training, you'd be a great addition to my act."

Steve slipped his arm around Lizzie and pulled her close as a cool breeze blew in their faces.

"I'm telling you, you're a natural," he continued with genuine enthusiasm. "The first day I saw you, I knew you could do it. All you have to do is work at it. I can see it in your style, your feet, the way you move your body, and even the way you conduct yourself around other people. The most important thing is that you're naturally coordinated and you have a fear. Take that TV newsman who went up on the wire with me. He could never be a performer because he didn't have that fear. He got cocky up there. You're different."

The night before Steve's final appearance at the mall, Lizzie couldn't find him anywhere. One of her friends said he had seen Steve and Richard walking over to a tavern across the highway from the mall. There, she found Richard sitting with her friend John, the security guard, but Steve was nowhere to be seen. The two of them were hopelessly inebriated.

"Why do you care where he is?" John shouted. "He met some chick in here and they went back to his trailer. Anyhow, I told him you're only seventeen and you're jail bait. He's just trying to get into your pants, Liz, can't you see that? Once that guy leaves this town, you'll never see him again."

"And there's no damned way you're going to Jamaica, either," Richard chimed in. "Besides that, I'm going to drop Steve—he can find another promoter. He's a has-been."

Lizzie burst into tears and retreated to the bathroom. When she returned, a couple of husky motorcycle gang members had John and Richard pinned against the bar, telling them in no uncertain terms to leave her alone.

"Hey, man, we don't want any trouble," Richard said. "We're just trying to warn the girl that there's somebody out to get her, that's all."

"It's okay, really," Lizzie told the bikers, who released their grips. "They're not going to hurt me. They just had a little bit too much to drink."

John and Richard chugged down their drinks and hurried out the door. Lizzie slowly walked back across the parking lot, trying to decide whether she should disturb Steve and his newfound friend at the trailer. She decided to walk by and see if there were any lights on.

Through the screen door, she could see him sitting on the couch, looking at a magazine. He was bare-chested with a towel draped around his neck. Lizzie knocked gently on the door and Steve looked up.

"I'm not interrupting anything, am I?" she asked.

"Heck no, Liz. Come on in. I could use the company."

"I thought maybe you had already had enough company for one night," she said.

"What's that supposed to mean?"

"Oh, I heard about your little get-together with a certain girl from the bar across the street."

Steve straightened up on the couch and gave Lizzie a blank stare. "Where'd you hear a story like that?"

"Richard and one of my friends told me about how you picked up some girl and brought her over to the trailer to get your kicks, I suppose," Lizzie explained.

"Did you believe them?" Steve asked.

"Why shouldn't I?"

"Because I've never been in that bar in my life. And by the way, I haven't been with a girl in a long time, either, in case that's what you're wondering."

Lizzie accepted his words at face value and proceeded to fill him in on what had happened to Richard and John. Steve began laughing.

"Hey, it's not funny!" she said. "Richard said he's going to fire you."

"Don't worry about him. He does that all the time. He's a diabetic and shouldn't be drinking in the first place. How can he fire me? He's working for me! Now, about something a little more important. Are you going with us to Jamaica, or not?"

"I've decided I'm just not ready," Lizzie said. "I really appreciate the offer, but I need some time to think things over. This has been a very strange week for me."

Steve sat looking at her, and Lizzie began to feel guilty as if she had let him down.

"You're the only one who can make that decision," he said. "I'd like to take you with me, but I would never try to tell you what you should do. We'll be back in the states in a few weeks and I'll be in touch."

Just then, the door flew open and Richard crashed into the trailer, collapsing on the floor as he tried to catch his breath. "The bikers are after me! They're gonna kill me!"

"What bikers? What did you do to them?" Steve asked, playing innocent.

"Nothing! Those guys are crazy! They're just picking on me and some guy from the mall. We were just having a couple of beers, minding our own business, when one of them followed us out into the parking lot of this bar and started pushing us around. I just took off running and..."

# HIGH WIRE ANGEL

He stopped in mid-sentence when he finally noticed Lizzie sitting on the couch.

"She's the one who put 'em up to it," Richard insisted, sitting down and pulling back the curtain so he could peek out the window like a frightened child.

"I did not," Lizzie said firmly. "I don't even know those guys. I never said one word to them. They just didn't like the way you were talking to me."

Lizzie checked her watch and realized the bus would be pulling into the mall in a few minutes. She left the trailer, resigned to the fact that Steve would be leaving without her.

The next morning, she got to the mall early so she could say good-bye. Steve was milling around outside of his trailer, taking down the awning and preparing to leave. Lizzie gave him a kiss on the cheek and handed him a slip of paper containing her address and phone number. Steve folded it and placed it in his wallet.

"I'll see you again. I really will," Steve told her. "You're a very special person to me."

"I believe you," Lizzie said. "Just keep in touch. Don't let me down. Like I said, I'm a little confused right now."

Within a couple of minutes, Lizzie was jogging across town to join some friends at a swimming area called "Heaven's Hole."

"Are we ever happy to see you!" said Cassie, one of Lizzie's co-workers at Dipper Dan's. "We thought you would be on your way to Jamaica with those circus weirdos by now."

"I decided not to go," Lizzie explained. "I'm just not ready to give up everything—yet. We'll see what happens."

John, the security guard, was lying facedown on a towel, soaking up the warm rays of the sun. "What happened to you and your old lover boy, Liz?" he asked. "I thought he was going to turn you into a tightrope walker and take you around the world with him."

"Why don't you shut up, John?" Lizzie shouted. "Don't you have a hangover to take care of? Maybe you better run home to your mommy so the bikers won't get you."

Lizzie's other friends snickered. They tried to convince her that she had made the right decision. Lizzie wasn't so sure...

Chapter 4

# 'HE DOESN'T KNOW YOU'

Lizzie couldn't get Steve out of her mind. She would see little things he had pointed out to her, or hear a certain song, or walk along the same area they had strolled and he would instantly pop into her mind. She admired his intelligence and his special performing talent, and envied him for having so much free time and being able to travel around the world, in contrast to her own situation—stuck in a dead-end job with no real prospects of going anywhere but back and forth to work.

Steve was like no one she had ever met, a marvelous mixture of man and boy, knowledgeable about the ways of the world but still impulsive and unpredictable. He had nerves of steel and a mental toughness, though underneath it all she could recognize a kindhearted, sentimental man who yearned for emotional support, understanding, and acceptance.

During their discussions, Steve had loaned Lizzie several books, including *Jonathan Livingston Seagull*, and had recommended that she read and think about them. In his absence, she kept studying them, looking for clues about who Steve really was. The more she read, the more fascinated she became. Each time the phone rang, either at home or at work, she wondered if it was him. She called Mary Ellen every afternoon to see if there was a letter for her. Each time, the reply was, "No, not today."

Through this period, Mary Ellen became bolder in expressing her concern about Lizzie's growing fascination with Steve. She thought her young friend was making a big mistake by becoming involved with a man who was twice her age and from a questionable background. Whenever Mary Ellen raised these issues, Lizzie would attempt to allay her concerns by insisting she was more fascinated by the high wire than by Steve Wallenda himself.

Two months passed with no word from Steve. Lizzie called Richard's business phone in New Jersey but received a tape-recorded message telling her that the number was no longer in service. Gradually, she resigned herself to the fact that she would never see Steve again.

That all changed one afternoon when she was wiping tables at Dipper Dan's and overheard a couple of customers in the adjacent booth mention the name "Wallenda." Lizzie interrupted. "Excuse me, did I hear you say something about the Wallendas?" she asked the young man who was having a sundae with his father.

"I did," said the father.

"That's funny," Lizzie said, "because I'm friends with one of the Wallendas, but I haven't been able to locate him. Have you ever heard of Steve Wallenda?"

"Yeah," the man replied. "We were just talking about him. My son and I are taking our snack cart up to Suffern for the Rockland County Fair. That Wallenda guy is supposed to do some kind of show or something there tomorrow night and we're peddling our snacks there. You've got a poster about it on the wall right out in the hall."

Lizzie dropped what she was doing and hurried out through the doorway. There in plain view was a poster with a pencil-sketch of Steve on the high wire, along with photos of Chubby Checker, Louise Mandrell, and some of the other performers who were scheduled to appear at the fair.

Lizzie decided on the spot that she would empty her meager savings account, take a bus to Suffern, and confront Steve. It was important for her to find out how he felt about her after many weeks of being apart. Lizzie also believed he owed her an explanation for his silence. The long bus ride afforded her a chance to mull things over. She kept wondering why he hadn't bothered to call when he learned he was going to be back in the New York area.

As soon as Lizzie walked onto the midway of the fair, she spotted the colorful logo on the side of the Wallenda trailer where Richard and Jelly Belly the clown were seated on lawn chairs by the door.

"Hey, doll, what are you doing here?" Richard said, in sharp contrast to the belligerent tone he had used the last time they spoke.

"Take a guess," Lizzie said sarcastically. "I'm looking for Steve."

"Well, he's had an accident. Didn't you hear?"

"Oh no! Did he fall off the wire?" Lizzie asked as her body quivered.

"No, nothing like that," said Richard, "but he slipped on some wet grass or something and smashed his head on the pavement. He just got out of the hospital, but he doesn't know a damned thing. I'll bet he won't even know who you are."

An accomplished wire walker falling while he was on the ground? A case of amnesia? Lizzie found the story far-fetched, especially since Richard didn't want Steve to have anything to do with her from the start. At first, she suspected that the three of them had concocted an elaborate scheme to get her out of the picture. Then she realized they would have had no reason to go to such extremes, when Steve just as easily could have told her he wanted nothing more to do with her. If that was the case, Lizzie decided, she wanted to hear it from Steve himself.

Just then, Jelly Belly noticed Steve standing by himself near a group of teenagers, about one hundred feet in the distance.

"Go walk by him and I'll bet he won't recognize you," she said, grabbing Lizzie's shoulder and pointing toward him.

Steve was leaning against the wall of a refreshment stand, smoking a cigarette and watching the crowd. He hadn't shaved in a couple of days and he looked like he hadn't slept much either. Lizzie casually walked over and hung around the ferris wheel, close to where Steve was standing.

He gave her a brief glance, but nothing seemed to register. Lizzie stared right at him and he made brief eye contact with her, only to turn away, drop his cigarette onto the ground, stomp it out and plant himself on a bench behind the concession stand.

Lizzie was fortunate enough to come across Matthew, the younger member of the snack vending duo she had met the day before at the mall. After she told him of her dilemma, Matthew agreed to strike up a conversation with Steve and remind him who she was.

Lizzie stayed back by the ferris wheel and watched. The men talked for three or four minutes, looking in her direction from time to time. Then they shook hands and Steve walked toward his trailer. Matthew shrugged his shoulders as he approached Lizzie.

"He said you look familiar, but he's still trying to piece things together. He's very disoriented and confused, kind of spaced-out I guess you could say. He did say that he would meet you here at seven o'clock tonight. You'll just have to take it from there."

"Do you think he'll even bother to show up?" Lizzie inquired.

"I guess you'll find out at seven o'clock," said Matthew. "I do have my doubts. I'm not even sure he'll be able to remember that much. I'm telling you, this guy is pretty messed up."

Lizzie checked into a hotel room to rest while the time passed. Lying in bed, she began to prepare for the worst by giving herself a pep talk: "There *will* be other men; there *will* be other opportunities. I have my whole life ahead of me. Just like I've done so many times before, I'll accept events as they happen and adjust to them."

During her walk back to the fairgrounds, she became caught in a heavy downpour, leaving her long, blonde hair dripping wet and her clothes thoroughly soaked by the time she reached the fair. To Lizzie's delight, Steve was waiting for her, right by the ferris wheel. He had showered and shaved, and looked much more like the man she had gotten to know so well back at the mall. However, the first words out of his mouth were ominous.

"Man, you look like somebody dumped a bucket of water all over you. You are Liz, aren't you?"

"Of course I am. Don't you remember me?"

"I'm trying to," he said apologetically. "I had this fall and things are just

HIGH WIRE ANGEL                                                    31

beginning to make sense to me again. It's all coming back, but I've got to be
patient. Please, just bear with me."

Steve pointed to a large lump on the side of his head, ample evidence that
he had sustained a serious injury. Lizzie suggested they get away from the noise
and the crowd on the midway. As they walked a grassy hill that overlooked the
fair, she patiently reminded him of the experiences they had shared. The slow,
lethargic way he spoke made Lizzie wonder if he would ever be the same.

"Your face looks familiar," he told her. "I wish I could remember more.
I can't remember where I met you. It's so damned frustrating to me."

The longer they talked, the more he came to life. The turning point came
when Lizzie told him she had read his copy of *Jonathan Livingston Seagull*
several times. Steve brightened up and launched into a lengthy discourse about
how the author, Richard Bach, toiled so hard to choose every word with care,
then endured unrelenting criticism from book reviewers who considered his
work to be shallow and simplistic.

"It's beautiful because of its simplicity," Steve said. "It reminds me of
walking on the high wire. Your fate is in your own hands. It's just you and the
wire."

As he spoke, Lizzie looked directly into his eyes. They were dark,
compelling, controlling. She looked away and began drawing a picture of a
seagull on a small sketch pad she had in her purse. Above it, she wrote "Follow
Your Dreams." She thought about how this summarized her approach to their
relationship. It was so unlike her to drop everything and pursue a man like
Steve, especially when her friends were so convinced that he could only lead to
trouble.

"Why don't you hold on to this?" Lizzie suggested, handing him the
sketch. "It will give you something to remember me by." Steve smiled as he
inspected the drawing. "It's good," he said. "I like it. I'll put it somewhere very
special. I have just the place for it."

When Lizzie could jog his memory by mentioning something that had
happened back at the mall, Steve was able to fill in the blanks. She mentioned
that she had walked on the high wire with him.

"That's right," Steve suddenly recalled. "You chickened out right in the
middle before I could take you across. If you give me another chance with you,
we can work on that."

Things had not gone well for the Wallenda entourage in Jamaica. Steve
believed that Richard and Jelly Belly were riding on his coattails and he was on
the verge of breaking away from them and handling his own promotion, even
though he knew it would be difficult. He had never bothered to learn the
administrative aspects of show business. Still, he was nearing the point where
he was willing to take a chance.

Steve kissed Lizzie firmly on the lips as they parted, catching her off-guard
since he had never been so bold with her before. "Listen," he said softly. "I'm
going to have to go back to the trailer to rest. I get these headaches and the only

thing that makes them go away is to lie down. I do a lot of sleeping." They slowly walked back to the trailer and Lizzie continued on to her hotel. She tossed and turned in the loneliness of the room that night as she tried to sort things out.

The following afternoon, the fair kicked into high gear. It was a hot, muggy day and the midway was packed. Lizzie, dressed in a skimpy, cotton, tiger-striped outfit, visited a facepainting booth where a makeup artist etched some matching tiger stripes on her face. She looked in the mirror and began to worry that her silly outfit might seem too childish to Steve.

Matthew, the snack vendor, needed someone to help him sell peanuts during the main entertainment, a live performance by Chubby Checker and his band, so Lizzie volunteered. About midway through the lively, fast-paced show, the music suddenly stopped.

"Come on up here, you tiger, and let's see you do the twist," Chubby Checker shouted cheerfully, pointing down toward the crowd with his microphone. Lizzie glanced all around, then looked back up before she realized he was talking to her.

"Oh no, I've never danced in my life," she said to Matthew as her face turned red. She wanted to walk away, but the crowd was pushing her forward. Soon, she reached the stage as the band started playing the background music for "Let's Twist Again." Chubby greeted Lizzie with a huge smile and motioned for her to join him.

She had no idea how she should move her body to the beat, so she imitated Chubby's actions, with not nearly as much animation or confidence. Eventually, he started calling other members of the audience to climb up to the stage, and Lizzie found herself in the midst of about twenty twisting and shaking women. She took that opportunity to slip through the chaotic dancing scene and return to Matthew's peanut booth while the show rocked on.

Steve was forced to cancel his wire walk that afternoon because he still felt groggy. After the concert, Lizzie walked over to his trailer to see how he was feeling. "Did you get to see me on stage?" she asked as he opened the door.

"I already heard all about it," he replied. "Everybody was talking about it, telling me 'Your girlfriend was all dressed up like a tiger and dancing with Chubby Checker.' I'm glad you did it. I've told you before that you could be a real performer because you've got what it takes."

"What's this stuff about your *girlfriend* being dressed up and dancing? Is that what I am now, your *girlfriend*?"

"I guess that is kind of simplistic, now that you mention it," Steve said. "Who cares about labels like that? I know you're a very important person in my life. Let's just leave it at that."

As it turned out, Steve and Chubby Checker were good friends. Too embarrassed to admit that she had never heard of the singer until that week, Lizzie feigned excitement when Steve asked her to walk over to Chubby's trailer for a more formal introduction.

Steve and Chubby talked for a long time while Lizzie nervously sat across the room, leafing through entertainment magazines that were strewn on the couch. Eventually, she pulled Steve aside and said she wanted to spend a few minutes alone with him before returning to Mohegan Lake.

"I can't quite figure out where you're coming from," she said as they walked arm-in-arm toward the doorway of his trailer. "There's so much I don't know about you, but I want to know more. I feel like I have to know about your family, your life, your career. Who is this man that suddenly means so much to me?"

Steve disappeared into the bedroom of the trailer and emerged a moment later with a thick, red scrapbook and a glossy folder. "This will tell you some of what you want to know," he said as he dropped the material on the couch. "This publicity folder is what Richard sends out to all of the agencies that are interested in booking an aerialist. The scrapbook will let you know a little bit about my family and some of the things I've done. Things are still a little foggy to me because of my fall. You might learn more from these than from what I could tell you right now. To tell you the truth, I don't like to dwell on my past. I did not have what you would call an ideal childhood."

"You're not the only one," Lizzie said.

She had started to leaf through the scrapbook when Richard appeared at the door and said he had some important things to discuss.

"It's good news, for a change," he continued. "I've got us some jobs, if you're up to it. It's a whole series of appearances around the New York and New Jersey area for celebrity parties, more summer fairs and that kind of stuff. We have a lot of things to go over but we have to move quickly. The first one's tomorrow night and it's a three-hundred mile drive."

"I'm sorry, Liz, but it looks like I'm going to be tied up for a while," Steve said. He motioned to the scrapbook and folder. "Keep them for a while. I'll get 'em the next time I see you. I'm sure there's going to be a next time."

Richard frowned when he heard that. "Come on, Steve. We gotta get going. See you around, kid. Have a nice ride back home," he said smugly.

Steve walked Lizzie out to the road to stand with her while she waited for the cab that would take her to the bus depot. They huddled close together to fight a harsh wind that had kicked up. Steve said he would soon be breaking his partnership with Richard and he promised Lizzie he would contact her after that.

"One last thing," he said as he kissed her on the cheek and laid her suitcase on the back seat of the cab. "You're going to learn the wire."

Chapter 5

# WORLDS APART

Lizzie couldn't wait to pour through the scrapbook and learn more about Steve and his famous family. She visited three libraries to gather up everything she could find on the Wallendas, from magazine articles dating back a half-century to circus books and the autobiography of Steve's famous granduncle, Karl Wallenda.

Spellbound, she devoted every spare minute to studying this material. A story of dedication, determination, and daring emerged as she continued reading and piecing the information together with some of the things Steve had told her about his past. Her main concern was to determine how her special friend fit into the family puzzle.

At first glance, the paths that brought their lives together seemed as different as night and day. Yet, as Lizzie continued to uncover clues about Steve's life, she began to recognize fundamental similarities that would help bridge the vast chasm between their worlds.

Since his birth, Steve had been showered with material goods. His world-famous name and his family's lucrative involvement in show business virtually guaranteed that he would be well cared for.

Later in life, if there was something he wanted—sports cars, designer clothes, jewelry and so on—the money was available. There was a time when he would fly from Los Angeles to San Francisco because he liked a certain restaurant's food. For years he traveled from city to city, visiting show business acquaintances or looking for fun. In recent years, Steve had a more modest lifestyle, spending money as fast as he made it. He had no long-term goals. Steve Wallenda lived one day at a time, believing that tomorrow would take care of itself.

In contrast, there was nothing famous about the name Elizabeth Eve Pintye. She was lucky to have enough money to buy her lunch at school. Lizzie's idea of a treat was a roll of Life Savers. A typical Christmas morning found her unwrapping a candy cane—never any toys or nice clothing. Year after

# HIGH WIRE ANGEL

year, Lizzie wished that Santa Claus would remember to stop at her house, just once.

Steve's life of luxury masked the absence of some key elements throughout his childhood and well into adolescence. Shuffled from home to home at the whim of feuding relatives, more interested in their own careers than their children, he was denied love and stability. Even in adulthood, Steve had unfilled voids in his life.

Likewise, rarely in Lizzie's childhood was she provided with any outward expressions of affection from her parents. Family members never gave or received hugs or kisses. She was never told, "I love you." Her early years were spent shielded from her bizarre family circumstances by a series of foster homes. Despite their best intentions, the families always made it clear to her that she was an outsider and not "one of the family."

At the time they met, Steve and Lizzie were each still seeking the same things—love, companionship, spiritual growth, and a sense of purpose in their lives.

Steve Wallenda had already established himself as one of the world's all-time greatest aerialists. His name remains in the Guinness Book of World Records for the longest-ever walk on a high wire. One of the first things that struck Lizzie about him was his level of dedication to his profession. She recognized it in his facial expression when she first saw him walking across the wire. She heard it in his voice and saw it in his eyes when he talked about the high wire.

Family history practically dictated that he would become a high wire performer, yet it took a great deal of commitment and sacrifice on his part to pursue it as a career. He had left the business on several occasions, but something always drew him back.

His father, Gunther Wallenda, was a famous high wire performer himself who later became a circus history teacher in Florida. Now retired, he lives with other members of the extended Wallenda family in Sarasota, which is widely regarded as the circus capital of the United States.

Steve's mother was the former La Gay Fort, who was an equestrian and an aerial performer herself until she retired. At this time she was recovering from open heart surgery in Pittsburg, California. A woman of uncommon attractiveness, La Gay won many beauty pageants and was later chosen to perform as an Earl Carroll Vanity Girl.

Not long after she and Gunther Wallenda exchanged their vows, it became evident that she was still much too independent to be restricted by marriage. Even the arrival of Steve failed to settle her down. By the time he was 15 months old, she had left Gunther in Florida and returned to California, where she moved in with her parents. Still restless, La Gay left Steve behind with her parents so she could get on with her life.

La Gay's brother, Leon Fort, is still a highly-regarded circus trainer who has worked out of the "Circus of the Stars" complex at Universal Studios in

Hollywood for many years. He was an important figure in Steve's early life. An accomplished aerialist in his own right, Leon performed, along with Gunther Wallenda, Karl Wallenda, and four others, as the internationally-acclaimed Wallenda Seven-Man Pyramid, a high wire act that is still considered the standard by which all others are measured. The performing troupe earned worldwide acclaim by walking at the edge of the void, protected only by the combination of their skill, balance, and courage.

Steve was just three years old when he began his training under Leon's expert guidance. Steve has memories of riding the old-time circus trains before trucks took over the transition from city to city. His time with Uncle Leon and this early exposure to the world of entertainment provided him with a sense of purpose that was otherwise lacking.

Steve was reunited with the Wallenda side of the family for brief periods, living in Florida and Mexico. His father had remarried, having fallen in love with another aerial performer, Margarita Caudillo. She took an immediate interest in Steve and worked very hard to establish a close relationship with him whenever her busy performance schedule allowed.

Any chance they had of growing closer ended in 1959. Family members looked on in horror as Margarita fell during an aerial ballet act in Mexico City. She died several weeks later from injuries sustained in the fall.

This accident took a toll on both Gunther Wallenda and his son. For the father, it signaled the beginning of a terror that would eventually drive him away from the business. He had seen death from the high wire before, but he had never felt its sting until the woman he loved more than anything else in the world perished. To Steve, Margarita's death meant further upheaval in his life, as well as the loss of another maternal figure.

In 1962, the most notorious accident in aerial performing history occurred during a Shrine Circus appearance in Detroit, Michigan, when the Wallenda Seven-Man Pyramid collapsed, killing two members, paralyzing a third, and injuring three others.

Gunther was the only member who was able to maintain his balance and remain on the wire when the pyramid collapsed. "Pure luck, not skill," he would later describe his good fortune that day. However, he was all but convinced that he should pursue a safer line of work.

Steve was attending school in California when news of the accident spread across the nation. School officials called him down to the principal's office to share the news. They knew very few particulars, only that an accident had occurred with at least two fatalities. For several hours, Steve did not know whether his father was alive or dead.

Finally, a radio broadcast provided the information: Gunther was not only alive and well, but he was being hailed as a hero for helping save the life of another family member.

A little over a year later, the indomitable Karl Wallenda insisted on recreating the great pyramid for an NBC television program, but this time at a

Karl Wallenda's Seven-Man Pyramid (Circus World Museum, Baraboo, Wisconsin).

height of just ten feet. During a practice session in Sarasota, with the TV cameras rolling, the wire slipped and the pyramid collapsed, hurting no one seriously, although Gunter lost several teeth when he clipped his chin on the wire while going down.

Steve was in Florida visiting his father at the time. He did not witness the accident firsthand, but was in the living room of his father's house when the group gathered to watch the NBC-TV program that featured the footage. After the show aired and the performers were relaxing over drinks and snacks, Gunther stunned his colleagues by declaring he was finished with the high wire.

Steve could hardly believe those words had come from his father's mouth.

"This time I mean it," Gunther insisted. "I've lost my teeth. What will I lose next? There has to be a better way to make a living."

"But Gunther," his Uncle Karl chided, assuming his nephew was merely overreacting to the recent accidents. "You don't walk the wire with your teeth!" The group erupted in laughter. Gunther took the comment in stride, not at all ashamed about his own sense of self-preservation. At the same time, he understood the force that drove the others on to their next challenge.

"I'm scared silly every time I go on the wire," Gunther told a reporter, confirming reports of his early and unexpected retirement. "It's the kind of fear that shatters my confidence. It makes me believe that somebody's trying to tell me something—it's time to hang it up."

His father's departure from the business left Steve with his own feelings of self-doubt. These were only intensified when tragedy struck again in 1963. Another family member, Rietta Grotefent, affectionately known as "Aunt Yetty," fell to her death from a sway pole in Omaha, Nebraska.

Since Steve had been close to her in his early childhood, her sudden death was a crushing blow. It came at a time when there were serious questions about where Steve was going to be raised, and by whom. During his early days in Florida, Aunt Yetty had tried to adopt Steve. After she perished, he returned to his grandparents in California once again, and all contact between him and his father ended. He was left with the distinct impression that Gunther was eager to rid himself of his past, which included his own son.

Despite the tragic accidents and the rising body count, Steve had come to appreciate the Wallenda family philosophy, which centered on the worn cliche, "the show must go on." He was not about to follow his father's lead.

One close call in 1966 did give him second thoughts. It occurred when he was riding a bicycle on the high wire, under his Uncle Leon's watchful eye. For some reason, panic set in when he was about halfway across and he stopped in his tracks.

Aerialists must adapt their bicycles to the wire by removing the tire and innertube, allowing the wire to slip into the curved crevice of the tire rim. As long as the rider can keep his balance, he can keep the bike on the wire, even while holding fast in one place.

# HIGH WIRE ANGEL

On this perilous trip, anxiety overtook Steve and he began to imagine the bodies of his departed relatives lying on the ground under the wire. This image flashed on and off several times, causing him to stop riding and close his eyes in an attempt to regain his composure.

"Forward! Forward!" Leon shouted from below. "Are you all right?" That snapped Steve back to reality and he managed to peddle to the safety of the opposite mounting platform.

Because there was no life net below the wire, a fall from that height could have been fatal. This family tradition of not using a net has its roots in a number of long-held beliefs among aerial performers. Obviously, it adds to the drama of wire-walking by injecting an authentic element of crowd-pleasing danger. In addition, the presence of a net is no guarantee of survival in the event of a fall. But, most importantly, professional aerialists have found that the presence of a safety net can give them a false sense of security. It sends the message that it's okay to fall. This can hinder the concentration that is necessary for a performer to fully develop his skills.

A combination of youthful restlessness and Vietnam Era patriotic fervor drove Steve to leave school and abandon his budding career to join the U.S. Army. Still in his teens, he got his wish: deployment to the Vietnam War with the 101st Airborne.

Returning to the U.S. after receiving his honorable discharge, Steve spent time in college, studying pre-med and ocean ecology before he was lured away by the opportunity to become a stuntman with the Hollywood studios. He became a regular on "The Mod Squad" and "Mission Impossible," while also appearing in "Mannix," "The Young Lawyers," "The Rookies," and other prime time TV series. He earned a reputation of being a daredevil who would take chances that few other stunt men would even consider.

Doing stunts in Hollywood, at least at that time, was not as glamorous a job as many people believe. The pay was lousy, job security almost non-existent, and the work extremely dangerous. Steve had a close call while he was trying out for "The Rookies," practicing a stunt that involved a back flip off a trampoline. He came down slightly off-balance and smashed his head into a pipe, opening a huge gash that required 120 stitches to close.

Soon afterwards, actor Peter Graves, who was starring in "Mission Impossible" at the time, helped Steve decide to escape from the Hollywood scene. The two had become friends after meeting on the set of the popular TV series. One afternoon, Steve, who had just finished filming a stunt involving a leap from the roof of a burning building, was limping badly from a sore ankle.

Peter called him aside and bluntly opined that Steve's wire-walking talent was being wasted while he continued to risk life and limb for the meager pay from the TV studios. One more serious injury could ruin him as an aerialist forever. Not long after that conversation, Steve left the business and began to look for work with a circus.

Yet another member of the extended Wallenda family lost his life in 1972. Karl Wallenda's son-in-law, Chico Gusman, was electrocuted when his balancing pole hit a live electrical wire during an aerial performance in Wheeling, West Virginia.

Steve had his own brush with death later that year when he fell from atop a military tank, crashing to the pavement below. He broke bones in his neck and back. At first, doctors said he could be paralyzed for life. Weeks later, he was back on his feet.

Soon afterwards, he was practicing on the wire with his Uncle Leon again, despite the doctors' suggestions that he find a safer line of work. They said any aggravation of the injuries could cause Steve to suffer permanent paralysis.

On March 22, 1978, the nation looked on in shock and sorrow as 73-year-old Karl Wallenda fell to his death during a high wire walk between two hotels in San Juan, Puerto Rico. The television cameras brought the fall to the nation's attention in graphic detail.

Steve was living in Concord, California at the time. He was already beginning to build a solid performing reputation of his own and had most recently been hired to walk the tramway that ran sixty feet high over Nolan State Park in Oakland.

News of Karl's death sent Steve into a deep state of depression. Karl had been the patriarch of the family, its most identifiable figure, and the one Wallenda who was totally dedicated to skywalking and show business. Steve had the highest respect for Karl's ability and his commitment to the profession.

Memories of his granduncle flooded back to him as he watched the evening news' close-up footage from the accident. He recalled how, as a teenager, he had been riding in a car with his Aunt Verlee (wife of his Uncle Leon) and Karl Wallenda. Verlee playfully teased Karl that young Steve was becoming quite accomplished and might one day go down in history as the greatest wire walker of all time—even better than Karl himself.

"Perhaps you will," Karl replied in the German accent that he never lost. "But you're going to have to work for it, son. You're really going to have to work for it."

Just four days after Karl's death, suffering jet lag after a hastily-arranged New York to California flight, Steve slipped while he was walking the tramway cable in Oakland. He was able to catch the wire with his right armpit and climb back on top.

The accident proved to be considerably more serious than the initial diagnosis had indicated. As the days passed, Steve lost most of the feeling in his right arm. Significant nerve damage had occurred in his arm, affecting his equilibrium and prohibiting him from carrying his fifty-five pound balancing pole. He was grounded for several months while he underwent rehabilitation.

In the interim, while waiting for the feeling to return to his arm, he got a job as a private investigator and worked as a security guard for Paramount Studios.

# HIGH WIRE ANGEL

Karl's accident had focused renewed attention on the Wallenda family. The national media discovered that there was another Wallenda who was talented at walking the wire. As soon as he was able to perform once again, Steve appeared on ABC-TV's "Good Morning America" for a wire walk. He was also featured in People magazine that same week.

Such recognition enabled him to realize that he had a highly marketable skill. His long absence from the high wire made him that much more anxious to build upon his reputation when he returned. The attention also provided Steve with something that every performing artist needs: a feeling that all of his commitment to developing a special talent is appreciated.

He would go on to perform some aerial feats never before imagined and, in the process, raise thousands of dollars for worthwhile causes. He had recently concluded a tour as part of a patriotic extravaganza featuring the Osmonds when he pulled into the Westchester Mall with the Wallenda traveling museum.

Chapter 6

# MEANT TO BE

Did fate dictate that Steve would walk into Lizzie's life as she busily went about her duties at Dipper Dan's Ice Cream Shoppe? Their diverse backgrounds, the difference in their ages, and the profound impact they would have on each other all combined to suggest that they did not come together merely by chance.

There also may have been an element of predestination at work in the union of Lizzie's parents. Unfortunately, they did not live happily ever after. When Elizabeth Eve arrived on March 20, 1968, she was the sixth of seven children her parents would try to raise.

Her father, Frederick Pintye, had escaped the communist takeover of Hungary when he was a teenager, crossing over into Austria and soon traveling to the Dominican Republic. There, he discovered that the government's offer of property at bargain prices was too good to be true. The land he acquired consisted of swamps and bogs, suitable for neither agriculture nor any other productive use.

His dreams of operating a small farm in Latin America shattered, Frederick eventually decided to seek fame and fortune as a professional athlete in the United States. He thought the streets of America were paved with gold, but he discovered that the Europeans' game of "football" (soccer) bore little resemblance to the professional football of the United States.

So, this 20-year-old Hungarian immigrant, who spoke little English, found himself stranded and virtually penniless, in New York City. He was lucky in one respect: he had learned to shift for himself at an early age and was self-educated in the world of street survival.

His father died at an early age and Frederick was raised by his grandmother in the same kind of strict environment that he would later insist upon in his own household—with no toys and little social life. To his grandmother, life revolved around school, chores, and reading. Frederick's outlet was soccer, and he played it with a vengeance.

Hannah, the woman he would marry, escaped from Hungary with her family, moving to Brazil in the late 1950s. She was the youngest of ten children. Her teenage years were a nightmare as both of her parents battled alcohol problems that drained the family's finances and filled the home with tension.

Hannah was a talented artist who specialized in oil realism. She loved to paint city scenes that featured unique architecture, or ocean settings with subtle color patterns, particularly in the sky. Many of her works were prize-winners, but she had to sell them to keep food on the table.

She also earned money by singing in the Rio de Janeiro nightclubs. Hannah fell in love with a club owner who fathered her first child, Charles. This Brazilian businessman abandoned her a few weeks after the baby was born. She eventually rejoined her parents, who had relocated to the Hungarian section of Tarrytown, New York.

Frederick was working as a locker boy in a ritzy suburban New York country club when one of his friends introduced him to Hannah. She looked vaguely familiar, but he could not place her until they started talking. He was stunned to discover that he had been at her house and had actually met her back when they were teenagers in Hungary.

Within a matter of months they were married, and both went to work at the General Motors factory at Tarrytown, where Frederick still works today. They moved with the baby into a house in nearby Ossining, and Frederick accepted Charles as if he were his own son.

Away from the Hungarian community, their ways seemed strange to their new neighbors. They spoke in their native language and their customs were strikingly different. They had hoped to raise a huge family, but their first effort to have a child failed when a baby boy was stillborn.

This proved to be a searing and indelible experience for Hannah. She cried for days on end and eventually suffered a nervous breakdown that forced her to quit her job, the beginning of a battle with emotional problems that would continue for the rest of her life. After numerous therapy sessions and other treatment, she attempted to settle in as a homemaker while her husband supported the family, often with double work shifts.

Children arrived at a pattern of about one per year—first James in 1964, the following year Mark, then Ernie, Jeannie, and Elizabeth. As the family grew, so did the financial and social pressures. Hannah was hopelessly overwhelmed by the many responsibilities of caring for so many children. She often neglected their needs and secluded herself in her bedroom where she cried herself to sleep or buried her head in her pillows. To top things off, she discovered that she once again was pregnant.

Due to his short temper and his own upbringing, Frederick never hesitated to use severe discipline on his children for the slightest misbehavior. When Charles' teacher noticed belt marks on the boy's arm and was informed that these had been inflicted by Frederick, school officials notified the Child Welfare Department that all was not well in the Pintye household.

So began a long involvement between New York State social workers and the Pintyes. It only took a brief interview to tell the investigators that Hannah Pintye was unable to take proper care of so many children. Legal authorities threatened to seize all six children and place them in foster homes. But Frederick Pintye was a proud, self-reliant man who resented any intervention by the government. He reached a compromise with the Department of Social Services which would allow his children to remain at home as long as a county homemaker stayed there during the days.

In-fighting among the older boys and further evidence of excessive discipline by their father led social workers to seek a court order to remove the children. Frederick became aware that the petition was in the works and immediately moved the family just over the state border to a house in Danbury, Connecticut. The New York State child welfare officials could not intervene because the family was now outside of their jurisdiction. They apparently made no efforts to alert their Connecticut counterparts to the Pintyes' unusual family situation.

Frederick had rented a huge truck and hired two men to handle moving arrangements while he remained in Ossining to sell his former home. One of the movers was Kenny, a rough-looking man in his late twenties, who took a romantic interest in Hannah. After all of the furniture had been moved and the truck returned, he persuaded her to allow him to sleep over that night.

Any progress she had made in coping with her problems was erased as Kenny took advantage of her vulnerability. His stay grew from one night to several weeks.

He spiked her drinks with large doses of LSD, rendering her nearly unable to function, and became a terrible influence on the children. While smoking marijuana and snorting cocaine, he often forced the children to join him. Lizzie and her sister Jeannie were still much too young to smoke by themselves, so Kenny would place the marijuana joint, ember first, in his mouth and then blow into it, sending a stream of smoke into their faces allowing them to inhale it.

Frederick continued working and looking forward to the time when his family would be together again. He naturally assumed that Kenny and the other mover had deposited the furniture and gone on their way. He continued to send his wife money to buy food and pay other bills, but Kenny confiscated it to buy beer and drugs.

Connecticut social workers were not alerted to the family's bizarre circumstances until James and Mark brought thermos bottles full of blackberry brandy to school to drink with their lunches. That evening the house was rocking with loud music when a woman from the child welfare agency knocked on the door. Receiving no answer she peered in the window, and was shocked to discover that all of the home's occupants were nude.

Later that night, uniformed officers charged into the house, their guns drawn. The terrified children cried and threw things at the officers while Kenny and Hannah were handcuffed and held at gunpoint. Lizzie started to run away to hide under her bed, but an officer scooped her up and held her under his arm. Several policemen loaded the children into two cars and took them away. All six children were placed in a temporary shelter and then transferred to separate foster homes in nearby communities.

Now in the latter stages of pregnancy, Hannah suffered another breakdown from the ordeal and was hospitalized once again. Kenny would never bother the family again. Jailed on drug charges, he committed suicide by hanging himself in his cell. When Hannah gave birth to another son, Thomas, he was promptly seized and placed in a foster home.

Lizzie was thrust into a foster home setting where her emotional scars and inability to communicate were immediately evident to the foster mother, Lynn Sandbank. The separation from her brothers and sister was painful for Lizzie. She cried for a major portion of her first few days with the Sandbanks. Aggravating her situation was a language gap. For the most part, Lizzie spoke Hungarian and was unable to convey her thoughts or understand what her foster parents were saying.

At the age of three, she was relocated to another home in Carmel, New York. Her new foster parents, John and Pat Wilson, welcomed her with open arms. They had just lost two other foster children unexpectedly, and were anxious for another child to help them get over the heartbreak.

They did all they could to make Lizzie feel at home, and she adapted well, partly because she was rapidly learning how to speak English. They were kind, wholesome people who treated her as a part of the family. From the start, the Wilsons insisted on being called "Mom" and "Dad." Lizzie made rapid progress in developing her social skills, and showed few ill effects from the tumultuous scenes that marked the first couple of years of her life.

However, shortly before her fourth birthday, just as the Wilsons were making plans to adopt her, the child welfare agency informed them that Frederick and Hannah Pintye had patched up their differences and were anxious to resume life with their children. Tearfully, John and Pat Wilson said good-bye to Lizzie, promising they would always care about the little girl whom they had grown to love like a daughter.

Chapter 7

# BACK HOME AGAIN

Two social workers took Lizzie to a cold, empty room at the top floor of an office building so she could meet her family. Seated off in a corner, she started fidgeting with the leaves of an artificial rubber plant, scared and worried about what was going to happen.

Across the room was her sister Jeannie, the only person she recognized. Seated next to her was a woman from the social services agency who was holding little Thomas in her lap.

The door swung open and a man and a woman walked in. She was petite, attractive, and well-dressed, with nice blue eyes that crinkled as she smiled. The man's light brown hair was shining as he followed along a step behind, almost as if he were hiding. He looked troubled, even frightened.

The man who was in charge of the reunion leaned back in his chair behind a huge, empty desktop and chose his words carefully. "Well, everybody, we are here for a very happy occasion today," he began. "If that man and woman over there are strangers to you, they won't be for long. You see, Jeannie, Elizabeth, and Thomas, these are your parents. They're your mommy and your daddy. And today is a very special day for all of you, because today you are going to be going home with your mommy and daddy. You're going to live with them and they're going to take very good care of you."

Lizzie felt special—most girls her age only had one mother and father, but now she had two of each! The three children clumsily piled into the back seat of their parents' car for the short trip back to Ossining. Frederick Pintye was clearly nervous as he drove. He kept looking in the rear-view mirror, trying to reacquaint himself with the two young girls who had been away from him for so long. Finally, he invited Lizzie and Jeannie to climb over the seat so they could take turns sitting on his lap and pretending that they were turning the steering wheel as he drove.

Lizzie, Jeannie, and Thomas quickly became pals. Having two children who were close to her in age helped assuage Lizzie's loneliness. She soon felt the sense of security that could only come from being with her real family. Her half-brother Charles was back home by then, quite a bit older than the rest of the children and decidedly standoffish, even mean at times. Within a year, the three brothers, Mark, Ernest, and James, had also returned home.

Soon after they were all settled in, Hannah Pintye suffered another breakdown and was forced to undergo additional inpatient treatment. She had sustained serious head injuries in an automobile accident while all of the children were away, which exacerbated her condition. The added pressure of seven children and an ornery husband to care for snowballed for this unfortunate woman.

Lizzie's excitement over being back home was muted by her mother's absence. She was too young to understand, but the words of her father explaining that "Mama has to go away for a while so that doctors can make her all better" rang in her ears.

He realized that the social workers would be keeping close tabs on his family, so he hired an extremely overweight black woman named Mrs. Bush as a maid. The children became attached to their housekeeper because of her sincere friendliness and understanding. From her loud floral-print blouses to her cheery disposition, Mrs. Bush became an oasis of warmth and kindness to the Pintye kids.

She took them for walks to the store or down by the river to feed bread to the birds. Occasionally, she would slip the children a quarter apiece and allow them to buy their own candy bars, as long as they promised not to tell their dad.

Their mother returned from the hospital after a stay of about three months and was like a new person—full of life and happy to be back home with her family. She took pains to make certain that the children were well-fed, well-dressed, and clean. She even played tennis and other games with them. Her dream was that she could have a happy marriage and a pleasant home atmosphere. Happiness was an element that had long been lacking in her life. Unfortunately, the romantic family portrait that she tried to create did not last.

At the hospital, Hannah Pintye developed a close friendship with a volunteer social worker named Bill O'Grady. An elderly Irish widower, this retired Naval officer became known as "Uncle Bill" to the family. Bill was robust, warm, and happy-go-lucky. He seemed to sing his words in a jolly Irish brogue, his voice loud and confident. Bill could bring a whole room to life just by walking through the doorway.

He often took Hannah and all the children to the local Naval Officers' Club where he'd buy them Shirley Temples and plug quarters into video games. Sometimes they all would go to the history museum or feed the pigeons in the park. Bill frequently tried to encourage the Pintye children to discuss their future. "You can do anything you set your mind on doing," was one of his standard lines. Lizzie took his message to heart. In the years to follow, as she continued to mature, she would not be afraid to take chances or try new things.

After witnessing the warmth that flowed between their mother and Uncle Bill, the children yearned to see some signs of affection between their parents—touching, smiling, and laughing. It never happened. Their father had a hard time showing signs of love or happiness.

Hannah was never allowed to develop any friendships, with the exception of her relationship with Uncle Bill. Frederick would never take her out of the house to mingle. The highlight of her week was her trip to the grocery store every Saturday morning, or a walk down to the curb to get the day's mail. Uncle Bill could only rarely visit because of his advancing age and the long distance he had to travel from his home in Boston.

The only attention the children usually got from their father was discipline. His favorite punishment was push-ups. If he dozed off on the couch and one of the children woke him up, he would order all of them down onto the hard wooden floor to do push-ups. It didn't matter who was the guilty party. If he was mad, they all paid the price. Pleas for mercy went unanswered as Frederick stood over his charges like a drill instructor. Woe to anyone who tried to question his authority or judgment. On those rare occasions when his wife tried to intervene, he ordered her out of the room—and she always acquiesced.

It all traced back to his own childhood. He was taught that children were to be seen and not heard, and that toys were a waste of time and money. Lizzie and her siblings made their own playthings out of old milk jugs and egg cartons. They pretended they were running a grocery store and used toothpicks or pebbles for money. A dumping ground in the woods near the house was a virtual treasure trove to the Pintye kids. They sorted through the junk that people had thrown away, retrieving worn-out toys and other things to play with. Through it all, Lizzie was learning valuable lessons about appreciating those few possessions she did have and adapting to her circumstances, as meager as they might be.

Her father's attitude was particularly hard on the children at Christmas time. Others in the neighborhood would wake up and find bicycles, games, or pretty clothes that Santa Claus had left for them. For the Pintye kids, Christmas consisted of a tree with candy hanging from it. Their mother would make the best of it, gathering her children around the tree to sing Christmas carols and traditional Hungarian songs she had learned when she was a child. She had a beautiful singing voice and knew all the words by heart. A special smile on her face when she sang suggested there was nothing in life that made her happier.

Frederick Pintye did have a nice side to him, but his children rarely saw it. Every once in a while, he brought home a watermelon to share with the family or he took the children to Echo Lake to watch the ducks. Occasionally, he would let them sit along the shore while he was fishing. They could skip rocks or dip their bare feet in the cool, refreshing water.

There was a clear motive behind Frederick's decision to move his family to Mahopac in Putnam County, New York. Child welfare workers had been

# HIGH WIRE ANGEL

paying close attention to his family once again. Concerned that they might be planning to remove some of the children, Frank recognized that the move would place his family in another jurisdiction, covered by another agency.

The improvement in Hannah's emotional state proved to be only temporary. About a month after the family moved, she had the most serious of her breakdowns. She was wiping the kitchen counters when she suddenly fell to the floor and started crying uncontrollably, as Lizzie and Jeannie looked on in terror.

With his wife back in the hospital, Frederick was obviously in over his head as he tried to run the household. Not only was he working overtime at General Motors, but he had also taken a part-time job overseeing the wing of a school for wayward boys. More often than not, his own children were home by themselves with no supervision.

Many months passed before their mother returned. She had lost the spark of life that had been so evident the last time she returned. Although she tried to cook the meals, clean the house, and do the laundry, these jobs were major challenges for her. She showed little emotion or concern for the rest of the family.

Her moods would fluctuate, keeping the children guessing what type of behavior to expect from minute to minute. Once in a while she would recite Russian folk tales for them or sing Hungarian nursery rhymes, only to stop abruptly—just when the children were beginning to have fun—and go off to do housework or watch TV.

She was even moody around Bill O'Grady, sometimes losing her temper and ordering him to go back to Boston and leave her alone forever. Bill never talked back to her, nor did he allow her outbursts to affect his sunny disposition. He made a point to tell Lizzie that she shouldn't let the things her mother did or said bother her, because she was a very sick woman and therefore needed to be shown a lot of love.

It was only a matter of time before the Pintye kids began to run loose. With no one keeping them accountable, they cut classes at school and hitchhiked into the business district to shoplift toys and candy, or they embarked on other adventures that the older brothers cooked up. This traveling band of juvenile delinquents remained safe as long as they returned home in time to cook dinner for their father. He came home only to eat and sleep and then he was right back out the door for his four-hour stint at the detention home. Many nights, as soon as he walked in the door, he lined up all seven of the children and hit them with his belt. He reasoned that they must have done something wrong sometime during the day. Striking them all was his way of making sure they were punished for it.

With few clothes to wear, the children went to school with the same outfits on day after day, often with dirty faces and hands. They hardly ever ate breakfast, and their father rarely gave them lunch money for school. The only meal they had with any regularity was dinner, which their dad insisted be ready by the time he got home from work. He would eat first, by himself, then allow the children to help themselves to whatever food remained.

Meal preparation responsibilities fell to Lizzie and Jeannie. Sometimes they would burn the food or use the wrong ingredients, which would make their father furious, but more often than not they would produce some semblance of a meal.

Through all of this, the Pintye children had no idea that their family situation was unusual. Lizzie and Jeannie didn't realize that other five- and six-year-old girls weren't cooking for their fathers or digging their toys out of the junkyard. Some of the neighbors would occasionally invite them in for sandwiches and hot chocolate, or stop the kids on their way to school to comb their hair and wash their faces. These neighbors and school officials were also in touch with the Putnam County Child Welfare Department.

Chapter 8

# WE'RE DIFFERENT

Throughout Elizabeth Pintye's life she has pondered the significance of an experience that occurred on Thanksgiving morning at her parents' house in Mahopac. Some people who have heard the story have passed it off as a fancy flight of her imagination. But she steadfastly insists that the experience was real.

Lizzie had locked herself in the bathroom, concealing a picture book, *The Tortoise and the Hare,* that she had taken from her kindergarten classroom. She glanced over to her right and saw a peculiar image standing only about three feet away.

It had the shape of a human being, but it was smoke-like white and Lizzie could see through it to the opposite wall. Her eyes first caught sight of it at floor level, where she could make out a robe and bare feet. As she started to trace this shape upward, she was even more shocked to discover that it ended around the waist. There was no upper torso.

The longer Lizzie stared, the more frightened she grew until she turned her head away and squeezed her eyes shut as tightly as she could. When she looked back to where it had been standing, it was gone. Lizzie went running into the living room where her sister and brothers were watching a parade on TV, and screamed, "Hey, everybody! I just saw Jesus's mother Mary, right in our own bathroom!" To this day, she has no idea where those words came from. She saw nothing that would have identified the apparition, and she had never been to church or learned about the story of Christ, other than to ask her mother questions about a cross that hung on the wall above the headboard of her bed.

Lizzie's description was so convincing that all of the other children went dashing into the bathroom to see this strange being. When they found nothing unusual, they chastised their sister for her mischievousness.

It was all Lizzie could think about for days. She marveled at its mystery and pondered its significance for the longest time, finally accepting it as an experience that suggests there is much more to life than meets the eye. She can still recreate the image in her mind in stark detail, as if it were standing next to her again.

This occurred during a time when the Pintye family was slipping deeper into poverty. One of the neighbors gave Lizzie and Jeannie a huge plastic garbage bag packed full of second-hand clothes. They dragged the bulging bag home and sneaked up to their bedroom to try them on.

There were long, lace-trimmed dresses and pretty blouses and sweaters of all colors and sizes. The sisters pretended they were wealthy princesses as they flitted back and forth in front of the full-length mirror. Suddenly, the door burst open, almost knocking Lizzie over, and their father stormed into the room.

"Where did you get all of that stuff?" he demanded.

"The neighbors gave it to us; honest, Dad," Lizzie answered. "They said they were going to put it out for the garbage if we didn't want it. Look how pretty we look."

"You two stuff these things back in that bag right now and take it all back! You've got enough clothes. What do you think we are, a goddamned charity case?"

"Can't we just keep one outfit each?" Jeannie pleaded.

"No! Get 'em out of here right now!"

The girls wept as they began gathering up the clothes, which had been flung all over the room in their excitement to try them on.

"I have an idea," Jeannie said. "Let's hide them. He'll never know we didn't take 'em back if we can find a good hiding place."

"That's right. He never talks to the neighbors anyhow. Let's stash them under the back porch and then we can change into them when he's not looking."

Each morning, Lizzie and Jeannie stole around the corner of the house and crawled under the porch to pick out something to wear to school. Then they hid behind the neighbors' shrubbery and changed.

This continued for about a week, until Jeannie confessed and their father made the girls take everything back. Lizzie tried to outsmart him by keeping a blue and white striped dress that she had fallen in love with. Jeannie eventually told about that one, too, which made Lizzie furious. When she got back from returning the dress, she slapped Jeannie in the face, resulting in a huge red welt under her eye. That was nothing unusual; even though Lizzie was younger, she frequently attacked her sister and brothers.

For some reason, their father insisted that Jeannie be very ladylike, but he wanted Lizzie to be tough. He was especially proud of her when she stood up for herself or helped anyone in the family avoid humiliation.

One time the children were standing in line, waiting to get on the school bus, when a couple of the neighborhood bullies cut in front of them and began picking on James. When they started pulling his hair and ripped a big hole in his shirt, Lizzie charged into both of them and knocked one boy to the ground. Then she started beating on his head with her book bag until he got to his feet and ran away. Blood was streaming from his nose and mud covered his backside.

That evening, while discussing the incident with the school principal, Lizzie's father started laughing. After he hung up the phone, he called her over to his chair and told her he was proud of her for sticking up for her family.

Violence was no stranger to the family. The children would hit each other over the head with broomsticks, vacuum cleaner hoses, or whatever else was handy. Occasionally, a meat cleaver or butcher knife would be hauled out of a kitchen drawer for emphasis. Within minutes of these flare-ups, everything would return to normal, and the kids would be plotting some scheme to acquire toys or candy.

This unlimited freedom for the Pintyes came to an end when they were apprehended for smashing a window and burglarizing their neighbor's home. Within a week, Lizzie and Jeannie were on their way to Lake Carmel, less than an hour from Mahopac, to live with another set of foster parents, Harold and Cynthia Earl. Their brothers were also sent to foster homes, except for Charles, who after an argument ran away from home and joined the Army.

Joining the conventional family setting with the Earls proved to be a difficult transition. Jeannie and Lizzie had been taught some very strange habits. For instance, their father had always told them to chew very loudly, with their mouths wide open, so he could be sure they were really eating. Of course, this is what the girls did at the dinner table with Mr. and Mrs. Earl and their two children. After a few meals, Mrs. Earl finally suggested that Lizzie and Jeannie close their mouths when they chew. "Why?" Lizzie asked. "How will you know if we're eating?"

"It's common courtesy," she replied. "There's a lot you girls don't know about manners, but we're going to teach you."

The Earls allowed Lizzie and Jeannie to accompany them on vacations to North Carolina to see the farm country and get a taste of rural life. Foster children weren't supposed to leave New York State, but the Earls took a chance. Lizzie loved the rolling countryside, with open fields and grazing cattle. She hadn't realized there were any places like that. All she knew was the hard concrete and patchwork development of the New York suburbs. She resolved that, once she grew up, she was going to live in the country.

Mr. and Mrs. Earl enrolled the girls in a Catholic school where the teachers took pains to instruct their female students on how to be proper young ladies. This involved a whole new mode of behavior for the Pintye sisters. For starters, Lizzie had to recognize that, notwithstanding her father's encouragement, hitting other people or hurting them in any other way was wrong.

Although they gradually started having "home visits" at their parents' house on weekends, the girls felt uncomfortable staying there for just two days at a time. Traveling back and forth became tedious. Things were particularly confusing at Christmas time. Lizzie and Jeannie spent the actual holiday with their mom and dad, but they also celebrated with the Earls.

The Earls bought both girls Christmas presents; at their parents' home, they received none. To cover up their embarrassment, Jeannie and Lizzie made up stories about all of the gifts they had received from their parents and had left back at the house in Mahopac.

Their mother seemed to be no better than she was the last time they saw her. She said things that made no sense and gave people blank stares, as if she were miles away. Frederick Pintye had grown protective of his wife. "She gets like that sometimes," he would tell the children. "She's taking a lot of medication. It's from the car wreck, you know. Just let her go and she'll be fine."

His overall disposition had improved and he started warming up to his family. For her eighth birthday, he gave Lizzie $15 and took her to a store so she could pick out her own gift. She grew ecstatic when she spotted a Shirley Temple doll, with soft, curly hair that she could comb. Shirley Temple had been Lizzie's early childhood idol. With old-time movies always on TV in the mornings, Lizzie sat in front of the set entranced by the way the child star danced and sang. She wanted to be "somebody" too. The Shirley Temple doll came to mean more to Lizzie than any toy she ever had. As dirty and battered as it became, she never parted with it.

As time passed, the Pintye sisters found it harder to conform their behavior to Mr. and Mrs. Earl's expectations. As they approached the early stages of adolescence, they grew stubborn and resistant. Each of the girls fueled this spirit of rebelliousness in the other. Eventually, Lizzie and Jeannie started refusing orders and telling the Earls how much they wanted to leave their home. Convinced that the girls had grown too difficult to control, the Earls set the wheels in motion for their relocation to another foster home.

Chapter 9

# A BAD GIRL

Foster parents are supposed to be closely screened to make sure that sex perverts, child abusers, and other unsuitable individuals are weeded out. The system doesn't always work as well as some people would like to think. Part of the problem is a constant turnover in social workers, which can be attributed largely to low pay, difficult working conditions, and job burnout. At least 15 different caseworkers were responsible for Elizabeth Pintye's well-being during her childhood. Just as one of them would begin to understand her needs and the bizarre circumstances of her upbringing, another one would be assigned to her case. But out of the holocaust of those abysmal days and nights came the recognition of an inner strength that was destined to sustain Lizzie in the more trying times that lay ahead.

Richard and Pat Brook had four children of their own when Lizzie joined their household. Richard, a truck driver who was on the road more than he was home, was quiet and unassuming. Pat was grossly overweight, in stark contrast to wedding pictures which revealed that she had once been a beautiful, shapely woman. She was consumed by household duties, trying to tend to kids while she worked around her husband's schedule.

Lizzie's successful adjustment to this new foster home was reflected in many ways. She became a straight-A student and looked forward to going to school each day, partly because she developed a close circle of friends and partly because she welcomed the challenge of her schoolwork. Mrs. Brook also enrolled her in Sunday School, another social setting in which she blossomed. Church members warmly embraced Lizzie.

Although her visits back home continued, Lizzie could feel herself growing apart from her natural parents. They were still trying to force the Child Welfare Department to return their children on a permanent basis.

Gradually, Richard and Pat Brook persuaded her to discontinue these home visits, pointing out that the social workers could not compel her to visit her parents if she refused.

"You know, they're just going to destroy you," Pat would tell her. "Your father's an evil man who wants to hurt you and your mother has lost her mind. You belong with us, where you're safe."

Pat secretly took the clothing allowance the Child Welfare Department supplied for Lizzie's needs and spent it on expensive, stylish clothes for her own children. Lizzie ended up with hand-me-downs that looked like they came from the bottom of the heap at a Salvation Army outlet.

Having grown dependent on Pat Brook for love and support, Lizzie desperately tried to do things that might make her happy. For two months straight, she carried books to the school cafeteria and studied, rather than eat during lunch period. She amassed a small fortune in unspent lunch money, all piling up in the pencil box of her desk. When she had enough money saved, Lizzie bought Mrs. Brook a box of expensive chocolates and a nice designer sweater. Pat had little reaction upon opening the packages, and the gifts made no difference in the way she treated Lizzie.

None of it made any sense at the time. Lizzie now realizes that the Brooks were making every effort to destroy her reputation and credibility so nobody would believe her if she tried to tell authorities the alarming truth about what was transpiring in the Brook household: Richard was systematically using the female foster children to satisfy his sexual desires and was photographing these young victims in the nude, then selling the photos through an underground "kiddie porn" network.

Lizzie herself became a victim of his black market photography business, but she never allowed herself to fall victim to his sexual advances—not that he didn't try. Each time he attempted to have his way with her, she resisted until he finally accepted the fact the Lizzie was not going to submit to him. Her resistance was a matter of desperation—she was on the verge of a nervous breakdown—and a manifestation of the lessons her father had instilled about standing her ground. Richard Brook was trying to take away a part of her, and she was not about to let him have it without a fight.

Lizzie found it odd that, whenever Richard and Pat decided to show what they referred to as "home movies," the children in these films were depicted in the nude. Now on the verge of adolescence, and in the process of forming her own concepts of human sexuality, she felt embarrassed when he ordered her to remove her clothes and position herself in various poses for a brief photography session in his makeshift studio, located in the basement of the Brook home.

The Child Welfare Department caseworkers are supposed to keep tabs on the relationship between the foster parents and the child. Pat also had this base covered. Because the Brooks had been looking after foster children for years, she had become close friends with the social workers—so close that one of them was bringing her own one-year-old son to be watched on weekdays.

Each time Lizzie was alone with a caseworker, she wanted to talk about what the Brooks had been doing to her, but something kept holding her back. The social worker was already scolding her for all of the terrible things Pat said

# HIGH WIRE ANGEL

she was doing. Lizzie was sternly warned that if she didn't behave, she would be sent to a reform school, where the truly "bad girls" go.

Increasingly, she began to believe that she *was* a terrible person. She avoided everybody, thinking that one way she could stay out of trouble was to go off by herself. Schoolwork became Lizzie's outlet and her only source of pride. She'd retreat to her bedroom to study or to escape into adventure stories she borrowed from the school library.

Sometimes, she picked wild strawberries in the field behind the house or went swimming in solitude at a small pond down the road. If Lizzie saw others coming, she would climb one of the tallest maple trees that flanked the pond and peer out through the leaves at the swimmers below, wishing she was like everybody else.

Lizzie felt alone in the world. She believed that everyone disliked her. She became nervous and awkward around other people because she wanted so badly to please them. The only place Lizzie believed she could ever feel comfortable again was at her parents' home, and she had effectively closed that door behind her. She had nowhere to turn.

Lizzie started plotting ways to run away, but each time she summoned the courage to leave, something held her back. She remembered the warnings that she would be sent to "bad girl" school if she ever got caught. At times, she believed that might be an improvement over the conditions with the Brooks.

Other foster kids came and went. On one occasion, a young boy who had just joined the household fell and cut his forehead. Pat Brook told the social workers Lizzie had pushed the boy. Another time, she told the caseworker and neighbors that Lizzie had tried to drown the Brook's young daughter.

A fourteen-year-old girl named Stephanie moved in with the Brooks and they went out of their way to be nice to her. The reason for this did not become obvious to Lizzie until one afternoon when she found Stephanie sitting on Richard's lap, his hand up under her blouse. She only stayed for about a month, which was long enough for her to tell Lizzie that Richard had taken nude pictures of her and had forced her to have sex with him several times. As shocked as she was by these revelations, Lizzie was also thankful that Richard had backed off when she stood her ground.

Throughout the remainder of her childhood, Lizzie remained silent about the Brooks' activities. To talk about it would have required her to think about it, and all she wanted to do was erase it from her memory.[1]

Particularly after hearing Stephanie's stories, Lizzie had a horrifying fear that Richard eventually would try to overpower her and refuse to take "no" for an answer. She started letting everyone know how badly she wanted to leave the

---

[1]In November 1991, Richard W. Brook, 52, was arrested in Hernando County, Florida, north of Tampa, after a raid on his home resulted in the seizure of pornographic photographs and videos. Police were tipped off about Brook's illegal activities by Henry Hurt, roving editor for Reader's Digest, after Hurt interviewed Angel Wallenda for a feature story and learned of her experiences at the home of Richard and Pat Brook in Carmel, New York.

Brook household, even if it meant joining all of the other "bad girls" in reform school. Once the caseworker realized how desperate Lizzie was, she began making arrangements to obtain a court order to send her to Saint Cabrini's Residential Treatment Center.

Part of the application process at Saint Cabrini's was a tour by the prospective resident. Lizzie found this quite discomforting. Three girls were crowded into each little dormitory-style room. A school within the grounds was surrounded by a high fence, topped by razor wire, much like a penitentiary.

"Hey, ladies, looks like we got some new blood coming in," said one of the sassy teenage girls who gathered in the doorway as Lizzie and the caseworker passed by. Another girl whistled and winked at Lizzie. "I'll see *you* later," she said in a disgusting voice that caused Lizzie to look away in fear.

Juvenile court proceedings would take several weeks, so Lizzie was transferred to another foster home to stay while the petition worked its way through the New York State legal system. It didn't take Bill and Joyce Barrett long to recognize that this was not the problem child Pat Brook had made her out to be. They got along great with Lizzie from the start.

Lizzie was supposed to be sent to Saint Cabrini's for two months, during which she would be evaluated before a decision was made about where she would be raised. The night before she was scheduled to leave the Brooks' house, Lizzie packed all of her belongings into a plastic garbage bag and quietly slipped out the back door. She headed straight for a phone booth and placed a call to her father. Two years had passed since she had seen either of her parents, so her dad didn't recognize her voice.

"Can I come home?" Lizzie pleaded. "They're going to throw me in reform school and I didn't do anything wrong."

She must have appealed to his sense of family pride. No matter what kind of trouble she was in, Frederick Pintye was not about to have his daughter confined to a juvenile detention center.

"You stay right where you are and I'll come and pick you up so we can get to the bottom of this," he said, hanging up the phone without waiting for a response.

Through all of the turmoil, Frederick and Hannah Pintye had always hoped to one day have their whole family brought back together under one roof. The first thing Lizzie did after she returned home in May 1980 was to write a letter telling the child welfare agency and the court that she wanted to live with her natural parents again.

An attorney had advised the family that this letter would carry more clout with the legal system than anything else. Without parental permission, the state was powerless to place a child anywhere except in a foster home, unless the child committed a criminal offense, was failing in school, or had shown signs of mental instability.

The letter read as follows:

# HIGH WIRE ANGEL

*To Whom It May Concern:*
*I want to live with my mom and dad from now on. I know they will take good care of me. I don't want to go to a reform school. Please let me live with them.*

*Elizabeth Pintye*

Things had changed a great deal at the Pintye household. Thomas, who was almost 11 years old, was the only child remaining at home. Lizzie felt sorry for her mother, who spent much of her time drinking coffee and staring off into space.

The familiar smells, sights, and sounds combined to provide Lizzie with a sense of belonging that had been missing for so long. Her parents still bickered over petty things, but beneath it all she could still see that they loved each other in their own strange way. And she still loved both of them, despite all that she had been through.

Lizzie soon came to feel as if she had been there alongside her parents for all of her life. She ended up cooking most of the meals and doing the housework. In her spare time, she would practice gymnastics, go swimming, or hang out with her friends from the neighborhood.

They would talk about what they wanted to be when they grew up— doctors, pilots, movie stars, nurses, stewardesses, and so on. Lizzie could never decide on any one thing that she wanted to be.

"I don't want to be limited," she would tell her friends. "I want to experience everything." The only deep interest she had was gymnastics. She used to pretend she was going for the Olympic gold medal while performing on the parallel bars at school and doing tumbling stunts in her parents' yard. Schoolmates would marvel at Lizzie's talents as she hurled her body around the monkey bars on the playground.

Her sister Jeannie and brothers James and Ernie also returned home. Their father was now responsible for a chronically ill wife and five children, most of them unruly teenagers. Slowly but surely, he returned to his old ways. There were no more push-ups or belt-whippings, but his disposition grew sour and he constantly yelled at the children or sent them to their rooms with little provocation. Frederick knew he had to be careful: he had been ordered to cease his severe forms of discipline. Caseworkers visited frequently to make sure he was keeping his word.

It was especially convenient for him to have Lizzie there, because she was the only child who was willing to take care of her mother and help with the household chores. Money was tight. The children grew frustrated at never having any cash to spend for movies, video arcades, or other activities that their contemporaries from the neighborhood took for granted.

Realizing their father would not be able to provide for these "extras," the Pintye children fell back on their own resourcefulness. Together, they started working for a man named Harvey who operated a candy and cookie sale promotion that was nothing more than a scam—not that the youngsters knew it at the time. They would sell snacks door to door, or hawk them from a table set up on the sidewalk, and tell everybody that the money went to benefit a charity called "Junior Careers." They turned all the money over to Harvey and he divided the profits with them.

Frederick assumed it was a legitimate business. He was proud to have his children working for charity and still making some money for themselves, especially since he insisted that they give him the bulk of their earnings to help cover household expenses. The sales job also allowed the kids to develop an appreciation for the value of a hard-earned dollar.

There was no such thing as "Junior Careers." Harvey invented the name as part of an elaborate scheme using big, attractive candy and cookie boxes that were examples of deceptive packaging at its best. They carried a message telling how Junior Careers could "open the door of opportunity for thousands of underprivileged children who want to pursue their dreams, but cannot afford to take that all-important first step." There was a pitifully small amount of candy underneath all that fancy packaging.

Harvey took advantage of the children's eagerness, and Junior Careers turned into a very lucrative operation. They were smooth talkers who found it easy to fool people and cash in on their sympathy. Lizzie was a particularly effective salesgirl who found it easy to converse with customers. She was among the best of the family con artists.

A few weeks after Lizzie's thirteenth birthday, Mark, Ernie, and Jeannie talked her into running away with them. They packed their clothes in plastic garbage bags and took all of the Junior Careers money that they had been secretly stashing away. They also stole their father's tent and the leftover boxes of Harvey's candy. Mark figured he could get a job and the rest of the family vagabonds would find other ways to make money so they could afford to rent an apartment and live on their own.

While Frederick Pintye was calling the police and cruising the streets himself trying to find his children, they were busy setting up his tent in a wooded area just off Interstate 95. Independent and adaptable, they had little trouble establishing a makeshift encampment. Mark and Ernie stole a new king-sized mattress from a delivery truck and brought it back to the campsite. The first night after they had settled in, the foursome made friends with an eighteen-year-old boy named Keith. He supplied beer from a tavern near the campsite. They spent their first few days in the woods sitting around the campfire—drinking beer, puffing on cigarettes, singing, playing cards, and smoking marijuana that Keith had supplied.

This was the first time Lizzie had ever experimented with alcohol or pot. She hated the taste of beer, but she felt grown-up and accepted as she sipped from a can of Miller High Life and puffed on a Marlboro. In the back of her mind, Lizzie was pestered by Uncle Bill's warnings about the perils of drinking

# HIGH WIRE ANGEL

and smoking. She recalled promising him she would do neither. But now, acceptance by her siblings and their new friends meant more to her than any promises made to an old man.

The temporary home in the woods served the runaways well for about a month. They slipped over to Keith's house to take showers and clean up when his parents weren't home. The tent was only a half-mile from a bargain store, so they came down out of the woods and hung around the parking lot, peddling what was left of Harvey's candy and earning tips by helping people carry packages to their cars.

Mark and Ernie scouted around the parking lot for a car to steal, but Lizzie talked them out of the idea. Mark got a job at a bakery while the other three also applied for jobs, only to be turned away time and time again because they were too young. Lizzie realized that it was just a matter of time before the authorities would catch up to them. They hadn't been able to save enough money to rent an apartment and the novelty of being on their own was wearing off.

One night, they walked down to the theater to sneak in and watch "Raiders of the Lost Ark." With about a half-hour to wait, Mark went across the street to a snack shop and returned with a huge ham and cheese submarine sandwich. The foursome was sitting on a curb, dividing the sandwich, when a police officer walked up behind them. Nobody saw him until he spoke.

"And what are you kids up to tonight?" he asked with a tone of suspicion in his voice.

"We're just waiting for the movies to open," Jeannie said. "What business is it of yours?"

The officer suddenly became more interested. When none of the children would tell him who they were, he loaded all four of them into the car and hauled them off to police headquarters. A phone call to the Putnam County Child Welfare Department yielded the necessary identification and the Pintye gang's month of freedom and adventure was over.

Chapter 10

# BORN TO BE WILD

When a caseworker brought Lizzie and Jeannie back to Bill and Joyce Barrett's house for a brief stay, the foster parents were shocked at what they saw. Gone was the little blond-haired Sunday School girl they knew. In her place was a sassy, street-smart teenager, dressed in jeans and a tank top emblazoned with a Budweiser beer logo. Lizzie was puffing on a cigarette and snapping her gum as she strutted across the living room in her wide-brimmed hat and boots and plopped herself down on the couch.

The Barretts blamed this "new" Lizzie on Jeannie's influence. They viewed Jeannie as a lost cause and asked the social services department to transfer her to another foster home. Lizzie said she would have no part of the arrangement. She threatened to run away at the first chance if she were separated from her sister. Within a matter of weeks, both Jeannie and Lizzie were sent to Saint Dominic's Group Home, part of the prominent Catholic organization.

Lizzie had heard a wide range of horror stories about Saint Dominic's, so she was pleasantly surprised to discover that the facility wasn't nearly as oppressive as she had been led to believe. The rules were simple and to the point: go to school, do your daily assignments, show up for dinner, and be back to your room by the ten o'clock curfew.

Unfortunately, Lizzie lost all interest in school. The teachers constantly harassed her about smoking in the bathrooms or out on the school grounds. She reached the point where she didn't care if they saw her smoking anywhere.

"Either the cigarettes go, or you go!" said the principal after calling Lizzie down to his office one time to discuss the problem.

"Fine," she answered, rising from her seat and marching toward the door.

"Your father is going to hear about this!" the principal shouted.

"Who cares?" Lizzie yelled from the hallway as she continued walking. "He won't do anything to me."

She went to find her sister in the school cafeteria. "I just got kicked out for smoking," she said to Jeannie, who had just sat down to eat. "You wanna go with me? I can't hang around this dump anymore."

"Sure," said Jeannie, pushing her tray to the center of the table and grabbing her purse. They left the school and walked across the street to a donut shop, where they each ordered a Coke and lit up a cigarette. Lizzie looked across at the school building and savored her new freedom.

Recognizing that they were now in violation of the group home rules concerning compulsory attendance of school, Lizzie and Jeannie did all they could to deceive the nuns. They worried that school officials would notify St. Cabrini's of their absence during the final two weeks that remained of the school year.

Each day after the St. Cabrini's bus delivered the Pintye girls to the school parking lot, they waited until the driver was out of sight and then hurried over to a park behind the donut shop to hang out. Truancy officers were nowhere to be seen.

This was a period of complete rebellion. At the group home, Lizzie listened to punk rock, especially the Sex Pistols, which the nuns at Saint Dominic's detested. She loved the way that the singer, Johnny Rotten, and the bass player, Sid Vicious, poked fun at silly American customs. Anything that was anti-establishment suited her.

The more the nuns complained about her music, the louder Lizzie played it. At the same time, she plunged deeper into the drug culture, chiefly marijuana, and hung rock 'n' roll posters on her walls, replacing them with new ones almost as fast as the nuns could tear them down.

The Pintye girls' wild ways rubbed off on some of the other residents. One night, Lizzie and Jeannie organized an overnight runaway. All twelve residents of the group home joined them in roaming the streets, throwing snowballs at cars and passers-by, shoplifting candy and cigarettes from a convenience store. They managed to arrive back at their rooms just before morning wake-up call without being caught.

Another time, Lizzie and some of the others who were chosen to help escort Terence Cardinal Cooke on a tour of Saint Dominic's, proceeded to empty each of the wine chalices after the Cardinal stopped to give a blessing at several points on the grounds. By the time the tour was over, the girls were thoroughly intoxicated and caused an embarrassing scene. The nuns were so angry that they took away all of Lizzie's privileges.

This defiant teenager wasn't about to live under those conditions. The first chance she had, she slipped through the gate and was gone. Hitching a couple of rides and walking for miles, she showed up on her parents' doorstep several hours later.

Through the window, Lizzie could see her father sitting in his recliner, his face buried in the sports section of the *Daily News*. Her mom was sleeping on the couch. Lizzie paced the floorboards of the porch, trying to decide what she would tell them. Finally, she took a deep breath, opened the screen door, and turned the knob on the main door. It was locked.

She gently knocked and heard her dad's gruff voice yelling, "Who's there?"

"It's me, Dad. Liz. Can I come in?"

He opened the door and stared. "What the...," he paused. "Are you in trouble, or what?"

"No, Dad," she said timidly, walking in and closing the door behind herself. "I left the group home. I just want to come back and live here. I'll do whatever you want me to do. Please, Dad."

He turned toward his wife on the couch and said, "Hey Hannah, get a load of this. We've got company. You ever see this gal before?" She turned around and shielded her eyes from the light. A smile came over her face as she rose to hug Lizzie. "Oh my! Oh my!" was all Hannah said as she clung to her child.

This was the first time Lizzie had seen either of her parents since she ran away to live in the woods. Her father agreed to let her live at home, as long as she promised to abide by all of the restrictions he placed on her. She was forbidden to have any friends over, was not permitted to smoke cigarettes, and she was required to obtain her father's permission each time she wanted to leave the house.

To satisfy the formalities, Frederick contacted Saint Dominic's, as well as the Child Welfare Department, and received the go-ahead to let Lizzie live at home again, subject to occasional visits by a social worker. Through the mercy of the school administration, she was promoted to the eighth grade, despite missing the final two weeks of the previous school year. When school started in the fall, Frederick made his daughter's orders clear: go to class in the morning, come straight home, do the housework, and take care of her mom until bedtime.

Hannah Pintye drifted in and out of reality. When she was stable, she was a warm and loving person. However, she often suffered through periods during which she was thoroughly disoriented. In those spells, she talked nonsense—forgetting who family members were, or alluding to events that had never happened. Sometimes Lizzie could steer her back to reality. Then Hannah would be ashamed and apologize over and over again for her confusion.

Hannah couldn't possibly handle the cooking and cleaning chores. She even neglected her personal hygiene and grooming. Lizzie had to order her to take a bath or comb her hair, a strange role reversal for a mother and her teenaged daughter.

The situation was bearable until Jeannie and Ernie moved back into the house. Each of them was allowed to smoke and do all of the things their younger sister was expressly forbidden to do, which made Lizzie so resentful that she started smoking again behind her father's back and looking for other ways to deliberately defy him. Their relationship gradually deteriorated to the point where Lizzie started telling her friends how much she hated her dad. She would not even talk to him if she could avoid it. Lizzie took solace in the notion that she would only have to tolerate him until her fourteenth birthday, after which she could follow the example of one of her friends and declare her "emancipation" under the New York State law. That had become a family tradition. Charles, James, and Mark were long gone. Ernie had left just a few weeks after returning home and Jeannie was thinking about running away.

Just before Lizzie turned fourteen, she was advised that the minimum age for legal emancipation had been changed to sixteen. She couldn't envision putting up with her father's unreasonable demands and spending every waking hour either at home or in school.

The harder Frederick Pintye tried to clamp down on his youngest daughter, the wilder she became. Lizzie was exposed to all kinds of drugs and soon became a regular user. She was getting high on her way to class, or even in the bathroom of the school—when she bothered showing up for classes at all. Sometimes she would come home after smoking pot or taking mescaline and start talking to her mother, trying to "connect" with the disconsolate woman lost in her own strange world.

Lizzie derived a naughty pleasure by having fun with her mother's illness. She'd say things like, "I'm not Liz. You don't have a daughter named Liz. I'm your Aunt Alice from Australia. Don't you remember me?" Her mother would become so confused that she just shook her head and drifted back into her private thoughts.

The only time Lizzie enjoyed the kind of clean, heathy fun that a young teenager needs was when Bill O'Grady came to visit. Uncle Bill was also the only person who would ever take her mother out of the house, whether it was a stop at the ice cream parlor or a walk in the park. If he was ashamed by his special friend's behavior, it never showed.

Bill seemed to pop into Lizzie's life during those times when she was depressed or immersed in self-pity. He provided her with a positive role model. She observed that he was always careful to avoid taking advantage of people, and he strictly adhered to the rules of common decency. He was always polite and full of joy. His mere presence was a reminder to Lizzie that, without all the petty annoyances and hassles, life really could be fun.

Lizzie felt terribly guilty each time she lied to Uncle Bill about her involvement with drugs, alcohol, and tobacco. Deep down inside, she had developed a strong moral code. She realized that things like indiscriminate sex, lying, and stealing were wrong. She also knew that there was plenty of love in the world—she was just one of the unlucky souls who would have to look extra hard to find it.

If her father had let her do what most kids her age were doing, Lizzie may not have been unruly in the first place. She didn't mind the cooking and the cleaning, or looking after her mother, but like any teen, she needed something else. Instead, she became her father's personal prisoner. He was desperate to assert his control over her, even if it meant severe punishment and unreasonable expectations.

Because she had no long-range plans or goals, school had once again become meaningless to Lizzie. She passed her courses and paid attention when she was in class, but many times she yielded to other temptations and played hooky. Finally, in her freshman year, the guidance counselor and principal placed her in an alternative school because of absenteeism and attitude problems.

Under that school's system, a student could work for half of the day and go to school the other half. This school was quite an institution of "higher" learning. Students constantly paraded into the bathroom to smoke pot. The teachers would pretend they didn't know what was going on, even though the marijuana smoke hung in the air.

Lizzie had just started a job at a Chinese restaurant for four hours each afternoon, which allowed her to earn some money and afforded her another opportunity to get out of the house. Whenever she had a chance, she met up with a loose circle of friends and continued to experiment with a wide variety of narcotics. She now credits a God-given inner strength for allowing her to overcome dependencies that nearly grew into self-destructive addictions. Deep down inside, she recognized that drugs were providing her with a false sense of security. She had seen poignant examples of contemporaries who had ruined their lives.

Most of her teenage acquaintances became junkies, alcoholics, prostitutes, criminals, and, in two tragic cases, suicide victims.

Chapter 11

# ON MY OWN

An argument with her father led to Lizzie's departure from home—this time for good. It started innocently enough one Saturday morning when she received a phone call informing her that the woman who usually gave her a ride to work was sick. When her dad refused to drive her, Lizzie became incensed. "Be that way!" she said smugly. "I'll just hitchhike."

"Like hell you will! If you walk out that door and start hitchhiking, don't bother coming home," he shouted.

Convinced that her father was merely trying to assert his authority once again, Lizzie decided she was not going to play. For the first time in her life, she stood up to him.

"Well, I'm still going to work," she shot back, tossing her purse over her shoulder defiantly and walking toward the door. At that, her father yanked off his shoe and hurled it at her. Lizzie heard the shoe thump against the wall as she slammed the door and began running in the direction of the highway.

She called home that evening after work and asked her father if she could come home. "I gave you your choices and you made your decision!" he responded.

"Fine," Lizzie said, and she hung up.

She leaned against the side of the phone booth and sighed. The realization that she was actually free to go wherever she pleased at any time of the day or night, with no one to look after her, was overpowering and frightening. All of her desires to strike out on her own were tempered by a realization that she was still a child who was ill-equipped to deal with such freedom.

She began running the streets until all hours of the night. Drugs, especially speed and mescaline, could be found everywhere she turned. Lizzie rarely refused the offers. She woke up in cars, on sidewalks, or sprawled on the couch of an unfamiliar home with people she didn't even recognize in the cold morning light.

Incredibly, through it all, Lizzie kept her part-time job as a waitress and even showed up for school more often than not. The desire to maintain these ties was one characteristic that set her apart from the oft-changing band of misfits and degenerates that formed her circle of friends.

She went back to her father's house early one morning and tossed pebbles at Jeannie's bedroom window until she got her attention.

"Throw down as many of my clothes as you can find," she said to her sister in a loud whisper.

"Where the hell have you been? Dad's worried sick about you! He needs you to help look after Mom, but he's too damned stubborn to come and see you at work or at school."

"That's his problem, not mine," Lizzie said. "Now throw some of those clothes down here before we get caught." Stuffing as many garments as she could fit under both arms, Lizzie darted away when she saw her father approaching a downstairs window.

Later that same day, she called home to ask Jeannie if she had gotten caught and was greeted with some sad news. "We just got a call from a funeral director in Boston," Jeannie told her. "Uncle Bill died last night. I guess he dropped dead with a heart attack. I don't think Mom understands what happened. It's really going to screw her up when she realizes he's gone. I mean, what does she have left?"

Lizzie was speechless. This was her first close-up experience with death. She worried about her mother. Bill O'Grady was her only real friend in the world. Even as his own health failed him, he would do anything for her, always patient and constantly wearing that Irishman's smile. After she hung up the phone, she started thinking back on Uncle Bill's words of wisdom. She wondered what he would have said if he knew how she was now living. He had always joked that he wanted to "live long enough to see little Lizzie graduate from high school and make something of herself."

A strange sensation came over her and she began to feel lightheaded. Bits and pieces of her life flashed before her eyes—the police breaking in to rescue her from Kenny, the beatings by her father, her treatment by Richard and Pat Brook, and many more unpleasant memories.

Lizzie had about a half-ounce of marijuana in her purse. Instinctively, she retrieved the familiar plastic sandwich bag and carried it into the bathroom. Then she knelt over the toilet and furiously emptied the contents into the bowl, watching as the seeds settled to the bottom and the tiny green flakes floated on top. After staring into the toilet for several moments, she pulled the flush lever and watched as the illicit weed collected in the center and gurgled down the drain.

She knew that the time had come to take charge of her life—no more drinking and drugging, no more running the streets trying to figure out where to spend the night. With that one small but symbolic act, she resolved to turn things around.

# HIGH WIRE ANGEL 69

Elizabeth Eve Pintye's life had been nothing but starts and stops, endings and new beginnings. She desperately yearned for a steady flow, a continuity. With nobody around to push her forward or support her if she weakened, she recognized that the odds were against her. That made her all the more determined to show everyone that she could make it on her own.

A plan emerged in Lizzie's mind: she would lie low until she was sixteen—"emancipation day"— so the state could not put her in reform school and her father could not send the police or social workers out looking for her.

As Lizzie searched for a job that would keep her out of the public eye, one of her friends, Tommy, mentioned that his sister needed someone to stay at her house in Mount Vernon and look after her three kids. Lizzie checked into the job and decided it was the kind of situation she was looking for. There was no way she could continue attending school at the same time, so she dropped out in her sophomore year, promising herself that this would only be a temporary break in her formal education.

Lizzie began trying to build a savings account by taking a part-time job working as a clerk at the Shopwell grocery store at night, but almost all of the pay went to help cover room and board. The situation soon became all-too-familiar to her. She had no time to develop new friendships or enjoy any social activities.

In addition, Lizzie had to contend with the relentless efforts by Tommy, the amorous brother of her landlady. He had "coincidentally" moved in with his sister a short time after Lizzie took the job. Although Lizzie had no romantic interest in him, Tommy could not accept the fact and continued to pursue her, once going to the extreme of buying her a diamond engagement ring.

One year of this existence was about all Lizzie could take. It bothered her that she was mired in near-isolation in the prime of her life, and she was getting nowhere, financially or otherwise.

One day when she was feeling particularly lonely, she placed a call to Michael Mihalchik, one of her best friends from the alternative school, and explained her dilemma. Michael said he would work on a plan to help Lizzie. Although she begged him for details, he insisted on keeping it a surprise.

Late that night, Michael called back to say that Lizzie was welcome to live with him and his mother, Mary Ellen (the Wallenda fan who would accompany Lizzie to her experience on the high wire).

When Tommy heard the news, he was despondent. "You'll never see me again. Nobody will ever see me again—alive," he vowed as he squealed his tires and sped away. He returned to his sister's house later that night, stumbling drunk, and accosted Lizzie in the hallway. Suddenly, he pushed her down and started slapping her face. She squirmed and turned her head to protect herself, but Tommy's weight on top of her was too much to handle.

Finally, his sister heard the ruckus and intervened. By then, red welts had already formed under each of Lizzie's eyes and blood streamed from her nose.

Mary Ellen Mihalchik's home had come to be known as a "flop house" in the Mohegan Lake area. If a teenager needed a place to stay during times of trouble, Mary Ellen would open her door and try to help. She was very sympathetic and understanding to teenagers, something Lizzie wasn't accustomed to seeing in an adult.

After her face had healed, Lizzie applied for work at the Dipper Dan Ice Cream Shoppe in the Westchester Mall and—after telling the owners that she was 20 years old—was hired as a waitress and cashier. To cover part of the room and board, she helped Mary Ellen get her kids off to school in the morning and cleaned the house once a week.

The ice cream shop was Lizzie's first full-time job, so she wanted to prove herself. She felt as if she had been given a new chance to make something out of her life. She hitchhiked or walked to the mall each day and worked hard to show her bosses that she could handle as much responsibility as they were willing to give her. In time, she became a "management trainee," and eventually was promoted to the position of store manager.

One afternoon, Lizzie was dutifully serving ice cream cones at Dipper Dan's when she heard a familiar voice shouting her name. She turned around to see the smiling face of her sister Jeannie, along with their mother, in the hallway. Lizzie dropped her ice cream scoop and ran over to her mother, giving her a big hug.

"I can't believe this," she said gleefully. "Jeannie, how'd you pull this off?"

"I just waited 'til Dad went to work and told Mom I wanted to take her for a ride. When I mentioned your name, her eyes lit up, so I thought I would take a chance and see if you were here."

Her mother was more alert than Lizzie had expected and was obviously happy to see her daughter again. She couldn't help noticing, however, that her mom spoke and acted like a young girl, as if she had reverted back to her childhood.

"What happened?" Lizzie asked.

"Just humor her," Jeannie smiled. "That's just the way she gets."

"What about Dad? Won't she tell him where I am?"

"No. We've worked that out already. She knows how mad he would get, so we're not going to tell him anything."

Jeannie went off to run errands, leaving her mother sitting at one of the booths, leafing through a magazine and watching Lizzie as she waited on customers. "Mom, when I get a minute, I'll run across the hall and get you a dress and some shoes," Lizzie said, trying to impress upon her mother the fact that she still cared about her.

"Very nice," she said, glancing up at Lizzie and smiling before looking away, ashamed of her limited ability to communicate. Lizzie slipped over to a fashion boutique across the hall and picked out a pretty blue dress and a matching tourquoise bracelet. Her mom was thrilled to open the boxes and discover these gifts. She was not accustomed to being treated with kindness.

# HIGH WIRE ANGEL

Lizzie was overcome by guilt as she thought about her mother's travails. Losing her own children and then having her best friend die must have left Hannah feeling abandoned. Lizzie felt ashamed that she hadn't visited her mother more often, as mad as she was at her father. She hadn't seen or talked to Frederick Pintye since their argument. Lizzie was still intent on teaching him a lesson about treating people like human beings, especially his own children. She also wanted him to realize that she didn't need his help to make it on her own.

Jeannie returned to the ice cream shop and grew impatient as Lizzie and her mother said their good-byes. Lizzie promised she would visit soon. Her mom kept looking back and waving as she and Jeannie walked away. After they disappeared into the crowd, Lizzie wanted to run after them and ask them to stay longer so they could all go out to dinner and talk the night away. Something about the way her mother looked at her as they parted made Lizzie think she would never see her again.

Less than a week later, Steve Wallenda walked into the Dipper Dan Ice Cream Shoppe and took a seat at a booth near the back.

# CHAPTER 12

## STABBED IN THE BACK

Lizzie's brief, albeit short-lived walk, on the high wire, the offer to travel to Jamaica; the experience with Chubby Checker and the rift she had caused between Steve and his agent—so much had happened to her in such a short period of time! She could hardly believe this was real.

But now, all she had to show for her relationship with Steve was an old scrapbook and a handful of memories. As she patiently waited to hear from Steve after their rendezvous at the Rockland County Fair, she grew increasingly concerned. Maybe Richard had succeeded in persuading Steve to forget about her and concentrate instead on his solo career. Maybe he had found another woman at one of the celebrity parties or fairs where he was performing.

Lizzie began to doubt his sincerity. "Why did I ever believe him when he promised me he would stay in touch!" she thought to herself. "Whatever possessed me to take this strange, deceitful man seriously when he said he would teach me to walk the high wire?"

She lost count of how many times she read through Steve's scrapbook of news clippings and publicity material. It now rested on the corner of her dresser, covered with dust. The circus books from the library had long since been returned.

"Oh, well. This isn't the first time in my life that I've been forced to pick up the pieces," she rationalized. "There will be other chances. I can watch the newspapers and magazines for circus advertisements and, eventually, I'll find somebody else who's willing to teach me to be a performer. After all, I'm a 'natural.' Or was Steve lying to me about that, too? Maybe I really was meant to be an ice cream dipper."

Lizzie was on her way out the door early one morning, heading for work, when Mary Ellen yelled to tell her she had a phone call. As soon as she heard Steve's voice on the other end, she knew something was wrong. He sounded deeply depressed.

# HIGH WIRE ANGEL

Steve said he was a patient in a hospital at Phillipsburg, New Jersey, and he wanted Lizzie to help him sneak out when nobody was looking.

"What happened this time?" she demanded.

"It's a long story," he replied.

"Why do you need me to get you out? Can't you walk?"

"They took my clothes. I'm fine, really. Could you please just bring me a set of clothes? I can't say too much right now. I'll fill you in later."

After finishing her work shift at Dipper Dan's, Lizzie bought Steve some jeans and a shirt and jogged over to the bus depot. All kinds of disconcerting thoughts crossed her mind. She wondered if Steve had fallen from the wire, or had gotten into a fight with Richard, or had been in a car accident.

Lizzie hardly recognized Steve when she walked in his cold, sterile hospital room and found him staring out the window. His face was a washed-out white and the gleam was gone from his eyes. After seeing him in his performing costume and his stylish street clothes, she could not believe this was the same man now draped in an oversized, faded, blue and white striped hospital gown.

In his hand he held the seagull sketch Lizzie had given him, with her phone number scribbled on the back. She kissed him on the cheek as he turned to greet her. Steve reached to hold her face close to his own. He was very quiet, in a serene frame of mind. Lizzie felt awkward to be invading his privacy.

Steve slowly explained that he had been admitted to the hospital after suffering from severe headaches, probably stemming from his fall. The headaches continued, but Steve had grown restless and nervous, and was desperate to be released. Still, the doctors wanted to keep him for observation and refused to return his clothes until it was time for him to be discharged. Steve closed his eyes, then squinted as if to block out the pain.

He reached to clasp Lizzie's hand as he gave her a penetrating stare. The look in his eyes and the tight grip of his hand told Lizzie she had an important role to play in his life. His crooked smile betrayed a little boy's fragility. Perhaps this famous aerialist needed Lizzie more than she needed him.

She was beginning to think that she truly loved him, even though he was still an enigma to her. Steve appeared to offer none of the security that she was seeking in her life. Yet Lizzie felt she could accept him for what he was because she also recognized what he could be. She admired his intelligence, his straightforwardness, his sense of humor.

"Why did you call me?" she asked him. "Why didn't Richard bring you some clothes so you could get out of here?"

"Oh, that's another thing," Steve said. "We had a big argument. He just wants to take advantage of me anyhow. I do all the wire-walking and take all the risks. All he does is take a cut of the money. I've got one more show next week near here and then we're finished."

Steve slowly made his way into the bathroom and dressed while Lizzie peeked around the corner to see if the coast was clear. The pants were a couple of inches too big around the waist, so she made a tuck with a safety pin.

They tiptoed down the hall and slipped out the side exit into the hard drizzle to check into a nearby hotel. Steve had a hard time keeping up with Lizzie as they walked. He had injured his knee during his fall and was limping badly.

"Slow down!" he urged. "It's not like they're chasing us."

Lizzie had no idea at this point what the future might hold, but she had such strong feelings for Steve that she decided to throw caution to the wind. While Steve stayed behind at the hotel, Lizzie returned to Mary Ellen's to get most of her things and stopped at Dipper Dan's on her way back out of town to announce that she was quitting.

At first, both Steve and Lizzie may have been trying to fill the emptiness they had felt throughout their lives with the warmth and intensity of friendship. But now, their relationship had blossomed into something more lasting and meaningful.

Steve had a performance booked for Byram, New Jersey as part of the Byram Day Fair. As much as his knee still hurt him, and as bitter as he had grown toward Richard, he still felt compelled to honor his commitment, if for no other reason than to earn enough money to live on.

"Are you ready to go up with me again?" Steve asked, catching Lizzie off-guard as they packed what few things they had to take on the trip.

"Do you mean walk the wire in front of all those people?" she asked, half-excited and half-scared.

"Of course that's what I mean. You've done it before. It's the only way you're going to learn."

"Well, if you say so, I guess I'll give it a try."

Steve was supposed to meet up with Richard at the Wallenda Museum trailer. It was set up in a large parking lot outside of a restaurant owned by Gus and Elsie Bichakis, a Greek couple who agreed to let Steve and Richard store their trailer there so they could be close to the fairgrounds and, at the same time, steer a little business toward the eatery.

Lizzie and Steve were approaching the trailer when Richard appeared at the door. "What the hell is she doing here?" he asked.

"She's part of the act now, Richard, whether you like it or not," Steve said.

Richard frowned. "This isn't going to work," he said, barging out the door and storming across the parking lot toward the restaurant. "It won't work! I won't stand for it!" he shouted over his shoulder as he continued on his way.

"Don't worry about him," Steve assured Lizzie. "It's none of his business what I do when I'm up on the wire. All he's responsible for is the bookwork."

After giving the matter considerable thought, she declined the invitation to return to the wire and persuaded Steve to perform by himself the first day. That way, Lizzie reasoned, she could observe him and build the courage to go up again.

# HIGH WIRE ANGEL                                                    75

The Byram Day Fair featured everything from clowns and a celebrity dunk tank to three-legged races and the greased pig chase. The entertainment consisted of a folk singer, a magician, and a clown act, but Steve was clearly the star of the show. Showing no signs of having banged his head or his knee, he put on a great performance.

The wire extended from the ground to the top of a crane. This was only a 45-foot ascent, but the steep angle made it a difficult walk. About one-third of the way up, he gave the crowd a thrill as he bounded onto his buttocks, and then back to his feet without missing a beat. Everybody—including the news reporters—thought it was part of the show. In reality, one of the men who was supposed to be supporting the cable with a guy wire from the ground had let go. The main wire shifted, knocking Steve onto his backside.

At the midway point, Steve took a bow. He leaned forward on his right knee while his left remained behind him. Farther up, he stopped and tossed a handful of coins to the crowd below. Kids swarmed in under the wire and eagerly scooped up everything Steve had dropped in a matter of seconds.

When he finally reached the top, he sat down atop the crane for a brief rest and then carefully walked back down. Steve was greeted by dozens of fans seeking autographs, as well as news photographers and a TV crew. Lizzie waited patiently as he took the time to talk with anyone who wanted to meet him. He was confident, but not cocky, as he answered a steady barrage of questions and posed for snapshots.

Steve emphasized that their walk together would require more effort than the performance at the mall, since the angle was much steeper and the cable was looser.

Lizzie had trouble sleeping that night as she pondered the next evening's wire-walk with nervous anticipation. When morning finally did arrive, she awoke Steve and suggested that he once again go back on the wire without her.

"I don't want to slow you down. You looked so impressive yesterday."

"Now listen," he said sternly. "I told you it was healthy to have a certain amount of fear and respect for the high wire, but not to the point where you're looking for excuses not to go up. If you're going to keep backing out, you might as well look for a job somewhere dipping ice cream again."

After they enjoyed a leisurely brunch, Steve and Lizzie walked over to the fairgrounds so he could check the tension of the wire and make sure the connections were secure. Then they took one last trip around the midway. Steve came to life as he talked about the high wire. He explained to Lizzie how she should try to catch the wire and hold on for dear life if anything went wrong. That made her feel uneasy.

"Are you telling me that it's actually possible we're going to fall?"

"Anything is possible," Steve said, looking at the passers-by on the fairgrounds and then back at Lizzie. "If you do what I tell you and promise to hold on, you'll be safer than you'd be if you were crossing the street. Believe it or not, I do know what I'm doing."

"Oh, I trust you. It's just a little unnerving to be told what I should do if we start to fall."

"I just told you that because you can never be too prepared. When it comes to the wire, I like to think of myself as a perfectionist. That's the way I was raised. It kind of runs in the family."

As they circled back toward the grandstand, a large audience was already gathered for the aerial performance. Steve slipped into a tiny dressing room at the fair office to put on his costume while Lizzie sat outside and watched the crowd. She could sense the anticipation as men, women and children looked up at the wire trying to envision how a person could keep his balance on so narrow a lifeline.

They were introduced as "The Great Mr. and Mrs. Steve Wallenda," since Steve believed that this presented a better image. Lizzie felt awkward being mentioned in the same breath as a performer with Steve's credentials.

He stepped up first and knelt down on the sloping wire so his partner could use his back and shoulders to pull herself up behind him. Even at ground level, it was important for Lizzie to mount the wire correctly to avoid upsetting Steve's balance since there was no chance to grab the wire for protection during a fall.

Fear did not begin to overtake her until they moved a few steps higher up the wire. Lizzie instinctively tightened her grip on Steve's shoulders and he sensed her predicament.

"Just trust me," he whispered. "If you hold on to me and keep your feet on the wire, nothing can go wrong."

"I don't know about this—this cable has so much give in it. I feel like I'm going to fall," she answered.

"Hey, you're with me, okay? And we're going all the way to the top, so just hold on, not that you're in any position to argue with me."

Lizzie could feel the force of gravity pulling her backwards as Steve moved forward and she followed. Her feet were slipping with each step, although she could put enough pressure on her toes to avoid sliding back more than an inch or two at a time.

"I'll provide the strength," Steve said out of the corner of his mouth as they neared the top of the crane and the applause began. "You just have to keep your feet on the wire. I'll do the rest."

It suddenly dawned on Lizzie that there was no way they were going to be able to reverse positions on the wire so that Steve could lead her back down to the ground. "Now what?" she said in a mounting state of alarm.

"No problem; just relax," Steve said, reassuringly. "We'll just back down."

"With me going first? What are you, crazy? You never said anything about this!"

"It's not as hard as it sounds. Just start backing up, one foot in front of the other, and I'll keep us both balanced."

# HIGH WIRE ANGEL

"I'm going to get you for this, Steve Wallenda."

Lizzie turned her head around as far as she could to watch where she was going. Steve stared straight ahead. She could feel his muscles tighten as they began their descent. He gently pushed her along. "You're doing fine," Steve said. "Keep it steady and we'll be down before you know it."

Lizzie wanted to stop, kneel down, grab hold of the wire and hang there until somebody could get underneath to catch her. The backward steps came easier as they moved closer to the ground. Lizzie hadn't lost her fear or her respect for the wire, but she was beginning to feel some confidence in her ability to remain balanced. As she had back at the Westchester Mall, she wondered if she would ever be able to do it without having Steve to hold on to.

As soon as Lizzie's feet were back on the ground, she felt a burning desire to go back up on the wire and recapture the indescribable sensation that came from being so precariously perched high above the ground. She recognized the incomparable satisfaction of conquering fear and accomplishing something that hardly anyone else in the world has even attempted.

While Lizzie was daydreaming about walking the wire alone, Steve and one of the Byram Day rodeo performers began a grand finale that would give the crowd something to remember. Steve walked back up to the midway point of the cable and carefully sat down, placing his balancing pole across his lap. He reached in his pocket for a newspaper, unfolded it, and held it between his hands.

The cowboy unrolled a long, braided, leather whip, which he proceeded to snap between Steve's hands, tearing the paper in half. Then Steve took one of the halves and bravely held that between his hands while the rodeo star took aim. Somehow, he managed to land the whip right in the middle again, barely missing Steve's hands. A tiny scrap of paper remained.

"Let's see how good you really are," Steve dared him, holding up the tattered remains for the spectators to see.

The cowboy waved him off. "Nobody's that good."

The crowd erupted in applause as Steve walked back down and draped his arm around the rodeo performer's shoulders for the photographers.

Following the formalities, Steve and Lizzie walked over to where Richard and one of the Byram Day entertainment organizers were talking

"Good news! We've booked you for a performance in York, Pennsylvania, for some big bucks," Richard said. "Terry here pulled some strings for us. There's a big fair going on and you'll be the opening act for a concert by Alabama. Let's forget what happened. We've got work to do."

"I'm not going anywhere unless she goes with me," Steve said, gesturing toward Lizzie.

"Just cool it! We can talk about that later," said Richard.

"For this show, you get your cut and I get mine. What you do with your share is your own damned business."

Terry reached into his shirt pocket and pulled out an envelope that had a pair of round-trip bus tickets protruding from the end.

"Bus!" exclaimed Steve, flabbergasted and insulted. He snatched the envelope out of Terry's hand and threw it on the ground. "What about a limo? What am I, a second-stringer?"

"This is the best we can do," Terry said. "Short notice, you know?"

"It's all right Steve," Lizzie interjected, trying to settle him down as she picked up the envelope and stuffed it in her purse. "We'll be together and we'll enjoy the ride. It'll be fun."

They were supposed to meet a monkey trainer named Roger, another one of Richard's clients, at the fairgrounds in York. He would have the rigging for Steve's wire-walk and the stereo system to provide the background music. They would stay in his trailer overnight and take the bus back to Byram the next day.

"Is this the way you always do things? Let Richard make all of your plans and then just show up?" Lizzie asked.

"Oh yeah. He's got a lot of contacts, like Terry there, all over the country. Let them hassle with the small stuff like paperwork and contracts. I'll do the hard part."

When they got to York, they quickly found the monkey cages and introduced themselves to Roger, a crusty circus veteran with a dark tan and deep southern accent. He recognized Steve without any introduction.

"So what can I do for you?" Roger inquired.

"Well, we're going to need some help to get the rigging set up, if you have a few minutes. I'd also like to go over the music and find something that's appropriate, kinda loud and dramatic if you have anything like that."

Roger gave him a blank stare. "What rigging is that?"

"Don't you have it?" Lizzie asked. "Steve is supposed to perform before the Alabama concert tonight. Weren't you supposed to meet us here?"

"I have no idea what you're talking about," Roger insisted. He paused and then, in his gravelly drawl, added, "I think you folks have been had."

Steve made no effort to disguise his mounting anger. "That son of a bitch! I'll break his kneecaps when I catch up to him."

"Maybe it's just a misunderstanding," Lizzie said. "They probably just got their dates mixed up or something."

Roger hurried to the fair office to call back to Byram and see what had happened. "Richard says there must have been a cancellation that nobody told him about," he said as he returned to the monkey cages. "He wants you to go back to Byram on the bus tomorrow to sort this thing out."

With nothing else to do, Lizzie and Steve roamed the fairgrounds and tried to ease their frustration by attending the Alabama concert. Lizzie felt like a teenage girl on her first date as she walked the carnival midway, clinging to Steve and watching the crowd. She threw darts at balloons and won a teddy bear in the ring toss.

As they rolled into Byram the next day, Lizzie was afraid the situation could erupt into violence. Steve was eager to have some answers. Anger turned to shock as they walked toward Gus & Elsie's parking lot; there sat the trailer, torn apart inside and stripped down to its basics. Their belongings were spread out on the ground.

A bunch of kids were playing with Lizzie's priceless Shirley Temple doll and some of her stuffed animals, dragging them in the mud and tearing out the stuffing. The Wallenda posters, old equipment, and other family souvenirs were nowhere to be found.

Gus spotted them looking over the trailer and came out of the restaurant to see what was happening. He was a warm and cheerful old man. "I didn't expect to see you again," he said as he offered a handshake to Steve.

"I can't believe this," Steve said. "Where are Richard and Terry? What happened to our trailer?"

"Oh, I thought you knew all about it," Gus said. "I bought this from Terry for eight hundred dollars. He and Richard said it was theirs. They had the title to it and everything."

"Those lying bastards!" Steve exploded, stomping his foot and throwing his head in disgust. "I never gave them anything." He smashed his half-smoked cigarette hard against the ground and kicked one of the tires on the trailer.

Gus felt terrible. He even offered to sell the trailer back to Steve for less than he paid. But he and his wife had done so much damage to the inside, trying to make more room so they could use it as a travel camper, that it would have been next to impossible to salvage it.

Now Steve knew how far Richard would go to take advantage of him. He and Terry had evidently cooked up the Pennsylvania scheme to get Steve out of the picture so they could make some quick money by selling the trailer before Steve severed all of his ties with Richard.

Steve finally caught up with Richard by telephone back in Asbury, New Jersey, where he maintained a large lot to store circus equipment and travel trailers. Richard claimed the fair promoters in Pennsylvania had never told him that Steve's wire-walk had been cancelled. He offered a feeble excuse about selling the trailer to help cover a long-standing debt. In addition, Richard boldly delivered an ultimatum: if he was going to continue to promote Steve's career, it would only be as a solo act.

"That's a bunch of bull!" Steve yelled into the phone. "Whether you like it or not, she's part of my life now, and she's going to be part of my act." Lizzie felt as if she were caught in a grueling tug-of-war between two strong-willed men. They argued for several more minutes, but Richard wasn't about to budge.

"This girl has what it takes and she's gonna make a hell of an aerialist when I can find the time to train her," Steve insisted. There was a long silence as he patiently listened to whatever parting shots Richard was firing, then slammed down the phone in disgust.

"What a jerk!" he said. "All he cares about is himself and his bank account. It's going to catch up to him one of these days. Somebody's going to do him in. I guarantee it. It might even be me."

Steve never saw Richard again. He died in 1988 from pneumonia. Just before Richard's death, Steve received a card from him apologizing for the way he had taken advantage of him and wishing both Steve and Lizzie the best life could offer.

The whereabouts of the Wallenda family souvenirs remain a mystery.

Chapter 13

# YOU'RE MY ANGEL

"Did you really mean what you said to Richard?" Lizzie asked as she and Steve sat in Gus and Elsie's Restaurant trying to sort things out.

"What are you talking about?" Steve said.

"The part about me being part of your life now, and performing together on the wire, and all that."

"Of course I meant it. You'll always be part of my life. I know this is going to sound contrived, but I'm going to say it anyhow. When I first saw you, I knew an angel had come down from heaven to save me—to save me from everybody who was out to take advantage of me, to save me from myself! I've been waiting a long time for you." He looked into her eyes. "I know it's going to take some time to get used to, but you'll always be Angel to me. I want to call you that from now on. Would you mind if that was your new name?"

Lizzie recognized that her relationship with Steve was, indeed, the start of a new life. Becoming Angel wasn't just a name change, it was the beginning of a new identity. She never did like being called Elizabeth, or Liz, or Lizzie.

"I like it; I really do," she assured him. "It's going to take some getting used to, but, sure I'll be Angel."

"There's something I've kept to myself ever since I first saw you, because I was afraid how you would react to it," Steve continued. "I didn't want to scare you off, but I've been dying to tell you about it for a long time."

He went on to describe a vision he had one year before they met, while he was touring the U.S. and Canada. "I was sitting on a pier along the Pacific Coast, watching the waves and seagulls and enjoying the ocean breeze. Then I closed my eyes and felt the sensation of my body being lifted. I was being carried into the clear blue sky, where I could look down on myself in life situations of the future. There were people with me I had never seen before. I could see myself off in a forest with a very attractive blond woman, and we had a blond, blue-eyed boy who was four or five years old. That's why I could hardly believe my eyes when I first saw you back in the ice cream shop. I knew right then that the young woman was you! The only thing missing now is the little boy."

After the experience, Steve said, he penned a short poem on the back of a restaurant napkin, titling it "To My Angel." He let go of her hand and reached into the inside pocket of his jacket, pulling out a wad of folded papers. Leafing through the addresses, business cards, and other material, he came across the napkin. The ink had been smudged and was barely legible, but Angel could read the title and the date that Steve had affixed to the bottom, right under his signature.

"That was quite a dream," she said.

"It was NOT a dream," he insisted. "Far from it. I think it was some form of assurance God provided for me during a period when I was very worried about the direction my life might turn."

Angel then told Steve about having seen the robed figure in her parents' bathroom as a child. "I never thought anyone would believe me," Angel said. "You're the first person who hasn't laughed at me!"

"I've kept my own experience a secret, too, ever since it happened," Steve replied. "I promised myself that I would never share it with anyone except the woman I saw in the vision. I knew you were the only one who would believe me or even care. Anyone else would think I was crazy."

They spent a long time discussing the meaning of these experiences, agreeing that, in time, they both would be able to understand why these episodes had occurred.

Inside, Angel was scared—torn between giving up everything she had built so she could be with Steve, or returning home and buying some time to think things over. Then she looked into his eyes and all of her doubts were erased. Steve was so tantalizing and irresistible, so blatantly honest in his words. His manner was low-keyed, not at all intimidating or intrusive. Yet, he had a firm hold on her heart and soul. She knew in that instant that they would be together for life.

Steve suggested that they gather up what they could from their possessions at the trailer and head for New York City to look for jobs and a place to live until he could sign on with another entertainment agency.

"What about Richard? Does he still owe you any money?" Angel asked.

"I really don't have any idea. We always spent it about as fast as we made it. I'd say, if anything, he might owe me a thousand bucks, maybe two. I doubt we'll ever see it."

The bus ride to New York was so relaxing that they both dozed off, Angel's head resting on Steve as he leaned against the window. She was awakened by a light tapping on her forehead.

"Hey Angel, I have an idea," Steve whispered. "Let's find one of those street corner marriage shops in New York and we'll make this thing official."

"Okay," she said, not stopping to reflect on the implications of his words. Angel drifted back to sleep without saying another word. They slept peacefully

# HIGH WIRE ANGEL

as the bus rolled along. She later awoke and stared at Steve as he slept. Suddenly, his eyes opened and met hers.

"Did I just have a dream that you asked me to marry you, or was it real?"

"Are you kidding?" Steve answered. "Of course it was for real. Did you change your mind? Don't tell me you're having cold feet already."

"No, I was just checking," she assured him.

He stroked Angel's long blonde hair and lightly kissed her on the forehead. "What do you want me to do, get down on one knee while I ask you again? Or should I call your dad and ask him if I can have his daughter's hand in marriage?"

"That's all right. It's just now starting to sink in. It's fine. I'd love to be your wife. No cold feet, honest."

The relationship between them was like that. Right from the start, they shared a silent understanding, giving them a special harmony.

They walked the streets of New York with no destination and nothing but a handbag of clothes and a small suitcase to call their own. Steve said he knew some friends who could put them up for the night but their phone numbers were unlisted, and he couldn't read the phone numbers from the tattered papers in his wallet.

Not wanting to risk a charge of kidnapping, Steve insisted on calling Frederick Pintye to confirm that Angel was not a runaway. "It's not that I don't trust you," he assured her. "I just want to make sure your father has no objections to you leaving the area. It's important for me to hear it from the horse's mouth."

Angel stood close to him so she could listen in through the phone receiver as Steve identified himself as a circus recruiter.

"Basically, Mr. Pintye, your daughter has decided to run away and join the circus," he said, trying to make his voice sound as serious as possible, despite the wide grin that had come over his face. "She's signed up to take lessons on how to walk the high wire and she is going to be an aerial performer. Also, Mr. Pintye, she has a new name now. She's the 'High Wire Angel.' Some day you'll see her on TV."

"What's this?" said the voice on the other end. "The circus, you say? Where is she now? Can I talk to her?"

"I'm sorry, Mr. Pintye, but I don't know where she is this evening. I just know I'm supposed to meet her at a certain corner here in the city tomorrow morning and we'll be heading down to Florida to begin her training."

"Could you give her a message for me?" he asked, his voice sounding desperate. "Could you tell her that I'd like her to call home before you guys leave so her mother and I can find out what the hell is going on?"

"I'll be happy to do that, and I'm sure you'll be hearing from her soon," Steve said in a very businesslike manner. "In the meantime, do you have any objections to your daughter leaving with us so she can begin her training?"

"It's her life. She can do as she wants. But give her the message, would you?"

Angel was warmed by the idea that her father missed her. She also appreciated the fact that he was not about to say or do anything that would further alienate her. In her mind, he had done enough damage two years earlier by drawing a line and refusing to budge, expecting that she would be the one who would give in.

Their next stop was "Eternal Bliss Personal Unions," a street corner marriage shop where they said their vows in a brief civil ceremony. Steve scouted around outside and found a young man who was willing to stand up for them as a witness, in exchange for a five-dollar bill.

Very matter-of-factly, the magistrate read from his handbook. No tears, no rice, no cake and no reception. "Some day when we're rich and famous we'll renew our vows at the Ringling Museum of Circus in Sarasota," Steve said with a wink. "Prince Charles can be the best man and Princess Diana can be your maid of honor. We'll have all the big-name circus stars in the world entertain for us."

Steve made a couple of phone calls and then suggested a plan. They would rent a car and travel out to Los Angeles to see his friend Gene, the stunt man. There were more performance opportunities on the West Coast than in the New York area, and Steve was sure Gene could help him make connections in Hollywood.

He suggested that Angel take a bus back to Mary Ellen's house at Westchester to get the rest of her belongings while he checked into a hotel to make arrangements for the trip and use the telephone to pursue some contacts for the resumption of his career in California.

"Just get what you're going to need and say your good-byes." Steve told her. "Tell them Mr. and Mrs. Wallenda are heading out west to pan for gold."

Mary Ellen couldn't get over the fact that not only had her tenant married a Wallenda and changed her last name, but she also had a new first name. She still called Angel "Lizzie," no matter how many times she was corrected. Mary Ellen was worried about her young friend's future. Although she had seen Angel develop from a bruised-face adolescent to a responsible adult, she had misgivings about the relationship with Steve.

"He's got no money to speak of, no job, no car, no insurance, and nothing else to offer you, Lizzie," Mary Ellen argued.

"I don't expect to you to understand," Angel replied. "Steve has a lot to offer me. I can't explain it, but I know I love Steve and he's the right man for me. We're going to build our lives together. We have a plan."

Angel returned to meet Steve at the hotel and found him to be restless and anxious to leave.

"How'd you make out?" she asked.

"Just so-so," Steve said. "The rent-a-car is all set, but as far as an agency,

# HIGH WIRE ANGEL

I have a few options, but nothing I'm satisfied with. Don't worry, though. There'll be plenty of chances once we get to California."

Frustrated by his lack of success on the phone, Steve said he had spent much of the time studying his well-worn Bible and underlining passages he was anxious to discuss with Angel.

Traveling across the country was more enjoyable and enlightening than Angel had ever imagined. Recognizing that there would be some lean times ahead, they were intent on enjoying themselves while they had the opportunity. There were no deadlines to meet and no other pressures.

Angel got a pretty good view of America through a car window. They headed south and then cut toward the Plains, sleeping in the car, stretching out on a blanket at a public park, visiting museums, and other historical sites, and being as carefree as their limited finances and common sense would allow.

Often they stopped at roadside rests or truck stops to take showers and eat. Angel got a big kick out of the smoke-filled diners and the characters who spend most of their lives behind the wheels of tractor-trailers. They showed her a side of life she never knew existed.

She felt like a foreigner as she and Steve passed through Tennessee. They went into a general store on the corner of a tiny crossroads community and she couldn't understand one word the cashier was saying because of his deep southern accent.

Despite all of the interesting sites, both Angel and Steve were relieved when their rent-a car passed the road sign that read "California." Each of them had grown weary of riding.

Before they pulled into Gene's, they drove over to the coast so Angel could see the ocean for the first time in her life. With one look at the rolling waves, she could appreciate what Steve meant when he said that he drew so much inspiration from the ocean. They spent the night on a blanket spread out beside the car, right at the edge of the beach.

The next morning, Angel awoke first and sat up to take it all in: California—land of sunshine and fast living. She felt the surging power of the Pacific, a force stronger than anything she'd witnessed before.

"What am I doing here?" Angel thought to herself as she watched the waves crash against the huge jagged rocks that protruded like stepping stones along the shore. "I don't know a soul in California."

It dawned on her that she was wholly dependent on Steve to help her find her way. This thought gave Angel an eerie feeling. She had always taken such pride in needing no one.

"What are you thinking about?" Steve broke her concentration. He squinted his eyes to avoid the early morning sun.

"I was just thinking about you, and how exciting it is to be in California." Angel didn't see any point in sharing her anxiety with him. Steve sat up on his elbow and reached his hand under her T-shirt to massage her back.

"You seem tense. I want you to relax," he said as his fingertips pressed on her firmly. He was such a strong man—raw and tough, self-assured about his own masculinity, and yet so passionate and gentle when he touched her.

Angel closed her eyes and absorbed the love that flowed between them as they listened to the seagulls cry and felt the tide rising closer and enveloping their feet. Steve lit a cigarette and held his wife close.

"I don't know about you, but I'm ready to get to work," he said, catching a strand of Angel's hair with his hand and twisting it around his fingers.

"I'm scared, Steve. What are we going to do?"

"First, we'll find Gene. He'll get us going in the right direction. He knows his way around out here, and I still have some connections myself. Don't worry."

They fought through the Los Angeles traffic maze and finally reached Gene's house late that afternoon. Things weren't quite as rosy as they had expected. Gene, an ex-football player, was drinking heavily and constantly arguing with his girlfriend, who was tiny compared to him. Although he was happy to see his old friend and willing to let Steve and Angel live with him, he rarely was sober enough to be much help.

Steve soon became disillusioned and displayed an ornery side that Angel had never seen in him before. The honeymoon definitely was over—too soon, it seemed to Angel. Steve grew depressed and would start arguments about meaningless things. Angel could not understand why her husband was so quick to flare up and get angry.

Gene and his girlfriend noticed it, too, and even Steve himself admitted that he was having trouble keeping his temper under control. Angel blamed it on the idleness and uncertainty over their future. Steve attributed his mood swings to his various physical ailments, particularly the chronic headaches which sometimes nearly caused him to lose consciousness.

After a long discussion at the dinner table, Gene and Angel convinced Steve to see a doctor, and he was admitted to a nearby hospital for observation.

That same night, Angel felt a dull discomfort in her chest and developed a cough. Noticing a terrible taste in her mouth, she went to spit in the dingy sink of Gene's bathroom and discovered that her mouth was full of blood. As soon as she told Gene about it, he panicked and called 911. Paramedics arrived in a matter of minutes.

The bleeding had subsided almost as suddenly as it started. After a thorough examination by the emergency responders, Angel promised she would go to the clinic just a few blocks away if there were further problems.

Gene's house was situated in the heart of Watts. Every time Angel walked out the door, she felt like a spectacle. Gene called her the "neighborhood honky," pointing out that the presence of a young, unaccompanied white girl in that area was a rarity. He warned Angel not to go out alone. She thought back to those times when her father had cautioned her never to enter certain

# HIGH WIRE ANGEL

neighborhoods because of what "they" would do to a white girl who dared to set foot on their preserve. She was not intimidated back then, and she decided to take her chances in Watts.

Never had she seen such terrible squalor and poverty. In an alley that ran by the house, winos and other homeless souls were lined up against the building. Each had his own little niche in the mini-village of street people and misfits. Grey-bearded, dirty men sorted through garbage cans. The pornography shop a few doors down on the corner did a brisk business, as did the prostitutes who plied their trade in the same vicinity.

Angel would often sit in the darkness of her bedroom at Gene's, next to the open window, and listen to the raw sounds of the city. One night she heard a series of gun blasts and screams, followed by the arrival of a half-dozen police cars just two houses away. Gene informed her that the place was a well-established "crack house."

Angel had to do something to keep busy and take her mind off the depressing surroundings, so one morning she picked up Steve's Bible and began reading through it, paying particular attention to the hundreds of passages he had underlined. Steve had scrawled notes in the borders of many pages, and she became thoroughly engrossed in it.

For the first time in her life, Angel began to understand some of the words that would become beacons leading her to a spirituality of her own.

She also started tinkering around with a wooden recorder that Steve had given her before he was admitted to the hospital. Never formally trained in music, Angel was able to play by ear and was soon tooting the melodies from several songs she had learned as a child, many of them the Hungarian folk tunes her mother had sung. Today, Angel counts the crude instrument as one of her most cherished possessions. Playing it reminds her of the period of great uncertainty and trauma that marked her life in California.

Steve didn't like the idea of his wife staying at Gene's house any more than she enjoyed being there. He called from the hospital to inform Angel that he had become friends with a fellow Vietnam veteran. The man had recently been discharged from the hospital and insisted that Angel move in with him and his wife up in the Big Bear City area about two hours off the mountains.

"That sounds fine with me, but how are you doing? Did they figure out what's causing your headaches?"

"I'm okay," he answered. "I'm getting used to it. With all I've been through, I've pretty much resigned myself to the fact that I'll never get rid of these headaches. They can keep doing their tests, but I think I'll just have to live with the pain."

He gave Angel the address of his friend and told her she was expected there that evening. Luckily, there was a bus stop just one block away from the house on the mountain. Angel left Gene a note thanking him for his hospitality, packed her things, and was sitting at the bus depot within an hour.

When she arrived at the house, she found an envelope with the name "Angel" on it, taped to the door. A note inside read, "Family emergency. We had to go to San Francisco. Help yourself to whatever you need." The key to the front door was taped to the back of the note.

Angel's deepening interest in the Bible sustained her through the idleness. The more she read and the longer she thought about it, the more she realized that the answers to the questions of how she should live her life, support her husband, and endure the uncertainty of their future were contained in one time-tested book of knowledge, wisdom, and advice.

Her studying was interrupted one afternoon by a loud knock at the door. Through the peephole she could see Steve's smiling face. He opened his mouth wide and leaned his head closer to the hole to make a ridiculously distorted image in the curved glass. Angel opened the door and greeted him with a hug and a kiss.

They found a tiny apartment to tide them over, and Angel began to look for any kind of work that would generate some income. Steve reiterated his commitment to take her under his wing and train her to become his high wire performing partner just as soon as he could make arrangements.

This bolstered Angel's spirits. However, a dark cloud was forming on the horizon. She was brushing her teeth one evening when she discovered that there was once again spots of dark blood in her saliva. As she crawled into bed, she mentioned it to Steve.

"You probably just brushed your teeth too hard and your gums are bleeding," he suggested.

"I'm afraid not," Angel said. "This blood is coming from somewhere deep down in my throat or lungs. It comes up when I cough. Something's wrong."

Angel finally told him what had happened back at Gene's place. She hadn't wanted to alarm him with her own physical problems when he had his own troubles. Steve grew deeply concerned and insisted that she see a doctor.

The following day, Angel underwent a thorough physical examination at Los Angeles County Hospital and went home to await the results. A day later, their telephone rang with shocking news from the examining physician: Angel was pregnant.

"What about the bleeding?" she asked. "Is that normal during pregnancy?"

"Probably just a ruptured vessel in one of your lungs," the doctor said. "Nothing to worry about."

Steve was at the other end of the apartment when she received the news. As he emerged to ask who was on the phone, Angel said it was a wrong number. Then she went into the bathroom to hide while she tried to figure out the best way to break the news to Steve.

"How can we possibly afford to raise a child when neither of us is working?" she worried. "Will this mean an end to my ambitions to become an aerialist? How will Steve react? We haven't even discussed having children!"

On what should have been a tremendously exciting morning, Angel was a study in abject despair. She decided that the proper thing to do was to just tell him and let the chips fall where they may. Steve was lying flat on the bed, smoking a cigarette and staring up at the ceiling as she approached him.

"Hey Steve," Angel said, trying to talk loud enough to interrupt him as he sang along with the song "Traveling Man," blaring from their little clock-radio.

"Isn't that Rick Nelson great!" he said, keeping the beat by pounding his fingers on the headboard of the bed. "He was an aerialist, you know. I used to know him and his brother Dave pretty well. It's too bad Rick had to die."

"Uhm, Steve, I'm not too interested in Rick Nelson right now. There's something you need to know."

"What's the problem?" he asked, turning down the radio volume and looking her in the eyes. Angel stuttered as she tried to form the words. Then she just let it come out.

"I'm pregnant."

"No!" Steve said.

At first, she thought he was mad. Then his face broke into a warm, wide smile. "That's fantastic, honey! Are you serious? You have no idea how happy this makes me!"

Angel was still trying to comprehend how the addition of a baby would affect them. If Steve was concerned, he showed no sign of it. He insisted that they go out to a fancy restaurant for a steak dinner to celebrate.

Pregnancy provided Angel with added incentive to establish a stable home environment. She wanted to rebuild—start saving money and plotting their lives through an organized plan. She had a strong belief that things would eventually work out for the best.

However, Steve appeared to have trouble focusing on any long term goals or strategy. Because of the disagreement with Richard, they no longer had any rigging to set up a practice wire. Steve talked about suing to recover the lost equipment and family souvenirs, or threatening Richard bodily harm if that's what it took to bring about justice.

"Don't lower yourself to his level," Angel pleaded. "If those are the things that mean so much to him, just let him have them. We've got plenty of time to start over."

It was just her basic confidence asserting itself—Angel's lifelong belief that she could achieve anything she set out to do.

Chapter 14

# SOMETHING'S NOT RIGHT

A burning feeling in her right leg began to nag Angel. It was centered near a rubbery lump that had formed on the front of the ankle after she bruised it six or seven years earlier while doing gymnastics. The lump had never gone away and now it was growing larger and firmer. The skin around it was turning yellow.

She tried to ignore it. There were already enough problems to contend with. Steve was showing little ambition. Angel began to question whether they were growing—moving toward something in their lives. Whenever she tactfully suggested that he look for more conventional employment until he re-established himself professionally, Steve cited his frequent headaches and said he didn't think he could withstand the rigors of a nine-to-five job.

Through it all, Angel's faith in God and her enthusiasm to learn more about the spiritual dimension of life were intensifying. She and Steve attended various churches in the Los Angeles area, but found most of them too ceremonial or conservative for their needs. At Bible classes, Steve wasn't afraid to take issue with interpretations he believed to be wrong. Often what he said made sense; in a lot of cases, he knew more than the teachers did. He liked to ask questions, but the ministers preferred dogma to giving satisfactory answers. Steve rubbed people the wrong way, and it sometimes embarrassed Angel.

They found themselves with a lot of idle time, so they studied the Bible together on their own when Steve was willing. He had some very deep and complex beliefs. Early in life, Steve had developed an intense interest in trying to unlock some of the spiritual secrets of the world, or at least being able to comprehend them. He was patient with Angel and was able to explain his thoughts very well; she found that she could listen to him for hours.

Despite all he had been through, he never lost faith that God was protecting him and would pull him back to the path of righteousness whenever he strayed too far.

Much to his wife's delight, Steve began laying the groundwork for a thrilling plan that attracted plenty of attention when he announced it to a newspaper reporter in Los Angeles. Karl Wallenda had perfected the Seven-Man Pyramid that had brought the family international acclaim. Steve decided that he was going to put together an Eight-Man Pyramid.

Karl had quietly developed the act more than 50 years earlier and family members had practiced it; however, the stunt was never performed in public. Steve believed a revival of the act and the accompanying publicity would be one way to pay tribute to Karl and focus attention on his own career.

"Karl was always working on something to stay one step ahead of everyone else," Steve explained. "He had the eight-man in the bag in case someone matched the seven-man. No one ever did, so Karl never had to pull it out."

Steve saw the Eight-Man Pyramid as a new challenge. And he never backed away from a professional challenge. Angel expressed great enthusiasm for the plan until she learned, much later and quite unexpectedly, that he wanted her to be part of it. She was standing at the sink, washing the dishes and marveling at the constant pushing and kicking of the baby inside her, when he casually dropped the bombshell.

"Hey Angel, how would you like to go down in the history of aerial performing?"

"That's a good one," she chortled. "What do you want me to do, be the first woman to give birth on the high wire?"

"No, not quite, but something like that," Steve said. "You do trust me when it comes to the wire, don't you?"

"Wire, yes. Childbirth, no."

"Seriously, after you have the baby, I'd like you to be part of the act. I'm going to call it 'The Eight.' Karl always referred to the Seven-Man Pyramid as 'The Seven.' You and I are going to be part of 'The Eight.' What do you think?"

"You're serious?"

"Absolutely!"

"What makes you think I'd be right for it? What if I lost my balance and made the whole thing come down?"

"We'd work on it, over and over, until we got it right. You'd be on the top, anyhow. You're light enough and you have enough body control to ride on the shoulders of the top man and just basically stand there. The rest of us would be doing all the work."

Because Angel realized that her pregnancy would keep her out of commission for a few months, she knew it was safe to tell Steve that she would be willing to try it once she was able. Actually her stomach grew uneasy just thinking about being part of it. Her mind flashed back to the countless times she had seen the videotape of "The Seven" collapsing as Karl Wallenda tried to recreate it for the television film crew.

Steve's new project was planned out in great detail. He would train a team of ten performers (two alternates) in the Big Bear Valley, where the new act would attract great publicity. He placed advertisements in Circus Report and Amusement Business, seeking physically and psychologically suitable recruits. Oddly, no mention was made of wire-walking experience.

"I want to train them my way," Steve explained. "If they're already trained, I don't want them because they're not going to be able to do it my way. We're talking about making history here, so I'm not going to settle for just anybody."

He approached the Ringling Brother organization, which had been working with the famous Carrillo Brothers of Venezuela on a seven-man pyramid until the act collapsed during a practice session on the low wire and the plan was scrapped. Following that accident, the Carrillos had contacted Steve about a joint effort, but nothing came of it.

As he expected, the Ringling representatives were interested in seeing what we had to offer. Inspired by that, Angel started making a list of the dozens of people who called in response to the ads. While all of this was going on, Steve began working on arrangements for another spectacular feat that he had wanted to orchestrate for many years: a skywalk on a 300-foot-long cable between two hot air balloons.

The tethered balloons would rise hundreds of feet in the air. Once they were steadied, Steve would walk across the wire. Because the performance would take place so high in the sky, where few people could see it, he would grant a television production company the exclusive filming rights.

Even though there was an element of danger in each of the plans, Angel knew that if Steve put his mind to it, he could put together the necessary components for an act that would be safe and commercially successful.

From the time she saw him walk the wire high above the crowd at the Westchester Mall, Angel recognized the seriousness with which he took his work. Steve paid very close attention to detail and would never consider performing a wire walk without recognizing all possible risks and taking steps to reduce them.

With Steve's name back in the headlines, his chief rival of earlier years, daredevil Evel Knievel, announced he was coming out of retirement to perform a stunt that involved jumping over 15 buses on a motorcycle. As he had before, Steve challenged Knievel to a motorcycle ride across a wire strung across Angel Falls in Brazil, at a height of 3,800 feet.

Why Angel Falls? "Because it's the highest waterfall in the world and it has the same name as my wife! Isn't that enough reason?" Steve told one of the newspaper reporters. Although Evel Knievel refused the challenge, he did attract media attention to his bus feat, just as Steve had predicted.

"I don't know why that guy gets so much attention," Steve lamented. "He's not anything special. A lot of people could do the stunts he does."

# HIGH WIRE ANGEL

While the pyramid and hot air balloon plans were in the works, Angel and Steve made friends with a couple who operated an all-terrain vehicle track called "Adventure Expeditions of the Wilderness." They were considering expanding their business and eventually putting in an amusement attraction where Steve could work as an aerialist. It wasn't an ideal situation, but it was a glimmer of hope.

The Wallendas started working there full time. Angel helped the riders find the flight suits and equipment and signed them up, while Steve taught them how to ride. They made many friends, including Peter Lupus Jr., whose father had starred on "Mission Impossible" while Steve was doing stunts in Hollywood.

Their next-door neighbor, a middle-aged widow named Bea, also became a close friend. She often invited Steve and Angel over to eat dinner and watch movies with her. Whenever Angel became upset over Steve's behavior, she knew that Bea had a sympathetic ear and a shoulder to cry on.

All the while she worked at the track, the pain in Angel's right ankle was worsening. Eventually, carrying the extra weight that seven months of pregnancy had added, she decided she couldn't stand the stabbing pain anymore. The lump had nearly doubled in size and it burned like fire. Nothing would control the suffering, so Angel made an appointment with a family doctor in the Big Bear area.

He looked at it only briefly and diagnosed it as a bad bruise that would begin to heal in a few days. Those days grew into a month, with little change in her ankle. The dark cloud had moved closer.

One night while Angel was watching TV, a terrifying feeling came over her. Numbness struck her hands and arms, then traveled up her neck to her face. She couldn't remember what day it was or even where she was. The whole room was spinning. When she tried to tell Steve what was happening to her, she couldn't form the words. Panicked and unable to help her, Steve ran next door to get Bea. The two of them rushed Angel down off the mountain to Loma Linda Hospital. Nurses there began pumping blood thinners and other medication into her, trying to bring her out of what the doctors had diagnosed as a transient ischemic attack—a "T.I.A." or "mini-stroke" is how they described it. Angel's ankle also hurt more than ever during this whole episode, but the doctors were not concerned about it.

In and out of consciousness, she could feel the nurses rubbing cold jelly on her abdomen, listening to the baby's heartbeat and watching its movement through an ultrasound monitor. "At least this way, the mystery is over," the nurse told Angel as she looked closely at the TV screen that showed a blurred image of the tiny infant in her womb. "Real soon now, you're going to be giving birth to a ... Do you want to know?"

Angel nodded anxiously.

"A baby girl," the nurse beamed.

"That can't be," Steve insisted. "I've known all along that this baby is a boy. You're not going to tell me any differently."

"Look for yourself at the monitor; you won't find any male plumbing there," the nurse responded.

"Your machine is wrong!" Steve protested. "All I can see is a blur on the screen. You can't tell anything for sure. I know it's a boy."

Because of the growing concern about Angel's physical condition and the health of the baby, the obstetrician said the best course of action at this late stage of pregnancy was to induce labor.

Angel knew nothing about how to have a baby, and nobody explained a thing to her. She had no idea that it was going to be as painful as it was. Steve came in and out of the room, trying to comfort her, but Angel was nasty to everybody. She shouted for a cigarette, then cursed at the nurses when they wouldn't give her one. After one of the nurses caught her trying to sneak into the bathroom for a smoke, she flung herself into the bed like a spoiled kid. A few minutes later, a nurse whirred her into the delivery room and summoned Steve.

Despite Angel's intense discomfort, she giggled at the sight of her husband dressed in the hospital "scrubs," complete with his green gown, mask, and booties.

"You don't look so great yourself," Steve laughed.

"I can't help it," Angel said. "What am I supposed to do? Wear a dress? Let's get this over with."

"This time you're pushing with your contractions," Steve replied, wiping the sweat from her brow with a moist towel. "This next time around, make up your mind that you're going to push with all of your might. The doctor says you're ready."

"What do you know?" Angel snapped back, grimacing. "You've never given birth before. It hurts like hell. You're lucky you're a man."

With the next contraction, she decided it was now or never. Breathing very heavily, Angel gave it everything she had. As soon as the baby's head emerged, the doctors motioned for Steve to step over and help. Together, they pulled the baby out and Steve cut the umbilical cord.

Angel sighed in exhaustion, not even thinking to ask whether it was a boy or a girl. "So much for your machines," a beaming Steve told the nurse. "It's a boy, Angel. We have our boy!"

Steven Gregory Wallenda II was just five pounds, eight ounces, with wisps of blond hair and deep blue eyes. Another part of Steve's vision had come to pass.

Chapter 15

# I CAN'T DO IT

Angel Wallenda was ill-prepared for motherhood. Never having even handled a newborn before, she was now responsible for nurturing one. She was too ashamed to ask Steve or anyone else for advice. Surely, she reasoned, her maternal instincts would take over.

The nurse tried to hand Steven up to Angel immediately after he was born, but she wasn't ready. "Not now; he's all messy," she said, before catching herself. "I mean, let me get my breath and rest for a minute." Her awkwardness was obvious to everyone. Angel felt overwhelmed by this tiny human being as he screamed and made strange faces.

More amused than disturbed by her attitude, Steve took the baby and held him, toying with his fingers and softly stroking Steven's face. Angel could sense the love he already felt for their little boy. After a while, he handed the baby over to a nurse, who said she would clean, weigh, and measure Steven before bringing him for breastfeeding.

"We did it," Steve said as he adjusted Angel's pillows. "I've never been happier in my life, Angel." She only hoped that it would last.

Once they brought Steven to her, Angel felt more comfortable in handling him. Steve parted the blanket so they could peer at their son's face.

"What a beautiful baby," Angel thought. "I can't wait to establish a relationship with him."

No one in her family except her sister had even known that she was pregnant. Jeannie had promised not to tell anyone anything concerning Angel's whereabouts, but this veil of secrecy was about to be lifted. She was thrilled with the news of Steven's arrival. "You have to let me tell Mom and Dad all about it," Jeannie insisted when Angel called her. "This is their first grandchild, and they're going to want to know."

Angel urged her not to. She had no desire to talk to either her mother or her father after what she had been through. Part of her derived a certain element of pleasure from keeping her dad in suspense about her life.

Just before Angel was discharged, she finally did call her parents' house. Her father answered in his typically gruff manner.

"I have good news for you, Dad."

There was silence on the other end.

"Is this Lizzie? Where are you?"

"I'm in a hospital out in L.A., Dad. I just thought you might want to know that you're a grandfather."

There was more silence.

"What's this all about?" he asked. Frederick may have been more surprised to hear from his daughter than he was to learn he now had a grandson. "What are you doing out there? Are you in the circus, or what?"

"No, not yet. But I'm working on it. I'm married now, Dad, to Steve Wallenda, from the famous wire-walking family, you know?"

"Wallenda, you say? Sure, Wallenda. I've heard of them. The circus people, right? Are you okay?"

"I'm fine and the baby's fine."

Frederick Pintye, never a man of many words, could think of nothing to say and seemed anxious to get off the phone, so Angel informed him she would fill him in on all the developments in her life by writing a long letter.

She hung up and stared at the half-empty pack of cigarettes lying on the table next to the telephone. Angel laughed to herself as she thought back to the time she quit school rather than stop smoking cigarettes. Now, despite an even deeper dependency, she was giving them up voluntarily. All of the literature she had read about the effect of cigarette smoke on an infant's lungs convinced her to quit.

That was one aspect of her personality in which Angel took great pride. She could easily respond to whatever personal sacrifices might be demanded of her. Steve couldn't bring himself to quit, but he did agree not to smoke near the baby.

After Steven was discharged, the Wallendas cashed in their savings on a used mobile home situated at Kriskay Lodge, a hotel next to the Adventure Expedition track. Even though Angel was still feeling drained and weak, she helped the lodge owners clean their cabins to earn enough extra dollars to buy a car.

Out of nowhere, Steve's Uncle Leon called to tell them they were welcome to have a small Toyota that Leon had inherited from Steve's grandfather. Steve was able to patch the body and repair the engine so that it would pass the California State inspection.

Angel and Steve started exercising in the pool at the lodge to help get their bodies back in shape for Steve's return to the high wire and Angel's long-awaited training. Steven would lie in his port-a-crib and keep himself entertained for long periods of time, affording his parents the opportunity for uninterrupted exercise.

Eventually, Steve acquired some cable and the necessary rigging to set up a practice area on the grounds of Kriskay Lodge. The wire was securely stretched between two trees. They started with a low wire, about three feet off the ground, which Angel could use until Steve was convinced that she could perform safely on the higher wire.

Angel could not believe the ease with which her husband glided across the low wire the first time he stepped onto it.

"You big showoff," she complained. "You look like you don't even need to practice."

"Don't let that fool you," Steve replied. "The biggest mistake anyone can make on the wire is thinking that he's too good to practice. The first time you let your guard down on the high wire, you'll be carried off in an ambulance, or a hearse. Believe me, I've seen it happen."

Soon it was Angel's turn. First, she stepped up behind Steve on the wire and walked across while holding on to his shoulders, much like their performances at the mall and at Byram Day. They repeated this process for several trips, then dismounted for a rest.

Steve handed Angel the balancing pole, which weighed a hefty thirty-five pounds, and instructed her to walk on the ground, trying to put one foot directly in front of the other over a distance of several feet, all the while getting accustomed to the weight of the pole.

He taught her how to walk and still keep her balance while constantly transferring her weight from heel to toe, which felt awkward. Angel experienced a deep sense of adventure as she came to appreciate the danger and recognize the skill required to keep from falling. And this was only on the ground!

For the first month or so, she could barely support her own weight on the wire. She worked hard to build her muscles through a daily regimen of push-ups, chin-ups, knee bends, and other exercises. None of these was any substitute for the strength-building that occurred by actually walking on the wire. Maintaining balance on such a slender surface requires the use of a set of muscles that can only be toughened by repetition.

Steve was impressed by Angel's ability to learn the basic walking techniques very quickly, thanks in large part to the body control she had developed while practicing gymnastics in her earlier years. As she grew stronger, practice became more enjoyable. Back and forth she went, sometimes holding Steve's outstretched hand as he walked along the ground beside her and, at other times, balancing herself only with the pole while Steve served as her "spotter."

There were falls, but Angel was always able to brace herself before she reached the ground three feet below the wire and she was never injured. Gradually, she relied less on Steve's support and more on her own skill.

Finally, she could make it all the way across unassisted if she walked very slowly and did not allow anything to break her concentration. Angel was able to block out everything—Steven's crying, wind, rain, aching muscles—as she moved across the wire.

Steve kept reminding her that proper control could only come by repeating the walking process over and over again, and that the overall goal was to make it look easy. He also explained how she should work to develop a steadier pace so that her steps appeared smoother and cleaner. Eventually, he gave Angel pointers on techniques that would allow her to squat and sit on the wire, then return to her feet and walk the remainder of the distance to the other end.

Angel's progress was hampered by a piercing pain in her ankle. She couldn't put her full weight on it or bend it very far because the area around the strange lump just above the shoe line had swelled and her entire ankle had grown stiff. She felt a throbbing pain with every heartbeat, yet Angel did everything within her power to hide her suffering from Steve. She was afraid he would order her to stop training until the pain went away. At times, she would grimace and find him looking at her skeptically.

As Steven grew more curious and demanding, their friend Bea agreed to babysit him so his parents could spend time practicing without any interruptions for diaper changes, feeding, and other baby duties.

One afternoon, Steve picked up his balancing pole and did a few quick passes on the wire while Angel sat cross-legged in the grass and watched.

"If you're going to sit and watch the show, you're going to have to pay admission," he joked. "Seriously, let's get going and take advantage of the chance we have while Bea's here."

Finally, Angel gave in and told Steve she could no longer go on. "I can't," she confessed.

"Why not?"

"My ankle. It's killing me. Look at it." Angel raised her right pant leg and held her bare foot in the air for Steve to inspect as he looked down from the wire.

"Oh, man. I didn't know it was that bad," he said, stepping onto the ground and walking over for a closer examination.

"I've been keeping it from you. I didn't want you to worry, but I've got to get something done about it soon."

Steve bent down and rubbed his thumb over the yellow lump to determine how big it had grown. Angel writhed in pain. "Please Steve, enough!" she said as tears came to her eyes. "Why aren't the doctors concerned? It just keeps getting worse."

She was hounded by the notion that something was seriously wrong. It had to be more than an aggravated bruise. Angel's concern grew deeper when, as they were talking, she felt a sudden congestion deep in her lungs. When she cleared her throat, she could once again taste the awful flavor of blood in her mouth.

Her mind began to race. It all seemed so unreal.

Unable to sense Angel's growing panic, Steve took hold of her hand and walked her over to a tall shade tree overlooking their practice area. He lay down in the cool grass and motioned for her to join him. Angel sat down and let him rest his head in her lap.

"I hope you're all right," he said softly as his eyes closed and his hand began to stroke her thigh.

"I'm beginning to wonder," Angel replied, trying to remain calm. "You see, there's another problem. I'm coughing up blood again."

Startled, Steve turned his body and rose to his knees. "Why didn't you tell me?"

"It just started again, just a couple of minutes ago."

"That's it," Steve said firmly. "You're going to get an appointment at Big Bear Hospital so we can find out what's wrong."

They walked inside and Steve headed straight for the telephone. While Angel shared the latest developments with Bea, Steve discussed her case with a family practitioner. The doctor scheduled Angel for X-rays and tomography, as well as tests for tuberculosis and several other diseases.

Once again, the medical professionals could find nothing inside Angel's lungs that might be causing the bleeding. They also assured her that the ankle injury was nothing more than a deep bruise that would heal itself with proper rest.

Chapter 16

# SOMEBODY DO SOMETHING

Angel and Steve left the hospital deeply depressed about the lack of a diagnosis and perplexed by the way her case had been handled. A week after that appointment, Angel suffered another T.I.A. that floored her. In the process of changing Steven's diaper, she felt lightheaded, then dizzy and disoriented.

"Steve!" she yelled in desperation, holding one hand against the baby to keep him from rolling off the changing table while she knelt and pressed her other hand against her forehead.

Angel's face went numb. Luckily, Steve was in the next room talking to Bea and came running when she called. Try as she might, Angel could not make her lips form the words she wanted to say. She was terrified.

Grabbing the baby in one arm, Steve told Bea to start the car as he helped Angel to her feet. As they rushed to the hospital emergency room, the dizziness and all of Angel's other symptoms went away. Steve was shocked when the emergency room doctor examined her only briefly and simply told her to return home and rest.

"Can't you people see that there is something seriously wrong with this girl?" Bea pleaded with the head nurse.

"I'm not the doctor," she replied, "but I think it's just stress. Look how thin she is. She probably hasn't been eating enough."

Angel believed that, if nothing else, she deserved to be treated with decency and respect by medical professionals. There was no question in her mind that she needed more than rest and relaxation.

While Steve and Angel were walking out of the hospital, the examining physician spotted them and called Steve aside. Bea had pulled the car into the entranceway of the hospital and Angel collapsed onto the front seat. In the doorway of the hospital, she could see the doctor talking while Steve appeared to be nodding in agreement. Her concern grew as she watched them, the hot afternoon sun pouring through the windshield to make her even more uncomfortable.

# HIGH WIRE ANGEL

"What could they possibly be talking about?" she asked Bea.

"Probably something about the bill," she offered. "You know these doctors—first things first." Angel closed her eyes for a moment and when she reopened them, Steve was walking toward the car, shaking his head.

"What was that all about?" she demanded.

"Wait'll you hear this," he said. "The doctor said you might have some psychological problems stemming from your troubled childhood. He thinks you could be faking some of your symptoms to get attention and..."

"What a bunch of bull!" Angel interrupted, reaching for the door handle with full intentions of storming into the hospital and giving the doctor a piece of her mind. She had never discussed more than scant details of her upbringing with him, and yet he had seized upon these few comments to accuse her of inventing her symptoms.

Steve grabbed Angel's arm and pulled her back into the seat. "I already told him he was way off-base," he assured her. "Forget him. There are hundreds of doctors around L.A. We'll just find one who is willing to listen and check this thing out. Let's see how you feel by tonight," Steve suggested. "We'll take it from there."

By dinner time, Angel was back to full strength except for the pain in her ankle, and the idea of follow-up medical care faded from their minds. They still had a modicum of faith in the medical profession. As long as qualified professionals examined Angel and determined that her problems were nothing to be concerned about, Steve and Angel felt inclined to accept their findings.

The Wallendas took advantage of an opportunity to move their trailer to the North Shore Mobile Home Park in Fawnskin. It was a beautiful setting. A warm, soothing wind blew in from Big Bear Lake and the scenery was spectacular, especially when the late afternoon sun skipped across the waves.

Steve immediately set up a low wire as well as a trapeze. He also began working on the rigging for the high wire, to be strung at a height of about fifteen feet. Angel's heart pounded as she watched, the shiny new wire far above her head beckoning to her. She realized that she must be patient.

Just a couple of steps on the low wire told Angel that her strange illness and the brief layoff had drained much of her stamina. It took several trips across the wire over a period of three or four days, with Steve walking on the ground holding her hand, before Angel's skills had returned to anywhere near their previous level.

"Your body is trying to get back to normal, so it's only natural that those same muscles are going to protest when you put them to use again," Steve assured her. "Your technique is super, Angel. God, you could be a great one. All you have to do is regain the control you had before."

After their practice sessions, they often loaded Steven in a backpack and walked along the shore barefoot, or they carried a picnic lunch down to the beach and took him wading. He couldn't walk on his own yet, but he could stand and take a few steps if he held onto somebody's hand. Occasionally he flopped into the water face-first, always giggling as he was pulled back out.

Angel loved to watch the boats bobbing in the current while Steve sang some of the old sailor's songs he had learned as a child. Like any adoring mother, she couldn't imagine that there could be a baby any more beautiful than hers. He had inherited his father's attractive physical features along with his mother's light blond hair and blue eyes. Steve felt shortchanged because Angel paid so much attention to the baby. She sensed this jealousy, but tended to attribute it to Steve's moodiness. Angel sometimes caught him cradling his forehead with his hands, trying to soothe the pain of headaches that continued to plague him.

Angel was never quite sure what to expect from Steve. One minute he could be quiet and introverted and, the next moment, he would be in high spirits and eager to help her practice.

He began to show her tricks that could be performed after she had mastered the basics: standing on one leg, kneeling onto the wire, or "bouncing" on it as if it were a trampoline. These all required great skill and new types of body coordination.

"Karl was an expert at this," Steve explained. "He would bounce on the wire and lean one way, like he was going to fall, and you could hear a gasp from the crowd. It must have given him a great feeling of satisfaction."

Besides contending with Steve's inconsistent disposition, Angel had to sandwich practice in between her cleaning job at Kriskay Lodge and taking care of Steven. She also took a part-time job working at a laundromat across town. They desperately needed money, and the burden fell on Angel. Despite his wife's pleadings, Steve was reluctant to look for a job.

"All I want to do is walk the wire," he once told her as they discussed their financial problems. "That's what I was meant to do."

"That's all fine with me," Angel retorted, "as long as you're willing to promote yourself or get hooked on with an agency that can get you some performing contracts. They're not going to come knocking down your door, you know."

Bea became Angel's sounding board as she grew increasingly frustrated by Steve's lack of ambition. The pyramid and hot-air balloon plans had long ago been shelved. Angel wondered if her husband—the "last of the Great Wallendas"—would ever perform publicly again.

As conditions worsened, they each retreated into a private world. Days would pass without any intimate or meaningful conversation. Angel knew that Bea was right: the only way she was going to be able to help Steve overcome his problems was to make him confront them.

She chose one of their drives high into the Hollywood hills to plead her case. "I love you very much," she said tenderly, "but it's going to be hard for us to put together a decent life or even stay together unless you can do more to help. We've got to move forward. I feel like I'm wasting my life away. If I'm going to be a high wire performer, I'm going to need a trainer who's as serious about his own career as I am about my own. If that's not going to happen, I'm going to find another career. And, another thing. I can't pay these bills alone. I need some help from my husband!"

Steve stared out into the lights of the city spread out below. He knew she was right. "I understand," he said, avoiding eye contact with Angel. "I'll try harder. I really will. I know I haven't been fair to you."

When Angel took Steven for his check-up at Big Bear Valley Hospital, she mentioned to Dr. Donald Elia, the pediatrician, that her leg was still throbbing and burning. He recalled having looked at it before the baby was born. All it took this time was a brief glance for him to notice how much the lump had grown.

"My goodness," he said, the furrows on his brow deepening as he closely examined the ankle. The doctor asked Angel about her other symptoms. He made no effort to hide his concern.

With the conditioning and training regimen that had followed childbirth, her strength should have improved, Dr. Elia noted, yet she was getting weaker. For periods of two or three days Angel would feel okay, except for the pain in her leg. But then she would hit a spell where she was so worn-out that she could hardly move. Something was draining all of her energy. Dr. Elia was quite certain the problems were not stress-related. He took a biopsy and sent the sample to a laboratory for analysis.

Angel tried to put it all out of her mind as she waited for the results to come back. When she wasn't working, she was practicing, heartened by what she recognized as a much better attitude on Steve's part.

Finally, Angel got a phone call from Dr. Elia, who asked her to see him early the next morning, before he made his hospital rounds. He said the findings were too complicated to discuss on the phone. At last, Angel thought, she would learn what had been bothering her for so long.

That night, she tried to avoid falling asleep, for fear that she would miss her appointment. Finally, sometime after two o'clock, Angel crawled under the covers next to Steve and let the sound of the breeze outside lull her to sleep. A couple of hours later, she was as wide awake as if somebody had grabbed her and pulled her onto the floor.

She sat alone in the kitchen, staring out at the moonlit lake until Steve emerged in the doorway.

"What are you doing up so early?" he asked.

"The same thing you are, I guess, I couldn't sleep."

"You're not worried, are you?"

Angel didn't answer him. Steve stepped closer and began to rub her shoulders and back as she slumped onto the kitchen table. "I didn't like the way he avoided me on the phone," Angel murmured. "I just don't know what to think."

They were interrupted by Steven's loud bawling at the other end of the trailer. Steve went to comfort him and returned to the kitchen cuddling their emerging toddler.

"You're going to drive yourself crazy if you keep worrying about it when you don't really have any information to go on." Steve said.

"I can't help it," Angel insisted. "I don't like the way the doctors talk about it. I think there's something seriously wrong with me, and none of them want to deal with it."

Her appointment at Big Bear Valley Hospital was so early in the morning that the hallways were nearly empty. Steve stayed in the lobby to watch the baby. As Angel peeked her head inside the door of Dr. Elia's office, she found him sitting at his desk, studying some charts.

"Hello," she said, jarring him.

"Oh, I'm glad you're early, Angel. Let's get right down to business."

He began reading from a clinically-detailed report, so full of medical jargon that it made little sense to Angel. Then he looked up.

"What you have is massive damage to your ankle, extending well into the bone. It's not a very pleasant situation."

"So now what do I do?" she asked.

"You have to see an orthopedic surgeon immediately, and he can take care of you from this point on. Something is going to have to be done about it. It's nothing I'm qualified to deal with." He referred her to Dr. Garrett Peters at a highly-regarded Catholic hospital not far from their trailer.

"Now do you see what I mean?" Angel said to Steve as they loaded their sleepy-eyed boy into his car seat and prepared to head back home. "I told you it was something serious."

"You don't know that. Stop thinking the worst! All he said was that you have to see a specialist, right? Don't read anything into it that isn't there."

"Well, they wouldn't have made such a long report about it unless it was something terrible. Maybe they're going to cut off my leg."

"Stop talking like that!" Steve urged. "We'll just have to wait and see."

A couple of days later, before her next appointment, Angel had another T.I.A. while sitting at a table penning a letter to Jeannie. Her fingers went numb and her mouth would not move. Instinctively, she shook her head and, within seconds, she was back to normal.

Angel looked at the illegible scribble that had flowed from her pen. The attack had come on so surreptitiously that she had continued writing several incoherent lines before realizing that something was wrong.

Steve was at the grocery store, so she was on her own. She searched her purse for Dr. Peters' number and managed to dial his office, despite an uncontrollable shake in her hands. The receptionist said he was unavailable, but she promised to give him the message and have him call back if he saw any reason for concern. He never called.

At Angel's appointment two days later, Dr. Peters reviewed her case history and discussed her symptoms at length before concluding that she never had suffered a T.I.A. Her physical problems had been the result of pregnancy

# HIGH WIRE ANGEL                                                        105

and the stress she had been under in recent months, he insisted.

"No way!" Angel protested, rising to her feet. "I heard that line back at Loma Linda, but they said my symptoms would disappear after the baby was born. I don't think I'm getting any better, do you?"

"There's nothing to indicate that you have any physical problems that would make you feel the way you describe," Dr. Peters continued. "Have you considered undergoing some counseling to see if this might be something psychological?"

That statement pushed Angel to the breaking point.

"Give me my records, I'm getting out of here!" she shouted, arousing the attention of three or four hospital staffers and a waiting room full of at least a half-dozen other patients. "I'm not one of your hypochondriacs. I'll just go find another doctor who knows what he's doing. Why don't you go back to medical school and learn how to be a doctor?"

Steve didn't say a word, nor did Dr. Peters. Angel scooped up the folder containing her medical records and whisked past the receptionist. Then she muttered some vague remark about suing the hospital, slammed the door, and continued out to the parking lot.

Having listened to everything the doctors said, followed their advice and put her faith in their judgment, Angel wasn't getting any better. It made her furious that another doctor had the audacity to suggest the problems were all in her head.

Steve drove Angel down to the huge San Bernadino County Medical Center, where she barged into the emergency room and begged one of the physicians to treat her. One young woman managed to settle her down and assured her that she would be thoroughly examined.

"That's good," Angel responded, "because I'm not leaving this hospital until somebody examines me."

Once she had regained her composure, Angel was introduced to Dr. Lawrence Jansen, a general practitioner who was on duty in the emergency room.

"It looks to me like you've been given the run-around for a long time." he said after Steve and Angel related the details of her treatment. "I can promise you that we will get to the bottom of this and help you, but you're going to have to be patient."

Dr. Jansen appeared to be not only straightforward, but also sincerely interested in her case, a refreshing change from the treatment that she had been getting elsewhere.

A week later, she was admitted for a thorough physical examination. A second ankle biopsy was performed—this one deeper—and the tissue was referred for study by specialists at the Mayo Clinic, a world-renowned medical center in Rochester, Minnesota. The days stretched to weeks as Steve and Angel fought to prevent the uncertainty of it all from eating away at them.

They continued to work on the wire whenever Angel could stand the pain.

Steven G. Wallenda II demonstrated his aerial skills at an early age.

With Steve now enthusiastically involved, the Wallendas became quite an attraction at the mobile home park. They even succeeded in getting Steven to hang from the trapeze, first with his father holding on and later all by himself. Steve would pick him up, hold him next to the bar and, by instinct, he would reach out and grab it.

# HIGH WIRE ANGEL

At first, Steve didn't dare to let go. But as he cautiously loosened his hold, Steven's grip on the trapeze bar tightened and he held on all by himself.

One afternoon, Steve was studying the *Guinness Book of World Records* and discovered there was nothing there to cover a young performer such as Steven. He decided to stage an event and see if they could place another Wallenda in the annals of history, as "the world's youngest aerialist" at 11 months old.

Working through the Guinness organization, they arranged for three official witnesses to look on as Steven did his thing. A large crowd from the trailer park and several newspaper photographers and television film crews were on hand, indicating that the Wallenda name still carried some weight with the news media.

This was quite a professional debut for the little lad. Steve held him up toward the trapeze and he grabbed hold of the bar and proceeded to hang for about a minute, picking up his feet, swinging back and forth, and smiling for the cameras. It couldn't have gone any better. Angel sent all of the sworn affidavits, photographs, and other paperwork off to the Guinness people. Weeks later, a letter arrived from England announcing that the organization's screening committee had turned it down, based on some tightened rules dealing with age categories in their prestigious book.

As sore as she was, Angel insisted on continuing her training. Steve began showing her the basic techniques needed to walk the high wire as a team. Simply following him, as Angel had done at the Westchester Mall, was easy. However, climbing smoothly onto his shoulders while he was so delicately balanced upon the wire was something altogether different. Leaning too far one way or the other could dislodge both of them. Gradually, Steve and Angel gained a sense of each other's movements and body control so that they knew what to expect. They worked on making the husband-and-wife walk look clean and smooth. At times, Angel's ankle throbbed so much that she bit her tongue to keep from telling Steve that she could no longer go on.

Eventually, she was forced to abandon her wire training once again. Getting on and off was next to impossible. There was no flexibility or control in her right ankle.

Chapter 17

# YOU'VE GOT CANCER

Angel was getting ready to step into the shower one morning when the phone rang. It was a receptionist from San Bernadino County Medical Center, who told her that Dr. Jansen wanted to see her right away. The shower could wait. She gathered up Steven and pulled into the hospital parking lot in a matter of minutes.

Dr. Jansen greeted her at the doorway of his small office. He seemed to be uncomfortable as he took a seat at his desk, across from where Angel was seated.

"The doctors from the Mayo Clinic are still not sure what we're dealing with," Dr. Jansen said in a calm, deliberate voice. "And to tell you the truth, I'm kind of stumped myself. They have suggested that we perform what's called exploratory surgery. It means we will make a small incision in your ankle and take a closer look."

The range of possibilities was so broad that Dr. Jansen was reluctant to speculate on what they might find. "However, to be perfectly honest with you, it does not look good," the doctor added.

Those words echoed in Angel's mind throughout the two weeks she had to wait before her next appointment. By the time she was scheduled to report for the operation, she had convinced herself that the problem could easily be remedied and she would be better in no time. As Angel was wheeled into the operating room, she was anxious to get this little inconvenience taken care of.

Therefore, when she awoke from the anesthesia, she was hardly prepared for the shattering news, or the callousness of the nurse who first broke it to her. It didn't take much "exploring" of the ankle to confirm the doctor's worst suspicions.

"Well, Angel, you have cancer and your leg will probably have to be amputated, but we don't know for sure," the nurse said in a very matter-of-fact tone. She might as well have been talking about the weather, for as much emotion or consideration as she showed. Angel became nauseous.

"We don't know if your leg is the only place you have it or what," the nurse continued, gathering up the blood-spotted towels and gauze pads from the foot of the bed. "We don't know how long you will live. We just don't know. The doctor will be in to see you soon. He can tell you more."

The only questions now were what type of cancer it was and how far it had spread. The dark cloud had moved overhead. Storm warnings that should have been heeded for months had been ignored.

Just as the nurse walked out of the room, Steve appeared in the doorway, holding Steven under his arm. Bea followed behind them.

"I heard," he said as he rushed over to give Angel a hug. He soon lost all control and wept on her shoulder, crushed by the terrifying thoughts that the word "cancer" brought to mind.

Angel turned away, trying not to cry, but she eventually dissolved into tears that drenched her pillow. She wanted to run away to a place where nobody could find her. The optimist in her rummaged through the debris of her ruins but found nothing of comfort. She said a silent prayer.

Another nurse who came in to check on Angel tried to comfort her. A gentle, smiling woman, she calmly explained that they had taken a small sample of the affected area on her leg for examination. The initial diagnosis was cancer, but depending on the results from tests on the tissue, Angel might be able to make a full recovery.

Steve gently stroked the strands of hair that had fallen over his wife's forehead. Her feelings turned to anger and bitterness. "How could all of those doctors have allowed this to drag on for so long without finding out what was really wrong with me?" she thought. "How could they have told me that it was 'all in my head'? Why didn't they look deeper? Maybe they're wrong. After all, cancer is a disease that strikes other people, older people."

"We're in this together," Steve whispered, trying to mask the look of worry on his face. "I told you up at the overlook that I'm going to be there for you from now on. I really mean that, Angel."

Suddenly, the shock, bitterness, depression, and confusion were inexplicably exorcised. A comforting wave swept over Angel and washed away the negative emotions and self-pity that had begun to wrap themselves around her. She felt a strange sense of calmness as she turned and began to toy with Steven's little hands, trying to make him smile. There were no more tears.

"Oh, well. That's the way it is, so let's get on with it," she said to Steve.

He was astonished by her mood change. "That's my Angel," he said. "Give her a cloud and she'll find a silver lining."

For about an hour, she sat upright in the bed talking—even laughing—with Steve and Bea, waiting for Dr. Jansen to arrive and deliver the particulars.

He finally came in and sat down. Angel could tell from the expression on his face that the message was not an easy one for him to deliver. He spoke cautiously and deliberately, as if he were handling one of his own surgical instruments.

"What you have, Angel, is a very rare form of spindle cell cancer called 'leiomyosarcoma.' There are a lot of things we still don't know about this case, but the one thing we do know for sure is that, to stop the spread of this cancer, we're going to have to amputate a part of your leg, right below the knee."

A pall came over the room as Dr. Jansen's words hung in the air. "I'm really sorry, but there's no other way out, Angel," the doctor said. "It has to be done."

Angel needed some time to think, so she stood up and excused herself, telling everyone she wanted to be alone for a few minutes. Reeling from the shock, Steve started to follow her, but was stopped by Dr. Jansen.

"Let her be alone for a few minutes so she can come to grips with this," the doctor said. Angel limped down the hallway to the solarium, where she found a seat in the corner and stared out the window, secluding herself behind a bookcase and watching the traffic buzz along the highway.

A jogger was chugging around the hospital courtyard, a glaring reminder to Angel that she would never be able to run or do gymnastics again. Obviously, walking the high wire was out of the question. She stared at the wall, not fully able to comprehend what was happening.

Bea peered around the corner and spotted her by the window. She brought Steven over and said, "Somebody wants to see you, Mama."

Angel took him in her arms. "If you only knew what your mama is going through," she whispered as he poked at her face with his index finger and giggled.

Cancer was a horrible unknown to Angel. She had never even met anybody who had cancer. The origin of her disease was a mystery. She wondered why she was singled out as a victim.

The Wallendas had a friend at the trailer park who frequently mentioned how wonderful the City of Hope National Medical Center was. The hospital is located in Duarte, just outside of Los Angeles, and specializes in cancer treatment. Founded by volunteers in 1913, City of Hope now has about 500 support groups throughout the country.

Steve and Angel decided that she should seek a second opinion from a specialist there. The San Bernadino County Medical Center people were very agreeable and understanding. Angel would have to wait two months to get an appointment with Dr. Daniel Riihimaki, a general cancer surgeon. In the meantime, he and other members of a panel reviewed her medical records, such as they were.

Steve's career was particularly important now that they knew Angel would be handicapped. If she couldn't have her old life back as a budding aerialist, she would become her husband's booking agent, Angel decided. She would turn her life in another direction and be strong and resourceful, just as she was when she was banished from her parents' house and forced to fend for herself.

It wasn't easy to promote a person who had been out of the limelight for so long. Steve's publicity material, a small locker once burgeoning with pictures and promotional text, was nearly depleted and had grown hopelessly out of date. However, with the Wallenda name and his impressive list of accomplishments, they had plenty to work with.

The telephone was Angel's most effective tool as she fell back on some of the salesmanship skills she had developed while selling candy for Harvey and his fictional "Junior Careers." Within a month, Angel was successful in landing Steve a pair of performance contracts for back-to-back skywalks in Savannah, Georgia

# HIGH WIRE ANGEL
## 111

and Jacksonville, Florida. This was welcome news to a man who had been looking for an opportunity to prove himself to his wife.

While he was away, Angel once again immersed herself in the scriptures. Her perspective on Jesus Christ's teachings had changed considerably since the cancer diagnosis reminded her of her own mortality.

Steve returned from Georgia with a crude, barely visible videotape of the Savannah walk. Angel was aghast when she realized all that it entailed. Kerosene-soaked cloth attached to each end of his balancing pole was set afire before Steve started up a long incline. Halfway to the top, he had to tip his pole until it was almost perpendicular to the ground so that one of the blazing ends could pass over a car that had been propped up on its back bumper, right next to the wire.

After Steve reached the top of the wire, he began his descent by walking backward. As he tipped his pole and edged his way past the car, he started bouncing the wire, keeping time to the song "Eye of the Tiger."

He had expanded his act with some extremely dangerous moves, after telling Angel that his high-risk wire antics were over now that he was settled down as a family man. She was glad to see that the performer's fire was still burning within him, but not to those extremes.

At the conclusion of the Savannah performance, the organizers dimmed the lights and stopped the music for a moment of silence on Angel's behalf.

Steve's return came on the day before Angel's first appointment at City of Hope. He was up early that next morning and out the door, telling Angel he had to take care of some business. She packed Steven's diaper bag and took a long shower while he napped. As she was dressing for the trip, Angel heard a car horn honking in the driveway. She hurried over to look out the door, and discovered Steve sitting in the driver's seat of a shiny red pickup truck parked behind their little sedan.

"What's going on?" she yelled out the screen door.

"If we're going to be traveling around the country so I can walk on a wire, we're going to need something to carry our equipment," he shouted back, barely audible over the revving engine. On the spur of the moment, he had gone out and bought a truck.

"You really did it, didn't you!" Angel said as she approached.

"I sure did. Like you said, 'Follow your dreams.' My dream is to have you and me walk the high wire together, so we're going to need the right kind of vehicle."

"Let's see, what else are we going to need?" Angel responded. "Oh yes, now I remember—a leg! I'm going to be losing one pretty soon, or did you forget about that part?"

"You don't know that for sure, Angel. Maybe they won't have to amputate."

Dr. Riihimaki was nearly two hours late for the appointment. Angel and Steve sat in his office, entertaining Steven and listening to the classical music that was flowing from two huge stereo speakers. A short, graying man, the affable doctor exuded confidence in his every mannerism, immediately putting them at ease. He apologized for his tardiness, explaining that he had been called in for an emergency operation.

He began the conversation by recalling how he had always admired the Wallenda family. Even as he closely examined the problem area on Angel's ankle, he spoke in detail of the Seven-Man Pyramid accident and other episodes of the family history.

"I can remember seeing Karl Wallenda on TV, the way his eyes lit up when he talked about the pyramid," the doctor said. "He called it 'The Seven' and he always paused when he said it. He seemed to speak with such reverence about it."

Steve and Angel exchanged smiles. It was a subject they had discussed many times in the past.

"Wait until you see 'The Eight'," Steve said. "Now that's going to be something to talk about."

"I'll bet it will," Dr. Riihimaki said, his voice trailing. He then changed the subject to the immediate problem at hand and offered a ray of hope—there was a possibility that he would not have to amputate.

"I wasn't there when you had the exploratory surgery, so I didn't see for myself, but there certainly is the strong possibility that you will lose your leg. I want you to be prepared in the event that it happens."

Dr. Riihimaki explained that the decision would be based on how far the cancer had spread into the bone. If it had not penetrated too far, he explained, the surgeons could try a rather complicated procedure that would involve restoring the area by taking bone chips out of Angel's hip and removing some muscle tissue out of her stomach area.

Steve and Angel talked it over without growing too depressed. "Even if they do amputate it, it's not the end of the world," Steve said. "You can still get around okay. They'll fix you up with an artificial leg and you'll be fine. You'll be a hell of a good promoter and business manager for me, too."

"Yeah, right," Angel said sarcastically. "There's nothing fine about having an artificial leg." Steve had recently developed a habit of trying to make Angel feel better by being optimistic. Sometimes she could see right through it, yet she still appreciated the fact that he was trying.

The plan was this: Dr. Riihimaki and the rest of the team would open up the affected area of the leg and see how extensive the damage was. If possible, they would perform the procedure using the bone chips and muscle tissue. But if it was as bad as the San Bernadino County Medical Center doctors believed, surgeons would amputate right then and there. Angel would not know what happened, either way, until she regained consciousness.

All kinds of thoughts crossed her mind: "What will life be like with only half of my leg? Will Steve take care of me through all this? How will it affect Steven, growing up with a handicapped mother? Will I ever be able to walk again? And, God forbid, what part of my body will they want to cut off next?"

Angel remained calm on the outside, but her heart was pounding against her rib cage and her mind was running at fast-forward. There wasn't a thing that anyone could say or do to slow it down, because nobody knew what would happen next.

She wished she could travel back in time and sit on the rocks to watch her father

# HIGH WIRE ANGEL

pull fish from the Hudson River, or climb the tree near the Brooks' house to hide out and watch the swimmers, or just pull the blanket over her head and make everything disappear.

Before long, Angel Wallenda found herself in the long hallway at City of Hope, being wheeled out of the operating room. Through foggy eyes, she watched the faceless hospital staffers pushing and directing the gurney that carried her.

The first thing she did was scream and curse. The pain was so intense and widespread that she couldn't tell where it started or stopped. She still didn't know if they had amputated her leg, but the first clue was that she didn't feel any pain in her hip or stomach.

"What did they do?" she asked Steve as she was pushed into the corner of a room with bright, colorful walls that were covered with drawings of unicorns and teddy bears.

"Why don't you look?" he said, pointing under the sheet.

"I don't want to see it."

"Don't worry, it's all bandaged up."

"Well, did they or didn't they?" Angel pulled away the sheet and could tell by the shape of the thick bandaging that her leg had been amputated.

"It feels like it's still there," she told Steve. "It doesn't feel like it's gone—it feels like my foot is hurting! I feel like I can wiggle my toes. God, that's weird!"

"Just remember what I said before," he reassured her, trying to divert Angel's attention. "We're in this together. This isn't going to make any difference in the way we live our lives. I love you, and I'm going to help you learn to walk again."

"What does that have to do with anything?" she snapped back in frustration. "I don't need to hear that. I just want my leg to stop hurting. That's the only thing that matters to me right now."

The shock of actually losing a limb had not yet hit. Angel leaned all the way back on her pillow and stared at the ceiling.

Because of a shortage of recovery rooms, she had been taken to a makeshift area of the pediatrics wing until she could be transferred to a regular hospital room. As she turned her head to the right, she came face to face with a young Oriental girl who was hugging a Cabbage Patch doll and staring at her.

"What happened to you, lady?" she asked.

"Oh, I just had a little operation, but I'm going to be all right," Angel replied, choking back the tears.

"So am I," said the girl, who was about eight years old. "I have cancer, but I'm going to be fine. I'm going to be just fine. My father told me so."

Chapter 18

# FIGHTING BACK

Once Angel was settled into her own room, Steve insisted on calling back east to tell her family what had happened. Naturally, Jeannie wanted to talk, but Angel insisted that Steve tell her she was sleeping. She didn't want to talk to anybody, her husband included.

Though Angel was on huge doses of morphine, the pain persisted. All she could do was complain; she was ornery every minute, snapping at everybody. Nothing anybody said made any difference to her. The only thing she cared about was getting rid of the pain. She didn't even want to see Steven, who clung to his father in puzzlement over his mother's strange behavior.

Steve kept trying to convince the doctor to increase the dosage of morphine or administer some other pain-killer. They finally gave her a muscle relaxant that did nothing to stop the pain, but did allow her to sleep for a while.

When Angel awoke, she had no conception of time. She felt as if she was having a nightmare, except that she could not wake herself up. It lasted for days on end. She wanted to die, just to escape the pain. Steve kept trying to lift her spirits, holding her hand and assuring her that everything would be all right.

"I feel so helpless," Angel told him, as he massaged her leg just above the bulky bandage that surrounded her knee. Steve leaned forward and kissed her leg where the bandage ended and the bare flesh of her lower thigh was exposed.

"We're in this together," he kept assuring her. Angel allowed those words to rattle around in her head, and in her heart, for the next couple of days. It gave her a warm feeling to know that Steve was accepting her as she was—her moodiness, her helplessness, and the grotesque stump that was once a leg.

On the fifth day after the operation, the bandaging came off so the leg could be fitted into a temporary cast. This would allow Angel to begin putting some weight on it. She was screaming at the top of her lungs as they squeezed and tugged to remove the bandages and fit a tight stocking over the end of her leg.

Angel tried to glance down in that direction without looking directly at it. In a way, she didn't want to see it, much less touch it. It felt so foreign. A pipe with an artificial foot was attached to her leg just below the knee. This was to allow her to stand up and begin growing accustomed to life without a right leg.

Over and over she tried to get up, only to drop back down into her wheelchair in frustration and exhaustion. A physical therapist who was working with her would then lift the leg onto a support rail to elevate it and prevent swelling while she rested.

Angel stared across the room at a mirror. So many thoughts tumbled around in her head as she focused on the gadget that had replaced her leg. She was unable to concentrate on anything else. Then she tried to read, but her eyes kept passing back and forth across the same lines while her mind wandered far from the text.

Angel was determined not to flounder in self pity or anger, yet she would lapse into periods of depression and outright brattiness. At other times, she was distant and unresponsive to anyone who tried to approach her. She was in the path of a hurricane of circumstances beyond her control; all she could do was hold on and hope for the best.

In the prime of her life, Angel knew that she would never be normal again. She feared that she would be so funny-looking or ugly that Steve would no longer find her appealing. People would stare at her. She wouldn't be able to wear pretty skirts or nice shoes, only sneakers and baggy pants that would fit around the leg.

The doctors assured Angel and Steve that the operation had stopped the cancer and it was not likely to recur. They also said Angel could learn to walk again and eventually resume a normal life with her husband and son. She wondered what they meant by "normal."

Much to Angel's surprise, her mother started calling on the phone. Hannah Pintye had a much firmer grasp on reality than before. However, Angel was skeptical when her mom said she wanted the three of them to visit as soon as Angel was feeling better.

"How does Dad feel about that?" she wanted to know.

"He wants to see you, too, honey. He'd never tell you that, though. You know how your daddy is. I'll write myself a note so I remember to tell him. I always seem to forget things."

Angel said she would discuss it with her doctors and call back when she was given the go-ahead. She was anxious to give both of her parents the opportunity to see their only grandchild. A part of Angel also saw the trip as a chance to become reacquainted with her mother and father.

As soon as the schedule of daily physical therapy began, she was discharged from City of Hope and transferred into one of the hospital's "Hope Village" apartments where she could stay with Steve and Steven while she underwent outpatient treatment.

The atmosphere helped in her recovery. She probably would have felt self-conscious appearing in public riding in a wheelchair, but around the apartment complex there were many people in wheelchairs. Some of the patients, including young children, had lost all of their hair because of chemotherapy. Some sat listlessly in easy chairs outside of their apartments, or they roamed the grounds as they recovered. Other people had problems that were much more serious than Angel's.

"Who am I to complain?" she said to Steve as he wheeled her past the other patients and into their apartment. "I should be thankful to be alive and well on the road to recovery."

"You still have your family," Steve reminded her. "We'll just make the best of things. You'll never have your leg back, but that doesn't mean you should crawl into a hole and die. We're going to rebuild."

For the next two months, Angel went to physical therapy almost every day, accepting it as a challenge. Her disposition improved as she grew to accept her limitations. Soon she was able to take several steps on the walking track between two parallel bars. Using her arms to support her weight, she dragged the artificial leg along, putting as much pressure on it as she could stand without losing her balance.

"I used to be pretty good at these parallel bars, you know," Angel said to Laura, the young therapist who was helping her. "It's a little more of a challenge now. I guess my days of gymnastics are over."

"Don't be so sure," said Laura. "I've seen patients do some pretty amazing things." A slender, brown-haired woman in her middle thirties, Laura took a particular interest in Angel's case. She taught her special exercises to maintain the flexibility in her knee and strengthen the remaining muscles in that area. Laura was full of praise and encouragement. In turn, Angel reached down for something extra to prove that she could do even more.

It wasn't easy to adjust. Little things that Angel had always taken for granted became major challenges. Even taking a shower in the specially-equipped bathroom proved to be an adventure after she removed the artificial leg; she had to hang on to a bar that stretched above the shower door and swing her body around and into the shower.

Occasionally, she would bound out of bed and forget that her leg was not attached. She ended up flat on her face on the bedroom floor. Usually rather than bemoan her fate, Angel reacted to those episodes with laughter.

When she was in physical therapy, Angel worked toward a clearly-defined goal and could derive a great amount of satisfaction from achieving it and then setting an even higher standard for herself. In her idle hours, she would sit alone, often lapsing into a quiet sadness. To overcome depression, she began to draw up a game plan to help Steve resume his performing career, with Angel serving more formally as his booking agent and publicist—a job she could perform regardless of her physical limitations.

# HIGH WIRE ANGEL

Steve's Uncle Leon had a friend who persuaded Steve and Angel to set up their mobile home on a huge ranch in southern California's high desert. They would have the place all to themselves, as long as they kept watch over the ranch. Vandals had repeatedly ransacked the property because it was left unattended. The owner welcomed an opportunity to have someone residing in the area.

This proved to be a good arrangement for Angel and Steve, as well. There was room for Steven to play without the worry of him wandering into traffic or being abducted.

Angel visited City of Hope three days each week for check-ups and therapy. As anxious as she was to be able to walk again, she gladly welcomed the first tangible sign of progess—her graduation from the wheelchair to crutches.

At night, she and Steve would sit outside the trailer and talk, the quiet of the desert interrupted only by the wind or the barely audible howling of the coyotes they could sometimes see silhouetted in the distance.

One of the Los Angeles television stations learned of Angel's operation and sent reporter Tim Malloy and a crew to meet Steve and her at City of Hope. They filmed an interview and showed it on the evening news, emphasizing that Angel's cancer was the latest in a string of tragedies to strike the Wallenda Family. She half-jokingly told Tim that, some day, he might see her up on the high wire as the first person to ever perform there on an artificial leg. In truth, the thought had never really crossed Angel's mind. She was having enough trouble learning how to walk on the ground. Soon after the telecast, their mailbox was filled with letters and cards from relatives, friends, and other well-wishers, as well as letters from other news agencies pleading with them to share their story.

The next stage of Angel's recovery involved removal of the temporary artificial leg and cast. Now, she had nothing below her knee. It was the strangest feeling she had ever experienced and the most emotionally-draining period of her recovery.

For three weeks, Angel had to put up with this. She covered it up with a blanket so she wouldn't have to think about it or worry what Steve might be thinking. Curiosity kept getting the better of her. She would pull back the blanket and take a quick glance, then cover it again.

She tried to avoid touching it or bumping it against anything. "I feel like half a person," she told Steve. "I know I'm unattractive to you."

"Not at all," he insisted. "When I look at you, I see the same beautiful woman I've always seen. I see your beautiful spirit. Nothing's going to take that away and, by the way, I think you're still a really sexy gal. A real knockout, okay?"

On her next trip to City of Hope, Angel was fitted once again with a length of metal pipe and hard rubber foot to hold her over until a customized artificial leg was prepared. As disgusting as this device appeared, it helped her get around on her crutches. Dr. Riihimaki said he was pleased with her progress and pronounced Angel sufficiently recovered to make the trip back east to see her family.

When Steve and Angel returned to their trailer, she promptly placed a call to her parents' number to make arrangements for the visit. However, she was greeted by a tape recording stating that the line had been disconnected.

"I'll bet Mom ran up a huge phone bill and Dad got mad and unplugged the phone," Angel sighed. "She does that all the time."

The next day, the telephone rang at the mobile home. It was her brother Mark.

"Hi Liz. I've got some bad news," he paused. "Mom's dead."

"What?" she asked, before his words had fully sunk in.

"Mom's dead. She died in a fire, at the house. She was trapped and she didn't make it out."

"My God," Angel said. "I just talked to her three days ago. I was coming out to visit her."

Angel was numb with disbelief as Mark filled her in on the details. Her mother had suffered smoke inhalation and the paramedics could feel only a weak pulse when they reached her in the smoke-filled house. She never regained consciousness. She was being connected to the life support system at the hospital when she slipped away.

Tears streamed from Angel's eyes, while her words stuck in her throat. Her mother's life had been so troubled. What a horrible final few moments she must have had. Angel had always hoped that, some day, she would be able to get to know her mom and understand her better. She was sometimes childish and difficult to comprehend, but Angel had always accepted her, even as her brothers ignored her and did not want to be seen with their own mother.

She had lived a hard, tragic life. How she must have worried as all of her children were taken away from her and placed in foster homes. How terrible it must have been to live with an alcoholic and abusive father, and then suffer through so many years of mental instability while living under her husband's domineering rule.

And now she was gone...

Angel nestled down into Steve's lap. She longed to be back home with the rest of her family members to share their grief. Life's circumstances had separated the Pintyes often, but upon this occasion, they mourned as one.

A few minutes later, the phone rang again. This time it was Jeannie. She took her mother's death the hardest of all. Jeannie had always believed that her mom would eventually be well and they would become a normal family. "Why did this have to happen to her?" she cried, her voice cracking with pain. "Why her? She never hurt anybody." Jeannie regained her composure as they spoke, especially after Angel promised her that she would come back home for the funeral.

# HIGH WIRE ANGEL

Steve was reluctant to accompany his wife and son on the trip, and Angel didn't press the issue. These were not the best of circumstances under which to meet the Pintye family. Angel viewed the trip as an opportunity to touch base with her past and temporarily escape the mounting pressure of her own situation—cancer, a baby, and her dream of a high wire career gone bust.

Jeannie and her boyfriend met Angel and Steven at the airport and drove them back to her apartment. Angel felt a special kinship toward her sister, especially on such a sad occasion.

"I've been crying a lot, which is strange for me, because I haven't cried in years," Jeannie said. "I can't stop running what happened to Mom through my mind. I can't help wondering what it was like for her. I hope she never knew what happened and didn't have to suffer."

As Angel retired for the night, she grew nervous about the prospect of seeing her father at the funeral home and not knowing what to say. At the breakfast table the next morning, Jeannie tried to reassure her that there was nothing to worry about.

"He's really mellowed out over the last couple of years," Jeannie said.

"Yeah, but it's been years since I've seen him. I keep thinking he's mad at me."

"He's gotten over that," Jeannie insisted. "He's really missed you, whether you believe it or not. He wants to see Steven. He wants to meet your husband. He's been concerned about your operation. Those kind of things. Give him a chance."

When Angel entered the funeral home she was caught off-guard by her father. "Hey, Lizzie, is that you?" he said, coming up behind her. Angel was struck by how much he had aged since she last saw him and how strongly he still carried his Hungarian accent.

Frederick Pintye was a far different man from the harsh disciplinarian who had beaten his children for the smallest indiscretions. This person was kind, smiling, and understanding. He also seemed more animated and genuinely human than Angel ever remembered him being. There was a warmth and softness that belied her childhood memories of him.

It was the first time he had seen his grandson, and the two hit it off from the start. Steven, more outgoing than ever, took a liking to his grandpa. As they got acquainted, Angel took the opportunity to hoist herself over to the casket. She leaned on her crutches and stared at her mother's body.

"At last she is at peace." Angel whispered to her brother Mark. "What do you want to bet that the first person to greet her when she passed over was Uncle Bill? Probably whistling some Irish song!"

She glanced back over in the direction of Steven and his grandfather, who were now engaged in a playful boxing match. It dawned on Angel that as much as the Pintyes had gathered to mark the passage of one life, they also celebrated the arrival of another. She felt good to be a part of that, even as she mourned the loss of her mother.

Her father kept trying to talk to her and didn't want anyone else to have her attention. It wasn't that he had that much to say; apparently, he just wanted to get to know his youngest daughter now that she was grown up. He was making up for lost time.

Everyone from the family was there, with the exception of Angel's half-brother Charles and her brother James. Family members had been notified by Army officials several months earlier that Charles had died in a trailer fire. His body had been burned beyond recognition, they alleged, and he was identified through dental records. Even today, his stepfather doubts that he was given the full story.

James' absence was due to circumstances beyond his control. He had been sentenced to a jail term of 15 years to life on a criminal homicide charge. James had found himself in the wrong place at the wrong time when one of his co-workers killed a man during a fight. Because James was with the murderer, he was arrested as an accomplice. Rather than face a trial and risk a life imprisonment sentence, James opted for a plea bargain that did not turn out the way his lawyer had promised. If all goes well for him, he could be a free man again soon.

The funeral was a traditional Catholic service, complete with all of the rituals. To Angel, it was like a capsulized look at her own past. Family members and former foster parents filed solemnly into the funeral home and took their seats.

There was Eileen Carver, one of the very first social workers who had taken a deep interest in all of the children and had tried so hard to pave the way for their return to their parents' house. Harold and Cynthia Earl were also there, happy to see Angel again and delighted to discover that she had emerged from her troubled childhood as a responsible adult. Sally Ulacewicz, a neighbor in Mahopac, arrived to pay her respects. She had often stopped Angel and Jeannie on their way to school in the morning to feed them English muffins and brush their hair.

So many people asked Angel about her operation, about Steve and her wire training, and about all of the other developments in her life since she had left for California. She grew tired of repeating the stories. At the same time, Angel appreciated the fact that these important people from her past still cared about her.

Little Steven received ever more attention. Having a young child around helped put people at ease during what was otherwise a very uncomfortable setting.

Angel kept asking her father and brothers for more details about the fire. No one knew how it started. Her mom was home alone and, within a half-hour of her brother Thomas' departure for work that morning, she was dead. Her body was found at the opposite end of the house from where the fire burned, right next to the doorway where Angel saw the strange vision of the robed figure when she was a child. Neighbors said they heard an explosion and caught a glimpse of someone leaving the driveway of the house in a car around the time the fire apparently started.

Angel and Jeannie had a lot of time to compare notes on their lives since Angel had left for California. Jeannie said their father was a lot more concerned about Angel than he ever admitted, beginning the very first night that she left the house.

"He was always too damned rigid and so set in his ways," Angel recalled. "I never thought I'd see the day when he would mellow out."

Jeannie could not believe all of the things that her sister had been through in the past few years.

"I always knew you'd be doing something that was risky," she said as she poured them each a big glass of Angel's favorite drink, strawberry daiquiri. "Even when you did your gymnastics routines on the monkey bars at the school playground, you always took stupid chances."

"I didn't have anyone to yell at me and tell me not to," Angel laughed.

"I wasn't about to do it. You probably would have beaten me up. I can't believe how we fought when we were kids."

"It's the way we were raised," Angel reminded her.

"How 'bout declaring a truce?" Jeannie asked, holding up her glass. Her sister joined her for a toast. It was as if they were finally saying good-bye to their childhood.

Chapter 19

# BACK ON THE WIRE

Throughout her stay, Angel tried to telephone Steve but repeatedly got no answer. Her concern continued to fester as Angel dialed the trailer over and over to no avail. Plans called for Steve to meet Angel and Steven at the airport early Saturday afternoon. She worried that he would not be waiting in Los Angeles, and she had no idea what she would do if they stepped off the plane and nobody was there to pick them up.

Before boarding, Angel promised her father that she would visit him again, with Steve and Steven, under more pleasant conditions. She kissed him on the cheek, the first time she could recall ever doing that. Angel sensed that her dad's life was now going to be on a more even keel.

Steven was tired from all of the activity and attention he received, so he slept with his head on his mother's lap for most of the flight. As she softly brushed her hands against the long, blonde locks of his hair, she wondered what kind of a life they might be returning to, and how their insecurity was going to affect her little boy.

As the jet touched down and eased toward the exit area, Angel was heartened to see Steve standing out by the gate, smiling from ear to ear and holding the string to a large helium-filled silver balloon he had bought for Steven. He looked good and he was in better spirits than she had seen him in a long time.

"I called and called, but you didn't answer," Angel said.

"It wasn't my fault," he assured her. "There was a big windstorm that knocked out all of the power for almost the entire time you were gone. The phone wasn't working."

"What did you do while we were gone?"

"Oh, I did a lot of reading and worked on the car. Nothing too exciting. You weren't worried, were you?"

"Not at all."

In December 1987, Angel was finally fitted with her artificial leg. It looked realistic, except for the pale color and the smooth exterior. She felt much more comfortable wearing it than she did with the pipe apparatus she had been forced to use.

It made her feel almost whole again. She could wear nice clothes, as long as she hid the area below her knee where the leg was attached. From a distance, it looked like a real leg. Angel was assured that, with enough practice, she would be able to walk normally.

Each time she visited City of Hope, Angel intentionally wore something that would display her artificial leg. Gradually, she was able to strike up conversations with the residents of the long-term care section and she and Steve both became friends with them. Angel tried to impress upon them that they could also improve their own situations if they made up their minds to do so.

One of the patients was Barry, a boyish-looking man in his early forties who usually sat and listened to the rest of the patients talking to Angel. One afternoon, he motioned her over and asked her to wheel him over to the other side of the room so they could talk alone.

"How do you do it?" he asked in a sheepish voice, looking into Angel's eyes like a confused child. "How can you be so full of life when you've lost your leg and you're fighting cancer?"

"It's no big secret," she told him. "I can't change what has happened, so I just make the best of it."

"Don't you ever ask, 'Why me?' Doesn't it bother you that you're the one who has to go through all of this, while almost everyone else your age can live a normal life?"

"I live a normal life, too. I don't consider myself any different than anyone else. Sure, I had my leg amputated, but I have another leg now. As far as I'm concerned, I'm right back where I started. You can't let those things that are out of your control get you down."

"I really enjoy talking to you. Would you ever consider marrying somebody who's paralyzed from the waist down?" Barry said with a wink.

"Well, I'm kind of spoken for, but I'll tell you one thing: If that's what you want out of life, to find the right woman and settle down, then go for it. Set it as your goal and put everything you have into achieving it. You have to have a goal. Focus on the positive things. Everyone has bad times, bad days. Just don't get wrapped up in them. Instead, be thankful for what you do have, or what you *can* do."

Barry smiled and reached to grasp her hand.

"Thank you, Angel," he said. "Thank you for talking to me."

"Hey, Steve," Barry shouted as Angel pushed him back over to where the other patients were congregated. "I tried to have an affair with your wife but—fool that she is—she wouldn't let me. She doesn't know what she's missing."

"Don't let her fool you," Steve kidded. "Some days, I couldn't give her away if I tried."

Steve made arrangements to visit his Uncle Leon at the "Circus of the Stars" complex on the grounds of Universal Studios, where he and Angel could watch the celebrities work out for their upcoming show on national television and scout around for a promoter or some interim performance opportunities. They recognized the need to get back in touch with the people who had connections before they could expect Steve's career to take off once again. Steve also wanted to begin breaking-in Angel as his booking agent.

Leon Fort is a tall, silver-haired man with dark skin and a muscular physique. He was obviously thrilled to see one of his star students again.

"Steve was one of my first projects," Leon told Angel as they were introduced. "He and I go back a long way—longer than either of us would like to admit."

"Wait a minute, Leon, you go back a lot longer than I do," Steve said. "Don't forget, I was three years old when we started."

"Yeah, but I was just a kid back then, too. Hey, isn't this the beautiful blonde I saw on TV a while back? She's even prettier in person. How did an old cuss like Steve end up with a doll like you?"

Angel could feel herself blushing.

Leon made a point of introducing them to some of the celebrities there. Among them were Ricky Schroeder, Mary Hart, "Tap Dance Kid" Alfonso Ribeiro, Leslie Bega, and Billy Barty. Steve and Angel were able to roam the grounds at will. Actress Ami Foster, who starred on the "Punky Brewster" show at the time, took a special liking to Steven and hoisted him up on the trampoline with her. After that, she held Steven up to the trapeze and let him swing by himself for a while.

"I think we have another Great Wallenda in our midst," Uncle Leon chuckled.

All around, performers in costumes or sweatsuits were busy on the teeter board, sway pole, and other equipment. Steve noticed the high wire was empty and he couldn't resist the urge to put on a pair of slippers, pick out a balancing pole, and show off a little.

"Watch closely, Leon," he yelled down. "You might learn something."

That special look of determination and concentration returned to Steve's face, the first time Angel had seen it in a long time. It made her feel good to watch him back up on the wire. She knew how impoverished and meaningless his life was without it.

"Now it's your turn, Angel" he said, motioning with his head to the low wire. "Why don't you give it a try?"

"Sure, Steve," she answered, assuming that he was kidding.

"Hey, I can see it all coming together now—'The Triumphant Return of Angel Wallenda'—what do you think?" he continued, breathing heavily as he climbed down and wiped the sweat from his brow with a towel.

"I think you better come back to earth," Angel said, holding up one of her crutches as a reminder of her limitations. But the more she looked at the low

# HIGH WIRE ANGEL

wire, the more she wondered if it might actually be possible for her to take a couple of steps on it.

"I'm going to try it," Angel said impulsively as Steve slipped his boots back on his feet and put the slippers back in the rack. "I'm serious. I'll see what I can do."

"All right!" Steve exclaimed. "Uncle Leon and I will be your spotters. We won't let you fall." Leon looked at his nephew skeptically, but said nothing.

Steve found a pair of slippers that he could fit over her feet and a light balancing pole she could use. With a nervous, fluttery stomach and shaking arms, Angel placed most of her weight on Steve's shoulders, stepped up with her good leg and lifted the artificial one up in front of it.

She teetered one way and then the other, causing her two spotters to raise their arms and prepare to catch her. To Angel's astonishment, she was able to stand still and maintain her balance without Steve or Leon holding on to her.

"Now I'm going to take a couple of steps," she said.

"I don't know about this," Uncle Leon laughed. "I'm not sure our insurance is paid up."

"Come on, Angel, you can do it if you really concentrate," Steve urged.

"Go get 'em, girl," Leon echoed.

Angel had to look down to where her feet made contact with the wire, rather than trust her instincts to tell her that she was properly positioning each foot. The first step was the scariest because, for an instant, she was balanced solely by her artificial leg.

Her second step was a different experience altogether. Angel had no trouble lifting the prosthesis and balancing on her good leg, but she was reluctant to push herself forward and apply any weight to her right foot.

"You can do it!" Steve encouraged her. "Tell yourself you can. It'll work. Think positively."

Angel managed one more difficult, but gratifying, step before she decided it was time to get down. She lowered herself into Steve's waiting arms, and he carried her over to a chair to rest.

"I think I must be the proudest man in the world right now," he said as he removed her slippers.

"I've seen a lot of things in this business over the years," added Uncle Leon, patting Angel on the back, "but that's the first time I've ever seen anybody do that."

Chapter 20

# SURGERY REVISITED

Arriving back from the circus training grounds, Steve couldn't stop talking about those few steps his wife had taken. "I think the fact that the TV station sent Tim Malloy over to interview us awhile back says something," he said. "You're quite a story, Angel. I'll bet if you could learn to walk on the high wire again with your artificial leg, we could put together the most spectacular aerial act the world has ever seen. And when Steven is old enough, he could also be part of the show."

"Yeah, maybe," Angel answered. "I might be willing to give it a try, but I'm not going to make any commitment right now. It sounds kind of dangerous." Having never really mastered the high wire with two good legs, the idea of walking on a narrow wire as an amputee seemed far-fetched to her.

"Well, I'll promise you something: if you're willing to try it, I'll do everything I can to train you," Steve assured her. "You could take as long as you wanted. You've already shown that you can keep your balance and take a step on the wire. That just proves you can do it."

That night, Angel felt a nagging soreness near the middle of her back. She thought she had pulled a muscle from the awkward movements on the wire. As the night wore on, fearing her tossing and turning would disturb Steve, she left the bedroom and ended up falling asleep in the living room chair.

When Angel awoke, she could barely move. An intense tightness twisted her chest. She decided to take a hot bath. That didn't help either. To top things off, she started coughing up blood again. Each attempt to take a full breath failed. Short gasps were all she could manage, and even those took a conscious effort.

"Steve, I've got a problem," Angel said as she shook her husband to wake him. "I can't breathe. And there's blood coming up when I cough. I don't like this, Steve."

"We better see what the doctors say," he said, sitting up on his elbow and rubbing his eyes. "And, this time, we're not going to let 'em screw around like

# HIGH WIRE ANGEL

they did before."

None of the doctors in the area could schedule Angel for an appointment that day. Despite at least a dozen phone calls, the earliest she could get an appointment was Monday, which was two days away, unless she went to an emergency room.

Angel desperately tried to pull air into her lungs. When she was lying down, she felt a bit more comfortable and her breathing was somewhat easier. But, as the chest pain became more intense, Steve insisted that they drive to the emergency room at Palmdale Hospital.

An X-ray there clearly revealed that Angel's left lung was collapsed. The emergency room physician told her he had to make an incision in her side to insert a tube. It would supply the right combination of air pressure and suction so the lung could expand back to its normal shape.

As soon as his instrument made contact with her skin, she felt as if she had been stabbed in the side by a butcher's knife. She closed her eyes and tried to separate her mind from her body's experiences, a technique she had learned through her reading. "It doesn't hurt if I don't let it hurt me," she kept repeating to herself, as she tried to take her mind on a journey far from the operating table.

The jarring experience of the lung popping back into shape was like a small explosion deep within her chest. A wave of nauseating pain washed over Angel, and she screamed until she passed out. She awoke to find the room spinning. A vague voice coming from somewhere in the distance told her that she had been heavily sedated. She fell back asleep and when she woke up again a half-hour later, much of the pain was gone.

The doctor tried to quiet Steve and Angel's fears by explaining that this type of lung malfunction sometimes happens for no apparent reason to teenagers and young adults who are particularly active. Despite what Angel told him about coughing up blood sporadically over the past several months, he believed the collapsed lung was not related to any other health problems. He said if this had been a sign that her cancer was spreading, it would have shown up in the X-rays or on the magnetic resonator scanner printouts as tumors on her lungs.

Angel was not fully convinced he was correct, but her skepticism was tempered by her very strong desire to be well. She was in the hospital for two days and discharged with assurances that her lung had returned to its normal condition.

A week later, the lung collapsed again. This time, Angel felt it coming on and recognized the symptoms right away. Steve was sitting next to her on the steps of the trailer. He saw her complexion turning white even before she could tell him what was happening.

When they got to Palmdale Hospital, Angel warned them, "No way. I'm not letting you shove that tube in me!"

"Why not?" said the youthful looking doctor. "You won't even feel it."

"That's bull. I sure did the last time. I was screaming my head off."

"Well, it shouldn't hurt. Didn't they numb you before?"

"No!"

He seemed surprised. "This time we will. Just relax."

A few minutes after the novocaine had taken effect, he inserted the tube. All Angel felt this time was was the jarring pop of the lung ballooning back into shape.

The doctors at Palmdale didn't have a clue about what could be causing the lung complications. They said Angel should undergo exploratory surgery to see what symptoms might be escaping detection by the X-rays. She called Dr. Riihimaki back at City of Hope to see what he thought.

"Isn't that considered major surgery?" she asked.

"If you want to put it in those terms, I guess you could call it major. I would call it that."

"Is there any chance that it could be cancer again?" Angel inquired.

"I can't say for sure until I see you. There is that chance, based on the fact we're dealing with your lungs. The cancer may have metastasized there. It's a possibility."

"Oh God, I can't go through this again," she thought to herself. "Maybe if I ignore it, it will go away all by itself."

"Why me?" Angel wondered aloud to her husband. Steve looked long and hard at her. "Why would God allow something like this to happen to me?"

"That's one of man's greatest questions," Steve replied. "I have my own ideas. It could be that He's strengthening us for something that is to come. As strange as it sounds, I have to believe that some good is going to come out of this. It's hard to look at it that way now, but I think it will be revealed to us eventually. We have to keep our faith."

Angel's sister Jeannie agreed to fly out from New York to help watch Steven while she was in the hospital.

A comprehensive battery of tests failed to show any problem except for a small hole in Angel's lung from which the air had been leaking. Dr. Riihimaki referred her to a lung specialist, Dr. Frederick Grannis, who reviewed her charts and promptly scheduled her for surgery to close the leak by reattaching the delicate lung tissue.

A pleasant man with splendid clear eyes and a beautiful white-toothed smile, he behaved more like a good friend than a surgeon. Angel marveled that, in a few hours, this same man would don his mask and surgical gloves to begin cutting away at her lungs.

She felt comfortable and optimistic as the anesthesiologist placed the mask over her mouth and nose and told her to begin counting backwards. Angel was long gone by the time Dr. Grannis carved through the delicate tissue and discovered that her left lung was in much worse shape than any of the tests had revealed.

While Angel lay on the operating table expecting to have a small operation, no more complicated in her mind than patching a tire, the hospital was assembling a team of highly-skilled specialists to perform a complicated lung operation.

It had become alarmingly obvious to Dr. Grannis, after he could actually see the lung, that the dozens of tiny blister-like growths that had shown on the readouts of the CT scans as insignificant blotches were, in fact, a source of major concern. Many people have similar-looking small, harmless growths on their lungs. Angel's were more deeply rooted.

The complicated operation involved removal of the lower lobe on her left lung, which left her with less than half of a lung on that side. They also had to remove about a dozen small tumor-filled wedges from the top of the lung and repair that area, a procedure known as "resectioning."

When Angel regained consciousness, Dr. Grannis and Steve were there to break the news. In this frightening and intense moment, she at first felt no pain and no emotion. Dr. Grannis was very solemn and Steve just looked at his wife. Angel couldn't talk and could hardly move. It was a battle for her to keep her eyes open. Then it hit her—the worst pain she had ever felt in her life. She was sure she was going to die. She spotted Bea and Jeannie, holding Steven.

"Everybody who cares about me is gathered around my bed and they're all silent," Angel thought to herself. "Am I dead? Is this one of those out-of-body experiences I've read about, my lifeless corpse lying on the bed while my soul departs to enter the afterlife?"

She was awake for only a few seconds before slipping back into unconsciousness. The next time she awoke, two nurses were there shaking her, saying, "Come on, Angel, it's time to get out of bed. You've got to start moving around."

Three days had passed. During that period, Steve nearly lost his mind worrying about whether Angel would ever regain consciousness. She had laid motionless on the bed, surrounded by an oxygen tent and connected to a respirator and a heart monitor with intravenous tubes in her right leg and both arms. Other tubes had been passed through her rib cage and between the muscles that had been slashed by the surgeon's knife. These chest tubes were inserted to drain blood and keep Angel's lung expanded.

The doctors had told Steve that they were not sure she would pull through, but tempered that gloomy prognosis by pointing out that she was at the right stage of life to heal rapidly.

"Where is my husband?" were the first words out of Angel's mouth as the nurses roused her.

"Probably in the lobby down the hall," one of them said. "He hasn't left here since you had the operation. Your sister and some other woman keep telling him to get some rest, but all he does is pace the floors."

Despite the pushiness of the nurses, Angel insisted on taking her time before rising from the bed. They had disassembled the oxygen tent and removed the monitor and respirator, along with all but one of the intravenous feeding tubes.

It took her the better part of an hour and still she could not get out of bed and into a chair. She would start to lean upward and then collapse back down onto her pillows. As slowly as she moved, every little motion caused the pain to intensify. Angel could barely breathe and she would tire easily. The nurses scolded her and told her she wasn't trying hard enough but she was doing the best she could.

Angel kept wanting to go back to sleep and make the pain go away. Finally, summoning every ounce of strength she had and pushing herself well past any involuntary pain threshold, she managed to pull herself up to a sitting position and quickly slip into the chair. Her upper body hurt so much that she thought she was going to black out.

The torture of uncertainty for Steve was eased when he came through the doorway and stopped in his tracks. "Oh my God, you're up!" he said. "I don't believe this. Why didn't somebody tell me?"

He came over to the chair and gave Angel a gentle embrace, mindful of the IV tube. She felt so sore and weak that she couldn't reach out to return his hug.

Dr. Grannis followed Steve into the room. "It's nice to see you with your eyes open for a change," he said, forcing some additional small talk to pave the way for what was coming.

"Angel, the results of the scan show that there is some cancer in your other lung," he told her. "I don't want to alarm you, because I don't think it's as serious a problem as you had in your left lung, but eventually we're going to have to go in and work on that one, too."

"When?" she asked, wincing from the pain that came from just saying that much.

"We'll worry about that procedure when you recover from this surgery. It will have to be pretty soon."

Steve asked, "Isn't there anything that can be done to stop it, instead of operating on Angel all the time?"

"This is a very rare form of cancer," Dr. Grannis replied apologetically. "There is no known treatment. The course of the cancer is unpredictable. I wish I could tell you more. There's just so much we don't know."

Steve tried to comfort Angel, but she was too weak to carry on a conversation with him. She sat in the chair, leaning against the bed mattress and wondering what could possibly happen next. While Steve and Dr. Grannis were helping her back into bed, she fainted.

In and out of consciousness, Angel could hear the voices of Jeannie and the nurses and could sense the presence of other people, but she kept her eyes closed and rested. Jeannie kept jumping out of her chair every time her sister uttered a sound, worried that she was choking or having a seizure.

"Can you hear me? I'm worried about you," she said on one of those occasions that she rushed to Angel's side. "I just can't believe everything that has happened to my only sister. I don't want to lose you!"

Angel opened her eyes and smiled weakly, trying to sound reassuring as she whispered, "You're not going to lose me. I'm going to be fine. I guarantee it."

"How much pain are you having?" Jeannie asked.

"I'm fine, really. It's okay," Angel said deceptively, believing that false bravado would at least put others' minds at rest, even as she suffered.

Her recovery period began as soon as her vital signs had stabilized. It involved exercising certain portions of her upper body to rebuild the damaged muscles, another extremely painful task. Her frustration often showed and she grew depressed and then angry.

Making matters worse, her left lung would not stay expanded. Whenever the tube was removed, the lung deflated and Angel screamed in agony, though she was barely audible because her voice was so weak. The nurse suggested she could help the healing process by trying to walk, and by taking deep breaths and lightly coughing as she exhaled. That was hard for her because it went against her instincts, which were telling her to avoid any disturbance in that part of her body. The pain would intensify whenever she coughed. Angel tried to fool the nurses by making a noise that sounded like a cough, but they could always tell and they often scolded her like she was a naughty little girl.

The slowness of her recovery was made graphically obvious by the spirometer, a device that gauges lung capacity by how hard a patient blows into a plastic tube. A reading of fourteen on the scale indicates normal breathing. Angel was only registering a three or four.

Another measure of her progress came in the form of continued blood samples that the nurses took from her arm to see how much oxygen was in her bloodstream. This was a particularly intrusive process. Angel finally started complaining about the nurses constantly poking her with needles, and she resisted them like a spoiled brat by burying her arms under her body. They reported this to the attending physician, and he agreed that she could forego the blood tests as long as she promised to take deeper breaths.

Despite the complex surgery and the long recovery period, the doctors were optimistic about Angel being able to regain normal use of her lungs.

"We've talked about Angel learning to walk on the high wire with her artificial leg and all," Steve told Dr. Grannis. "Is this going to affect that?"

"I wouldn't recommend that at all," the doctor said. "The pressure on the muscles around her lungs would be terrific if she tried to carry a balancing pole, and there could be terrible damage to her lungs if she ever fell. No, I think that's out of the question."

Jeannie had to return to New York while Angel was still in the hospital. "Keep me posted, will you?" Jeannie said as she gently hugged her sister.

"I will," Angel assured her. A lump formed in her throat and she tried to hold back her tears.

"I wish I could see you more often," Jeannie said. "The calls and the letters are nice, but they're not the same. I miss seeing you. Be tough, okay?"

"You know I'm tough. I've been tougher than you ever since we were kids—except now you can run away from me and I'll never catch you."

"Hey Jeannie," Steve interjected. "Bring us back the broom of the Wicked Witch of the West and we'll go see the Wizard of Oz so we can get Angel a new leg and an extra lung or two."

Chapter 21

# MEANT TO BE

Jeannie's departure left Steve to fend for himself and Steven in the Hope
Village apartments. Angel's medical problems and the intense child care
responsibilities were taking a heavy toll on him. At times his spirits soared and
he could be the most loving and supportive person in the world; then he would
turn almost belligerent and withdraw, or he'd take Steven and leave the room
for hours at a time without letting Angel know where they were.

When he was in the room, he had a faraway look in his eyes and he paced
the floor, his shoulders hunched. He'd put up a false front of being stable and
at ease. However, inside he was having great trouble accepting the realities of
his wife's condition. Occasionally, this distress would emerge and Steve and
Angel would cause a scene at the hospital, with Steve leaving the room in anger
and Angel reduced to tears.

In his absence, Angel had frequent visits from Doug and Karen, a couple
she had met at a church she had attended off and on before her lung operation.
Overtly kind toward Angel and Steven, Doug and Karen did nothing to hide
their distrust of Steve.

Angel spent hours in her hospital bed staring and thinking. She studied the
patterns of the wallpaper and tried to count all of the holes that dotted each of
the ceiling tiles. She became immersed in a sea of guilt and confusion. Her guilt
stemmed from the feeling that she was letting her family down.

Confusion clouded Angel's vision of their future as husband and wife—
and as parents. She couldn't expect Steve to support her completely when he
himself was suffering so. She knew her disease would drastically alter their
lifestyle, but she didn't want it to destroy their very special relationship.

When Angel was well enough to be discharged, she decided to accept
Doug and Karen's offer to let her and Steven stay with them. Ostensibly, this
arrangement was made because their home was much closer to City of Hope.
However, Angel also believed the separate living accommodations might make
it easier for Steve and her to sort out their differences. Rather than carry out this

charade and betray Steve's trust, Angel decided to share her true feelings with him.

She was pleasantly surprised when he offered no objections. "I don't want you to be worried," he said. "I want you to be comfortable. I'll just have to prove myself to you. Now that you're out of the hospital, we can start to follow our dreams and rebuild our lives, all of the things we've talked about. I'm a lot better able to accept things as they are now. I guess you could say that I had a little talk with the man upstairs. He's going to help me. I don't blame you for doubting me. I'll just be patient. You'll see."

Angel assured him that she would visit him at the trailer, as long as their old car held out. She said that once she was convinced that conditions were right, she and Steven would move back home.

Angel accepted the kindness of Doug and Karen as a gesture of Christian love, born out of a sincere desire to help her. Therefore, she found it odd that, two days after she and Steven moved in, they wanted her to sign a document that would give them custody of her son if she were to die or become severely disabled. Because Doug and Karen were so deeply involved in their church and so supportive, Angel did not initially question their motives. But as she pondered their actions, she suspected other intentions: unable to bear children of their own, they saw the possibility that they might be able to "inherit" Steven. If this meant helping to build a wall between Angel and Steve, that's what they would do.

Doug gave Angel a stack of pamphlets and a cassette tape containing sermons from a soft-speaking evangelist, explaining steps a person should take in preparing to die. Steve heard her playing the tape during one of Angel's visits to the trailer.

"It doesn't say anything on there about hope, or fighting to live," he said in obvious anger. "You don't need to listen to a tape telling you that you're going to die. You've got to fight this thing!"

He ripped the tape out of the player and flung it against the far wall, where it dropped behind a couch.

"Don't worry, Steve, I'm fighting," Angel assured him. "I have no intention of dying."

"I know you are, honey. I know you've been through hell, and I haven't been much help to you." Angel turned toward him and they kissed.

"Why don't you move back in?" Steve asked gently. "It's lonely out here alone. I need my wife and my son. And, you know, I'd also like to think that just maybe you both need me. I feel a little useless right now."

This was the first time he had pressured Angel about the issue. "It's still a little too soon," Angel said. "I'll know when the time is right. Believe me, it's not that we don't both need you. But, this time, I have to be absolutely sure we're not going to start arguing again. It's not good for Steven. Plus, it's a lot more convenient for me to be close to the hospital."

# HIGH WIRE ANGEL

Steve nodded his head in agreement. He said he had engaged in a great deal of self-examination. His time had been consumed with Bible reading and wire training. Angel worried that one day she would find him lying dead underneath the practice wire, since there was no one within miles to attend to him in the event of a fall.

While Angel continued her regular visits to City of Hope for check-ups and physical therapy, the specialists were putting the finishing touches on a new "permanent" right leg apparatus for her. Part of the prosthesis was a state-of-the-art "Seattle Foot," developed after years of research by Dr. Ernest Burgess, a surgeon from Seattle, Washington.

Modeled from castings of human feet, this device was equipped with special parts that supplied the natural lift and thrust that had been missing in previous artificial feet. Dr. Burgess had designed a sole that stored and released energy in unison with each step. The foot also had flexible toes that would allow the patient to walk almost normally.

Once this leg was ready for Angel, she was off her crutches for good. It was a vast improvement over anything she had worn before. The foot's responsiveness gave her much better control of her movements, so she felt more comfortable placing the normal amount of weight on the leg when she walked.

The second lung operation was scheduled for April 1988. Steve arranged to stay at the Hope Village apartments again and Angel allowed Steven to stay there with him, under the condition that the two of them spend most of their time with her. She was worried what might happen to Steven if his father was subjected to another long, living nightmare like her first operation.

Doug and Karen protested her decision. They again stressed how unreliable Steve had been, and how much better of an atmosphere their home would be. They also continued urging Angel to sign the adoption papers.

"What's going to happen to that boy if something goes wrong? Haven't you thought about that?" Doug asked callously. "Do you think he's going to amount to anything if he grows up with Steve?"

"Don't bury me yet, Doug," Angel said, catching him off-guard with her defiance. "It's not like I'm going to die tomorrow. You're not being fair. You don't even know Steve."

The second lung operation was neither as complicated, nor as painful, as the first one. The surgeons had a clearer notion of what the procedures would be and were better-prepared to locate the problem and deal with it. Angel entered the operating room with little fear and emerged from the surgery with much less pain than she had expected. About three-quarters of one of the lobes at the base of her right lung was removed by Dr. Grannis and his assistants. Once again, she was connected to life support systems until her vital signs were stabilized.

Because Angel was the lone occupant of a double room, Steve and Steven were able to sleep together in the other bed. Steve kept going back and forth to

Angel's bed, rubbing her back and telling her how much he loved her.

"It's time for you and Steven to come back home where you belong," he said on one of those bedside visits. Angel agreed with him and said she would move out of Doug and Karen's house as soon as she was discharged. She knew in her heart that she was not meant to live apart from Steve—she loved him. The void of his absence had been enormous. Angel also knew that Steve needed her.

Recovery from this operation bore no resemblance to Angel's long road back from the previous lung surgery. Within twenty-four hours, she felt well enough to get on her feet without any encouragement from the nurses. The pain was intense, particularly in those muscles that had to be penetrated so that Dr. Grannis and his team could reach the lung, but Angel did not let it bother her.

Eventually, she persuaded Steve to leave her side and drive out to the trailer with Steven. She reminded him that their free rent was contingent upon them tending to caretaker duties, something he had been ignoring.

Within minutes of Steve's departure from the room, Dr. Grannis arrived to give Angel a check-up. He was pleased with her rapid recovery and announced that she could be discharged.

"That's the way it works sometimes," Dr. Grannis explained. "You can come right out of surgery and be ready to return to normal living in less than a week, or you can be laid up for a couple of weeks just trying to walk. I've never been able to understand it. But I'd have to say that this is the fastest I have ever seen a patient recover from surgery as serious as this."

Angel felt shaky and lightheaded whenever she stood, but she wasn't about to let Dr. Grannis or any of the nurses know that. She signed all of the discharge papers herself and slowly made her way out to the car, stopping just once to lean against a tree on the hospital grounds and catch her breath.

When she pulled into Doug and Karen's driveway, they were seated on their porch swing and rose to greet her. Angel opened the door of the car and dispensed with the pleasantries.

"I'm here to get my things," she declared.

"Where's the boy?" Karen asked.

"He's with his father. I just got out of the hospital. They did the operation on my lung. You both have been very nice, but it's time for me to move on."

"Hold everything—they let you out already?" Doug said incredulously.

"Yep, it wasn't bad at all this time."

"I suppose the first thing you're going to do is move back in with Steve," he said.

"If that's what you're planning, why don't you at least leave Steven here this time, at least for a while?" Karen chimed in.

They started in again about what a terrible person Steve was; a "circus bum" was the way Doug described him. Angel politely listened, offering little response, and then went inside to pack her things. Reluctantly, Doug and Karen helped her load the car.

# HIGH WIRE ANGEL

"I appreciate all you've done for me, I really do." Angel told him. "I know you think I'm making a mistake, but I'm going to prove you wrong."

"I hope so," Doug responded, closing the door to the trunk. "We'll be praying for you, Angel, and for little Steven. I want you to know that you're welcome here any time and you can bring Steven around whenever you want."

Each of them gave Angel a polite embrace as she settled into the driver's seat and then drove out onto the highway. As she pulled around the corner of the dusty desert road that led to the trailer, she could see Steve was sitting on the front step, with Steven in his lap.

"What is this, a mirage in the middle of the desert?" Steve said.

"No, it's real. I'm home!" Angel shouted out the car window.

"Do you mean you're home for good, or just dropping by to visit?" Steve asked as he trotted toward her, swinging Steven and over his head so he could straddle his dad's neck with his legs.

"I mean I'm home to stay, back where I belong," Angel assured him, "I do love you. I've never stopped loving you. I don't ever want to be apart from you."

Steve pulled Angel against him with one arm while he balanced Steven with the other. She could feel a special warmth flowing up and down her entire body as he kissed her. The pull was irresistible. They held each other for a long time. All of the anger, the resentment, and the petty disagreements were put aside as they absorbed each other's love.

"I don't know what went wrong between us, Angel, but I do know we've both been under a lot of pressure," Steve said. "I think we need each other if we are going to be strong. I don't ever want to be apart from you again either. You're a part of me, Angel; you're the best part."

"There's something I have to tell you," Steve continued. "We're only just getting back together and now we're going to have to be apart again. I've got a job. Well, not really a full-time job, but something that will force me to be away for a couple of weeks."

Steve had answered an advertisement to work for the Jordan International Circus, but not as a performer. Hoping to re-establish some circus connections, he had accepted a job as a concessionaire on the troupe's West Coast tour that would end in Las Vegas.

"The money isn't much, but I can guarantee you that I will come home with a little black book full of important names, addresses, and phone numbers," he assured Angel. "After that, it's your job as my agent to start plotting my comeback. And when you're feeling better, we'll get you up on the wire, too."

Angel was happy to see some of Steve's old enthusiasm returning, even if it meant she would be left in the desert to recover all by herself. She was not about to fall back upon Doug and Karen and give them another opportunity to badger her.

Steve called home almost every night as the circus made its way up the California coastline. On the final night, he didn't call until late from Las Vegas.

"I was busy for a little longer than I expected to be," he explained. "Oh, by the way, I told Dick Clark that you said hello, and he said to tell you he is pulling for your recovery."

Angel thought he was making it up. Steve had long been an admirer of Dick Clark, stemming from his frequent visits to watch the taping of American Bandstand when he was a young boy living just down the street from the studio. Both Steve and Angel admired Clark for his ability to convey a spirit of joy and youthful enthusiasm to any audience.

"I don't really know what possessed me, but I just walked over to him and introduced myself," Steve related. "He recognized my name and knew who I was. I'll tell you, he's a very genuine, wonderful person, the same way he comes across on TV. I felt privileged just to meet him."

Steve couldn't get over the fact that Dick Clark already knew what had happened to Angel, evidently from the newscasts in Los Angeles.

"He told me to keep plugging away and not to get discouraged," Steve said, "and he wanted to be sure that I told you how much he admires you for your courage."

Chapter 22

# PUSH TO THE LIMIT

With Steve away, Angel needed to find something to keep her mind occupied, so she searched the want ads and landed a two-day-a-week job helping a woman clean her house and tend to her children. The wife of a Hollywood entertainment agent who was rarely home, she was forced to raise their eight children on her own.

As much difficulty as she had doing such physical labor after her operations, Angel took great pains to convince everybody that she was doing all right. She wanted so badly to be normal, to get on with life and show people that she really was no different than she was before the surgery. Throughout her life, Angel never wanted anyone to feel sorry for her.

Many times, she and Steve had talked about where they should settle down. Angel wanted to move back east and become reacquainted with her family. Steve had mixed feelings because he had spent so much of his life in California and believed there would be more performance opportunities there.

Frederick Pintye shocked his daughter one day by calling and practically begging her to move her family into his house at Mahopac until she and Steve could get a place of their own. As soon as Steve returned from the circus tour, Angel shared her father's offer with him.

"But I don't even know the man. I've never met him," Steve argued. "And from what you've told me about him, I'm not so sure it would work out."

"I think he's changed," Angel countered. "I saw a side of him I'd never seen before at Mom's funeral. I really think it would be good for us. After all, we can always come back out here if things don't work out."

After much discussion, they reached a compromise. They would move to New York on a trial basis, allowing her father's house to be their home base. Wherever Steve's career led them, they would follow.

The circus exposure had inspired Steve to devote much more of his time to practicing on the wire, another sign to Angel that he was serious about his commitment to get on with their plans. Professional aerialists and promoters he had spoken with were confident that if Angel were ever able to walk the high wire with an artificial leg, the three of them—Steven included—could conceivably put together an act that would write their names in the annals of entertainment history. They would also be carrying on the famous Wallenda name in a most unique and potentially rewarding manner.

"Do you really think I should give it a try?" Angel asked Steve as he shared the details of his conversations. "I don't see how I could have any control. If I couldn't feel the wire, how could I balance myself on it?"

"There's a simple answer to that, Angel: practice. I'm telling you, with your physique and your body control, I know you could learn to do it. There isn't a doubt in my mind. You start on the low wire, develop your technique, and then graduate to the high wire."

The next morning, Angel was up and out the door to the practice wires before Steve was even stirring. The cool desert air had begun to move out; the day was going to be a scorcher. Above her, the high wire glistened in the early morning sun. Two long balancing poles were stacked under a hand-built shelter, along with the slippers and moccasins, and the rosin that assured proper traction on the wire. Angel was sorting through the equipment when Steve joined her.

"You're up kind of early. What's the story?" he inquired.

"I've been waiting for you. I'm just getting my bearings. I'm not going to start walking on the wire without some help from somebody."

That brought a smile to Steve's face. Angel changed into her slippers and added some adhesive tape to her balancing pole.

"Let's go for it," she said, "but not too fast. Don't rush me. I might decide to call it quits as soon as I have one foot off the ground."

Steve clung firmly to Angel's hand as she took a deep breath and then stepped up onto the three-foot-high wire. Even a fall from that height could snap her artificial leg and cause untold damage to her recovering lungs.

It wasn't nearly as hard for Angel to keep her balance on the wire as she had imagined, but she was barely strong enough to carry the pole. Supporting the extra weight of thirty-five pounds also forced her to breathe harder, making her lightheaded, especially as the southern California morning sun rose higher in the sky.

Within two weeks, Angel made her first post-operation trip all the way across the low wire by herself. Steve clapped his hands in delight of her accomplishment and Steven joined in with a mocking applause from his playpen.

The hardest part for Angel was to rely on the artificial leg to support all of her weight. Her tendency was to speed up her movements whenever she came down on her right foot so that she could get her left foot back on the wire as quickly as possible. Steve kept emphasizing how important it was to establish a steady pace so she could concentrate more on her balance than on the mechanics of the movement itself.

Steven got a real kick out of playing on the trapeze and watching his parents work on the wire. There is plenty of Wallenda in that little boy. Sometimes his dad would walk with him on his shoulders and Steven would throw his arms out wide to "style" while his mother or father sang, "Taa-daa!"

HIGH WIRE ANGEL

That got to be his cue. Angel would say, "Do your 'Taa-daa!' Steven," and automatically he would spread his arms out to each side and smile.

Steven also found a special way to help his mom. After she removed her prosthesis to take a bath, go to bed, or just rest her upper leg, she would ask Steven to retrieve it. He'd scurry around the trailer looking for it, then come running in, saying, "Here, mama. Here's you 'egg'."

Producers of the ABC television show, "Incredible Sunday," learned of Angel's efforts to return to the wire. With the name Wallenda and the special circumstances of her case, she was seen as a natural for that kind of a TV show.

They made an initial telephone call, explaining that they wanted to cover Angel's first public performance whenever she was ready. Steve promised them that they could have the exclusive rights to the filming and told them to check back in a couple of months.

"Can you believe it?" Steve exclaimed after he hung up the phone. "This is it! This is the chance we've been waiting for." Angel was more nervous than excited because Steve had made a commitment that she was not certain she could honor.

There were things they had to do before leaving California, such as selling the trailer and the Toyota. Yet, everything seemed to fall into place. Within weeks, they were able to load everything they owned into the back of a small rental truck and bid farewell to California. Angel and Steven rode in the pickup, following Steve as he drove the moving truck.

During their rest stops, they talked about the idea of performing on national TV. Steve saw it as a great financial opportunity, as well as a chance to get the Wallenda name back in the public eye. He believed their career as a performing family could take off from there.

With a specific goal in mind, Angel could not wait until they reached her dad's house so their training could continue. The "Incredible Sunday" producers insisted that she do a solo walk on the high wire, so she would have no alternative but to practice hard and often.

As Angel drove, she started jotting down notes of the things she wanted to tell Steve at each stop, resting her little notebook against the steering wheel as she wrote. Steven entertained his mother by trying to sing along with the songs on the radio as they drove. When Steven slept, Angel changed the station to listen to the news and the radio call-in shows.

Jeannie was in the kitchen, preparing a welcome-home dinner when Angel and Steve pulled into her father's driveway. Angel shut off the engine and sighed, concerned about the awkwardness of moving back into the house with a husband, son, and all of their belongings. Frederick Pintye broke the ice as he walked out to the driveway to offer Steve a hearty handshake.

Then he hoisted Steven up to his shoulders. "There's my little tiger!" he said. "Do you remember your Grandpa?" Steven gave him a curious look and nodded his head affirmatively.

"Hi, Dad," Angel said nervously, finally stepping out of the pickup truck.

"How was your trip, Lizzie? Oops, I forgot, it's Angel. That's going to take some getting used to."

"I'm okay. It's a little strange to think about moving in here with my family and..."

"No problem, believe me," her father interrupted. "I've got plenty of room. I'm happy to have you here, especially after everything you've been through." Angel was overcome with joy as she recognized how much more personable her father had grown. Even more pleasing to her was the way he seemed to hit it off with her husband and her son.

Her brother Thomas had separate living quarters in the same house. As an independent stone mason, he was always on the run. Jeannie was married now, with a child on the way. Living not far from her dad's house, she was a frequent visitor.

Steve set up practice wires in the back yard and he and Angel started training, almost religiously, from the time they got up in the morning until dark. It became her obsession. Blisters developed where Angel's right leg met her prosthesis, but she pressed on even though no amount of salve would relieve the pain. If the blisters hurt too much or started bleeding, Angel would step down off the wire and work on the trapeze until her leg felt better.

She easily mastered the low wire after just a couple of days, but the fifteen-foot high wire, strung for a distance of about thirty feet, was something else again. Without a net below the wire, she had no margin for error.

Angel discovered that saying she would be able to walk the high wire, and actually doing so, were two different things. It was much harder work than she had ever envisioned. After stepping onto the wire and then retreating back to the platform several times, she began to doubt that she could ever make it all the way across.

Even as Angel dragged herself into the house, exhausted from the effort, she kept practicing wire-walking in her head. Sitting in a chair with her eyes closed, she could envision herself progressing across the wire. Angel sometimes moved her body while she reclined, recreating the weight shifts that were necessary on the wire.

During a rest period underneath the wire, Steve approached her with a frosty mug of lemonade and told her there was something inside the house he wanted her to see. "But first I have to ask you this: Who do you consider to be the greatest entertainer?"

"Whaddya mean?" Angel asked. "There are a lot of great entertainers. I suppose you think I'm going to say that you are the greatest."

"No, seriously, who's your favorite? Who's the best showman in the entertainment world today?"

"I have lots of favorites. As far as showmanship, I guess Michael Jackson is hard to beat."

"I knew that was what you were going to say," Steve replied with a grin. "Now come on inside and you can meet him."

"Yeah, right, and now you're going to tell me that Michael Jackson is sitting at the kitchen table."

"Well, not exactly—but he's in another room, kind of." Angel was befuddled.

# HIGH WIRE ANGEL

They walked into the living room, but the only person there was Steven, fast asleep on the couch.

"I thought you said Michael Jackson was here. I don't see him," Angel said.

"You will in a minute," Steve responded, stepping over to the television set and pressing a button on the VCR. "Now just watch. We'll talk in a couple of minutes. I just want you to see this and I'll explain."

The video was "Moonwalker," starring Michael Jackson. A few minutes into the tape, Steve leaned over and pushed the pause button.

"There's something I want you to notice about Michael Jackson," Steve explained. He sat down next to Angel. "Michael Jackson entrances people with his music and his body movements—even people from my generation—and the way he does that is he pushes himself to the limit as a performer. Now I want you to see something else, and really think about it."

With that, he switched cassettes. It was the videotape of Steve's performance on ABC-TV's "That's Incredible" show a couple of years earlier. He advanced the tape to the point where he was about three-quarters of the way up an inclined wire, a black blindfold enveloping his face as the fierce wind whipped at his body.

"See the tension in my body?" he said. "Now I'm not trying to compare myself to Michael Jackson, but it's the same kind of thing. I pushed to the limit. I was able to find the strength to reach that platform up in the sky. Each of us has something within us, just waiting for us to tap into if we truly need it. You're not any different, Angel. You can't get discouraged. You can meet it head-on and you can make it. I know you can."

Angel recognized that she had never really told herself she *could* do it. She had subconsciously been thinking of reasons not to. Something had held her back. She had never reached for that inner reserve.

Although the financial potential and career implications of this performance couldn't be ignored, Angel began to recognize another even more powerful motivation: her life's experiences could serve as an inspiration to others. That point was further driven home one Saturday afternoon as she was resting after a practice session. Angel pushed the button on her father's television set and collapsed back into his recliner. A local broadcast of the Special Olympics immediately caught her attention.

Hundreds of young children with all kinds of handicaps were engaged in a series of track and field events. Angel tuned in just in time to see the starter's gun fire for the wheelchair race. The camera panned in close on the faces of the racers. They were pushing themselves just as hard as their physical strength and endurance would allow.

The winner was a boy about ten years old, with a crew cut and soda bottle-thick glasses. Such joy was written on his face that Angel could feel the same emotions. She shut off the TV to ponder what she had just witnessed. These unfortunate victims of all kinds of disabilities had put aside their problems and had gone out to prove something to themselves and to others. They touched something within her.

Angel closed her eyes and pictured herself lifting the balancing pole and walking smoothly across the high wire. She had the power and the opportunity to teach an important lesson about determination to millions of others through her appearance on national television. She would work her hardest—yes, push to the limit—and perhaps bring some hope to other people, showing them that they, too, can overcome serious obstacles if they will only fight back.

Chapter 23

# AN INCREDIBLE SUNDAY

Even though the techniques used on the low wire and the high wire are virtually the same, there is a distinct difference in the sensations that an aerialist feels. The low wire helps a walker develop technique, while the high wire teaches control. Fear is another factor. As much as one can pretend that a fall from the three-foot-high wire is a real danger, the reality is that most people will not be injured if they come off the wire from that height.

However, there is a completely different feeling and considerable risk when walking the high wire. Angel's first time across took close to a half-hour, as Steve and Thomas looked on from each side below her. If she fell, there was a slight chance that one of them might catch her. She was so nervous at first that she began making up excuses not to do it. "The wind's blowing too hard," she would say, or "The neighbors over there are making too much noise." Finally, she steeled herself, gently bit her lower lip, took a deep breath and stepped forward.

Every time Angel mentioned any desire to stop, Steve reminded her how important it was for her to get all the way across. He inspired Angel to achieve more, to be a better performer, to grow. Once she was near the midway point, she realized that the easiest route to safety was straight ahead to the opposite anchoring platform.

Angel was soaking wet with perspiration and still trembling with anxiety, as she collapsed into her husband's waiting arms.

"Just relax and catch your breath," Steve whispered. "You made it! The hard part's over now. Take a little while to savor the moment and think of what you've done."

At long last, the hurdle had been crossed. Though Angel retained a healthy respect for the danger of high wire performing, the intimidating fear was supplanted by a great feeling of accomplishment.

That same afternoon, Steve placed a call to the "Incredible Sunday" producers and told them this latest member the The Great Wallendas was ready. They set the performance for October 5, 1988, just four weeks away.

When Steve told Angel about the call, she was furious. "It's too early for that!" she insisted. "I've walked the high wire a grand total of one time, and you're ready to put me on national TV?"

"Listen, you're over the hump now," Steve said. "You've conquered the fear and proven to yourself that you can do it. Trust me on this. The hardest part is over."

As Angel's practices continued, Steve taught her to start off with a power surge, like a baseball runner trying to steal a base, and then to develop an even rhythm for the remainder of the walk, ever mindful of appearing relaxed and comfortable for the audience. That is usually possible until around the midway point, when natural instincts say to slow down. The body becomes shaky, almost out of control. Then the tendency is to hurry to the other side and forget about outward appearances or technique. It becomes a matter of survival.

Often, the wire has the most slack in the middle. This extra bobbing and weaving can cause the feet to slip, which only adds to the nervousness. By the time the aerialist reaches the platform at the conclusion of a walk, the body is shaking. After that, the adrenaline is flowing and compelling the performer to do it all over again.

Each walk teaches more control. The aerialist gains confidence and a respect for heights. You come to appreciate the accomplishments of those performers who have polished their skills to the point where they look totally relaxed.

By the time the advance crew from "Incredible Sunday" arrived at Frederick Pintye's house to film some background footage for the show, Angel had taken another half-dozen walks on the high wire, each of them faster than the previous one. The cameras rolled for hours as Steve and Angel practiced, worked out, swam, walked hand-in-hand, and casually chatted.

They received a package in the mail containing train tickets—Angel could not travel by air, due to her lung operations—vouchers, identification cards, a stack of papers to sign, and other documents. The train ride was a relaxing change of pace after working so hard to perfect the wire act. Steve was upbeat, inspired by his success as Angel's trainer.

Angel spent much of the trip reflecting on her progress since she stepped onto the wire at the Circus of the Stars, more as a lark than anything else. Her reward was the opportunity to perform on national television. It had been a long journey from the foster homes of suburban New York to the bright lights of the Hollywood television studio.

After Steve and Angel met with the directors to review the script and discuss particulars, they were plastered with make-up and taken down to City of Hope National Medical Center. There, the TV crew followed them through re-enactments of their discussions with the doctors and through Angel's physical therapy. As awkward as the hospital personnel must have felt being thrust into roles as actors, the administrators welcomed the opportunity to gain such widespread and positive publicity.

# HIGH WIRE ANGEL

Angel felt particularly uncomfortable in acting out her own part in this television re-creation which barely scratched the surface of what she had actually been through. Her mind flashed back to the horrors she had experienced in real life at City of Hope during the not-so-distant past.

This trip was Angel's first exposure to the luxury that the wealthy enjoy. The hotel was filled with aging businessmen, well-dressed yuppies, and stunning women of all ages. Limousine drivers ushered the Wallendas wherever they wanted to go.

"This is what it's like at the top, Angel." Steve smiled. "It's all part of the game. You're supposed to feel like you're some kind of a big shot."

"Forget that," Angel told him. "I'm just plain old me. I'm not impressed with this kind of stuff. If you want to know the truth, I feel kind of silly."

The scene at the ABC studio was hectic. Directors, technicians, make-up artists, and others who work behind the scenes were scurrying around, making sure the cameras were properly positioned, the sound levels just right, and all of the make-up properly applied.

"Image! Image! Image!" said the woman who was working on Angel's hair in the crowded dressing room. "Don't worry about how you look to yourself in the mirror, just think of what it's going to look like to millions of people who are seeing you on the TV screen. That's what matters right now. Are you nervous?"

"Not at all," Angel replied.

"Well, that's different. Usually, they're so jumpy I can't keep 'em under the hair dryer."

Angel found out quickly enough that what ends up coming across on the TV screen can bear little resemblance to what is really happening on the stage. She assumed the audience reaction was spontaneous during live programs or tapings, and never realized the extent to which these responses are programmed. Members of the audience were told when to applaud, when to laugh, and which way to look when they were clapping, even when there was nothing to look at.

As difficult as it was for Angel, the wire walk that was featured on "Incredible Sunday" wasn't nearly as dramatic as it appeared on TV. The producers created this illusion by dubbing in background music that built to a crescendo as Angel neared the end of her walk and patching in some of the staged audience reactions.

This is not to belittle the difficulty of the walk or the significance of this very important occasion in Angel's life. She had never felt as much pressure to succeed at something as she did the moment she boarded that wire.

The program opened with black and white footage from the Wallenda Seven-Man Pyramid accident during the 1964 television performance, not long after the tragic collapse in Detroit. That was followed by the chilling tape of Karl Wallenda's fatal accident and a brief recap of Angel's medical problems. Next, the program reviewed her recovery and her wire-walking training, focusing heavily on Steve's encouragement and guidance.

At that point, the producers patched in the tape of Angel's walk in front of the studio audience. Dressed in a black sequined top with rhinestone-trimmed bows on the shoulders and shiny red pants, she spent several minutes atop the platform, staring out into the bright lights and the sea of anonymous faces. Steve and the host, John Davidson, were waiting for her arrival at the opposite platform, about 35 feet away. Two spotters were poised 14 feet below to walk beneath the wire, prepared to follow Angel's every step.

"Do you think she's nervous?" John asked.

"Not as nervous as I am," Steve replied.

The director gave Angel her cue to step out onto the wire. With her balancing pole teetering ever so slightly, she made steady progress until she was past the midway point. There, she began to struggle against the looseness of the wire. Angel had grown accustomed to a cable with much stronger tension. She had to adjust the pole up and down in each direction to regain her balance and complete the walk.

Hours before the taping, Steve had urged the set-up crew to attach guy wires to keep the cable from swaying, but they said the filming schedule was too tight because the studio had to be used for another show later in the day. Angel was afraid the directors would order her to make another walk since she did not move smoothly enough, by her own standards. However, everyone else was pleased with her performance. Both Steve and John greeted Angel with an embrace as she stepped to the platform.

"I saw you shaking," John said to her.

"That was me," Steve interrupted with a smile.

As an encore, Steve stepped onto the wire and Angel carefully mounted his shoulders for a walk back to the other platform. Near the end, she lowered herself off his back to the wire. With Angel clinging to Steve's shoulders, they covered the final few steps as a team. "Crisp, smooth and clean," Angel whispered to herself.

Steve let out a huge sigh as the two reached the platform. He kissed Angel and they turned to the crowd to accept their accolades. After filming the show, Angel and Steve reported to City of Hope for her check-up and further testing of her lungs. Angel had put her medical condition out of her mind for the entire trip. Now, while she was lying motionless in the tunnel-like chamber of the CT scanner, it all came back to her.

Readouts produced just after her final operation had shown some suspicious images in her lungs. Dr. Grannis said at the time that it was possible they were merely scar tissue. Angel's instincts had told her that Dr. Grannis was less than certain about his findings and was trying to put things in the best possible light.

The latest test revealed growth of these images over the past four months. The diagnosis was alarmingly obvious: the dark cloud that was cancer had returned to haunt her again.

A jolt struck Angel's body when Dr. Grannis said the word "cancer." The whole appointment seemed like a slow-motion scene out of a horror movie. The doctor explained that, even if the cancer remained dormant for some time, additional surgery would be needed to prevent it from spreading. He felt she should wait at least three months for another test to provide further information on the path of the cancer and the extent of the surgery.

"I'm not going to lie to you, Angel," he added. "This could be very serious. Unless we can stop the growth through surgery, or chemotherapy, or a combination of the two, we could be looking at a terminal situation. I don't want to alarm you. I just want you to have a clear idea of where you stand."

Angel looked at Steve. He was staring into Dr. Grannis' eyes, shocked by what he had just heard. His face reddened and his eyes widened.

"How can this be? She's so young," Steve finally said. "Did you say 'terminal'?"

"There's no rhyme or reason to it," the doctor responded. "We know very little about this type of cancer. I wish I had more answers for you."

"Faith, honey," Angel said softly, reaching to take her husband's hand. "Remember our faith." Behind this facade, she was having her own problems coming to grips with this latest setback. Just when she and Steve were about to launch a performing career as a couple, just when her husband and son needed her the most, her very life was in jeopardy.

Angel made up her mind that, once she returned to Mahopac, she would not even think about the cancer. She would work with Steve on the high wire as if they hadn't even been told about it. If, by some miracle, the cancer went into remission, they could follow through on their plans.

Throughout most of the return trip to New York, Angel stared out the train window deep in thought, oblivious to the passing scenery. She and Steve barely exchanged a word.

Copies of her medical records were referred to a New York hospital, where Dr. Evelyn McClintock would review them. ABC-TV sent a letter informing the Wallendas that the "Incredible Sunday" segment would air nationwide the following weekend. Out of curiosity, Angel checked the TV listings in the newspaper to see what they said about the show and was amused to discover that they had misspelled her name:

*"Angela Wallenda from the famous 'Flying Wallendas' takes to the high wire for the first time since losing her leg to cancer."*

Jeannie came over to her father's house so they could all watch the "Incredible Sunday" show together.

"Look, Mama, you're on TV, just like Donald Duck!" Steven exclaimed as the show came on. "That's my mama on TV! Isn't that you. Mama?"

Her life's contrasts were in clear focus. Former foster parents and anyone else who knew Angel over the years could see what had happened to this little tomboy who spent so much of her childhood desperately trying to be loved and accepted. How ironic, Angel thought, that millions of people were hearing and seeing her story and marveling at her recovery at the very time she had learned that the disease had returned and her prognosis was poor.

Chapter 24

# HELP WANTED

The televised performance helped Steve and Angel get back on their feet. They used some of the money to purchase additional equipment for their training and to rebuild their publicity packages with new pictures and updated promotional leaflets. They became "The Wallendas: Aerialists Supreme," including a little trapeze star, Steven, to make it a true family act.

Angel had fully expected the national television appearance to lead to some immediate job offers, but the phone was not exactly ringing off the hook. She was now witnessing first-hand what Steve had been telling her all along: it's hard for an aerialist to find steady work.

When he was younger, performance engagements were not nearly as hard to come by. However, America's entertainment habits have undergone drastic changes. Today, most professional aerial performers either end up going into another line of work, or they sign on with a circus, where the pay is lousy, the conditions almost unbearable, and the job security practically non-existent.

Even those jobs may someday be hard to come by. The circus is a disappearing part of the American landscape. Far from "The Greatest Show On Earth," it's now nothing more than a curious novelty to today's young people, and a taste of nostalgia to those over the age of forty.

People get their kicks from action-packed movies or TV. The circus doesn't always seem so death-defying in comparison with other entertainment today. Its special brand of excitement cannot be conveyed on a television screen.

This was also a period of realization for Angel that her handicap, while it made her actual performance a novelty, was preventing them from landing jobs. Promoters and agents believed Angel was too much of an insurance risk because of her artificial leg.

"I can never get my message across, let alone make a living, if no one will hire me," Angel lamented as she discussed the dilemma with Steve.

At least he was employable. Steve accepted an offer to perform a skywalk to highlight a dedication ceremony for the new Minneapolis Convention Center.

Originally, he and Angel were scheduled to perform there as a team. Later, the organizers said they would hire only Steve.

When he protested and demanded an explanation, they told him Angel's wire-walking was notable only if people were aware of the story behind it. They were concerned that this would divert attention away from the convention center itself. The sponsors also maintained that they had taken a chance by booking one aerialist and did not want to increase their insurance risk by hiring a second, especially one who walked with an artificial leg.

None of the Wallendas' verbal assurances or offers to sign a waiver excusing the sponsors from liability carried any weight with the Minneapolis people. Their offer became "take it or leave it." Reluctantly, Angel and Steve agreed that it would be in their best interests to at least get Steve's name back in the limelight.

The performance was classic Steve Wallenda. Ignoring the script, which called for a relatively uneventful walk up the wire and back down, Steve stopped to kneel halfway up the incline. Closer to the top, he spun on one foot for a difficult 360-degree turn on the wire and then continued on his way.

After Steve reached the top, he laid his balancing pole across the rails of a small platform and produced a pair of three-foot-long scissors. With the spotlight reflecting off the giant metal blades, he ceremoniously snipped the strings of a net. About 4,000 navy blue balloons cascaded down on the crowd as the emcee called for a champagne toast.

Steve also had a couple of offers to perform during county fairs in New York State, but was forced to turn them down because of the state's "net law." Out of a sense of family loyalty, Steve steered the offers to his distant cousin, Tino Zoppe, a rival performer who had invested in his own rigging and net.

Angel was reminded of her limitations every day. She would get tired easily and she had trouble catching her breath whenever she was doing anything strenuous, all of which made her even more anxious to have her next doctor's appointment so she could learn the condition of her lungs.

Under an arrangement with City of Hope, Dr. McClintock was to study the changes between Angel's most recent CT scan and a new scan that had been taken just before her appointment. This would measure the growth of the cancer and establish the necessary groundwork for any further surgery that would be necessary.

To Angel's amazement and utter confusion, Dr. McClintock announced that the latter tests didn't reveal any signs of cancer. Angel wanted to believe her, but she feared the news was too good to be true. Dr. Grannis had never led Angel to believe that her cancer would go into remission. Dr. McClintock was at a loss to explain the contradiction. She pushed aside Angel's questions and said she should schedule a follow-up appointment in about two months.

Steve was reading the newspaper one morning when he came across a story about the plight of a Mahopac family. Michael Bradley, age three and one-half, had sustained massive brain damage due to lack of oxygen at birth. He was blind, unable to talk, and was fed through a tube in his throat. His parents were unable to pay for his medication, equipment, and care with the available Medicaid assistance, even with Michael's father working two jobs. Medicaid officials had told the Bradleys that the only way the boy could qualify for the care he needed was by being placed in an institution.

"I wish there was something we could do," Angel said after she read the sad story. "When you read something like this, it makes you realize that, all in all, you don't really have it that bad."

"There is something we could do, you know," Steve replied. "Let's do a wire-walk for him. We can try to get the news media involved and set up a Michael Bradley Fund, just like I did a few years ago for a friend who needed a heart transplant. I think if more people find out about the problems the Bradleys are having, they're going to want to help."

Angel began calling community organizations, offering to donate an aerial performance if they would sponsor the event and provide a place for Steve and Angel to walk the high wire. She received such a runaround from so many people that she went to the newspaper offices to see if the editors would be willing to print stories about the campaign. Articles did appear, but nobody called and the performance never took place.

The experience left a sour taste in Angel's mouth. It opened her eyes to the fact that so many people in need of help go without because everyone assumes that "someone else" will do it. Angel received a letter from the Heaven's Children Organization, an affiliate of the Make-A-Wish Foundation, informing her that she had been chosen to receive a National Academy Award for the Handicapped. To receive the honor, known as the "Determination, Achievement, Courage and Inspiration Award," she and Steve drove to Boston for a dinner at a plush downtown hotel.

They were seated with the other recipients, including actor Billy Barty and former professional football player Darryl Stingley whose promising career had ended when he was cracked in the back during an NFL game a few years earlier, leaving him paralyzed from the neck down.

The program was a new effort to acknowledge the individual accomplishments of handicapped people who might serve as role models for others. Angel appreciated receiving the award, but she could not help but feel that the ceremony was more of an appeal for publicity to benefit Heaven's Children than a recognition of the recipients' determination to overcome physical setbacks.

Before Angel was called on stage, the host, actor Robert Fuller, gave an inspirational speech to describe her medical problems and her will to overcome these handicaps and return to the high wire. After Angel returned to her seat, three older women approached the table and asked Steve and her to sign their programs. Several other people followed and, before long, a line had formed.

This was the first time Angel had been besieged by autograph seekers. She found it peculiar, almost embarrassing. Angel never expected, nor even desired, special treatment. She and Steve talked about the phenomenon as they drove

The Wallendas are shown in this publicity photo to launch their career after Angel's leg amputation.

back home. Angel wondered what it was that drove a person to want someone else's signature on a piece of paper.

She also thought a lot about what a "business" charitable fund-raising had become: "Why should it take the involvement of people with recognizable names to motivate people to support a worthy cause? What about the Michael Bradleys of the world—those causes that don't have a poster child or the grandeur and opulence of a fund-raising gala?"

In May 1989, the telephone finally rang with a very promising performance offer. An advertising firm was looking for people with recognizable names to use in a series of commercials for a prominent hotel chain. The agency thought an appearance by "The Flying Wallendas," represented by Steve, Angel, and Steven, would make an effective commercial.

A trio of advertising consultants traveled to Mahopac to discuss the plan and watch Steve and Angel practice. Because of his famous last name and professional accomplishments, Steve was to be the main focus of the ad. The consultants liked what they saw and signed a contract.

The script called for Steve to jump up through a box, perform a flip, and land on his feet next to a hotel bed. This would be no easy maneuver. To prepare, he spent hours bounding into the air off a small trampoline, hurling his body head over heels and crash-landing into the ground, sometimes on his feet, sometimes not. Perfecting an act such as this, usually performed by younger, more experienced aerialists, became a mission to Steve, and accomplishing it after just a week of practice was his own personal triumph.

Steven's part was much easier. All he had to do was jump on a hotel bed while his father performed the flip. Angel was to stand by and have a small speaking part. The Wallendas' hopes were dashed quite unexpectedly when the producers decided instead to use the services of Tino Zoppe as a representative of "The Flying Wallendas," and buy their way out of the contract with Steve and Angel.

This episode was a bitter pill for Steve and Angel to swallow. It represented the latest example of the rivalries that have developed within the Wallenda family over the years. Steve doesn't believe in living off the Wallenda name; he has built a solid reputation as a world-class performer in his own right. He believes many other members of the extended family attempt to capitalize on the Wallenda heritage, but their own performance records do not live up to the name.

Angel and Steve's relationship had grown stronger than ever. Angel recognized some very positive changes in Steve. Not only was he committed to establishing a good home life for Steven, he treated Angel like a queen. When there was deep snow or ice on the sidewalk, he'd scoop her up in his strong arms and carry her so she would not slip and fall. As much as Angel protested, insisting she was capable of walking by herself, she appreciated his support and concern.

Whenever her spirits were down, Steve tried that much harder to be pleasant and optimistic. When her patience ran thin, he would say something that would make her laugh.

Steve had shed the guilt, remorse, dependence, anger, and resentment. Gone was the forlorn expression he wore so often throughout their ordeals. His once dark and angry eyes had turned soft and warm.

Although she tried to keep her medical condition out of her mind, Angel received a jarring reminder one morning as she was putting on her slippers for practice on the wire. Noticing an awful taste in her mouth, Angel spit out her saliva and was appalled to discover the grass splattered with dark droplets of blood. Feeling a mounting panic, she rushed inside to call Dr. McClintock, who told her to come right down to the hospital.

By the time she was examined, the bleeding had stopped. Dr. McClintock listened closely to Angel's breathing and decided there wasn't any need to admit her.

"If it happens again," she explained in the condescending tone that marked all of her conversations with Angel, "you can call my office and we'll make an appointment for a bronchoscopy and a more complete physical exam. I think you're going to be okay."

Chapter 25

# A PLACE IN PENNSYLVANIA

Most of the money from the settlement that ended the flap over the TV commercial went toward the purchase of a second-hand motor home that could accommodate the equipment of "The Wallendas: Aerialists Supreme" and still provide room for sleeping quarters.

Steve and Angel were anxious to get a place of their own. Ever since he was young, Steve had wanted to live out in the country, where he could raise his own livestock, fish for wild brook trout, and not have to worry about neighbors. Angel also liked the idea, as long as they were not too far away from her family. She had fallen in love with the mountains when Harold and Cynthia Earl took her along on their summer vacations through the Appalachians and into the tobacco country of Virginia.

In mid-June 1989, Steve, Angel, and Steven embarked on a tour of upstate New York and northern Pennsylvania, looking for a place to settle down. The motor home had everything they needed, as long as they found campgrounds to hook into the water and electricity.

They drove and drove, eventually ending up on US Route 6, which cuts through northern Pennsylvania in an east/west direction. The scenery was beautiful and the people seemed as down-to-earth and friendly as any they had met.

As Angel and Steve rolled into Tioga County they were struck by the mix of luscious farmland and charming rural villages. Tioga County is also home of the "Little Grand Canyon," a breathtaking mountain range that rolls on and on like blue ocean waves and cradles the beautiful Pine Creek.

"I have an easy way to make a name for ourselves in Tioga County," Steve joked as they stopped to study a roadside marker. "We'll string a wire for ten miles, from one side of the Little Grand Canyon to the other, and put on a show like these people have never seen before."

It didn't take long for Angel and Steve to realize that this was where they wanted to be. The next stop was a real estate office to look over the properties that were for sale. Money could have been a major obstacle, especially since they had agreed from the start that they would not go into debt. Steve told the real estate agent they needed a starter home, or an "as is" special that would hold them over until they could afford something nicer. Naturally, the agent said he had just what they were looking for.

He drove them over a series of bumpy dirt roads into the open country. Ragged, low-lying clouds hugged the mountains about them. The salesman presented a well-rehearsed speech on the area's rich heritage as he steered his four-wheel drive through the stands of maple, beech, black cherry, and birch trees, shading clumps of mountain laurel.

"Our white pine made this area the logging capital of the world back at the turn of the century," he proudly proclaimed. "Now, we've got a whole new forest, filled with deer, bear, turkeys, and you name it."

He drove up through a high, narrow ridge crowned by open woods where they reached a run-down trailer which had been used as a deer hunting camp by a group of men from suburban Philadelphia. Although the mobile home was beyond repair, it was situated on a nice woodlot.

The closer they looked, the more potential Steve and Angel could see in it. They would have to do a lot of fixing, cleaning, brush clearing, and landscaping, but they loved it. The property was surrounded by wildflowers and berry bushes. Fresh spring water was available at the turn of a spigot and the air was clean and pure.

Angel and Steve also liked the remoteness of this little piece of God's earth, with only two other homes along the same road. "We'll take it," Steve told the agent without even dickering over the price.

Owning their own home meant a great deal to Angel and Steve. They finally had a chance for the simple lifestyle that both of them had wanted. Angel recognized that they were exactly where they had to be in order to experience and learn what they needed to know to make them whole in body, mind, and spirit.

The trailer was barely habitable, but the setting was perfect. There was plenty of level space to set up the practice wires and trapeze, additional acreage to raise livestock, plus a number of trees they could harvest to supply the wood stove.

Angel and Steve returned to Mahopac for their belongings. When they shared their news with Frederick Pintye, he was inordinately proud to see his daughter fulfilling one of his dreams.

"None of the other kids have ever had a place of their own," said this Hungarian immigrant who had made his own way in the world and expected nothing less of his children. "You can't go wrong buying a good piece of land."

Right from the start, people in Tioga County made the Wallendas feel that they were welcome. Those folks who recognized Wallenda as a world-famous name did nothing to make them feel ill at ease. Steve enjoyed talking to the natives about his family's heritage.

Angel tried one more time to see Dr. McClintock. The pain and discomfort deep in her chest told her that something was definitely wrong. Dr. McClintock's latest excuse was that Angel could not receive treatment in New York because the Wallendas were no longer residents and therefore were ineligible for Social Security coverage.

Reluctantly, Angel was forced to retain the services of an attorney, who pointed out in a terse letter to Dr. McClintock that her explanation of Social Security regulations was seriously in error. Angel also sent her own letter to the hospital administrators, not showing nearly as much restraint as the lawyer had.

Before she sealed the envelope, Steve suggested that she put the letter aside and give the matter some more thought. "No way. I'm mad!" Angel said. "It's my life that's at stake, and all I'm hearing are excuses. I'm not going to take it."

Besides allowing Angel to vent her anger, the letter demanded that her medical records be sent to Robert Packer Memorial Hospital in Sayre, Pennsylvania, which was much closer to the Wallenda's new home.

At Robert Packer, she underwent a series of tests and returned home to await the results. A couple of weeks later, the oncologist, Dr. Bruce Boselli, called and asked Angel to return to Sayre to discuss the findings. Not expecting a very eventful appointment, she made the trip alone. One look at Dr. Boselli's grim face told her that the news was not good. Leaning forward, his arms folded flat against his desktop, he hesitated before revealing his findings:

"Angel, your condition has become more critical since your last scan at City of Hope. The cancer is present in both of your lungs, and has spread considerably over the past few months. The only thing that will save you is further lung surgery."

Angel's heart started to race and her hands became drenched in perspiration. She had never expected her diagnosis to be that bad, especially since Dr. McClintock had led her to believe for so long that her condition had improved. Dr. Boselli said the cancer had apparently been growing, unchecked, since Angel had left California several months earlier.

"I won't have any more surgery on my lungs," was her first reaction. "I don't want to go back and have another operation and then be laid up for the rest of my life."

Dr. Boselli made no attempt to mislead her. "There's no way of knowing what your condition will be following surgery," he explained. "But further surgery is a small aggravation compared to the gift of life that the operations can give you. Basically, we're talking about increasing the number of years you have left."

"How long can I go before I have the operation?"

"I would say that four or five months is the longest you should wait. Even that might be too long. This is a slow-growing form of cancer, but it is going to continue to get worse as long as you postpone the surgery."

The drive back to Tioga County was a long and lonely one. Angel tried to

# HIGH WIRE ANGEL

Angel does chin-ups and trapeze manuevers outside of the family's home in Tioga, under the watchful eye of husband Steve (photo by B. Mark Schmerling).

get her mind off her problems by enjoying the brilliant orange, red, and yellow autumn foliage that covered the mountains on both sides of the highway. She was worried about how Steve would react to the news, so she started rehearsing different ways to break it to him.

Steve was chopping firewood while Steven was making a pile out of the scraps when Angel pulled into the driveway. A neighbor had dropped off a gallon of home-squeezed apple cider and some donuts that Steven had obviously been enjoying. The powdered sugar was mixed with sawdust all over his face and bare chest.

"How'd it go? What'd he say?" Steve demanded as he jogged over to the car.

"Oh, it's a long story," Angel said, trying to avoid sounding uneasy. "They're going to have to do some more tests before they know anything for sure. You know, that kind of stuff."

With that, she headed toward the trailer, the chickens scattering as she neared the doorway. Angel opened the windows to usher in the cool mountain air. Then she started doing the dishes and tidying up, trying to avoid Steve until she could regain her composure. He came in a few minutes later and sat down at the kitchen table, watching her every movement.

"What do you mean, more tests? You've already had all kinds of tests. Don't they know anything yet?"

Angel guiding Steven across the wire. Steven made his first solo walk at the age of five (photo by Paul W. Heimel).

"I guess not," Angel replied, walking into the bedroom.

Suspicious that he wasn't hearing the whole story, Steve followed her and sat down on the bed. "Is there something you're not telling me?"

Angel eased herself down next to him and Steve put his arm around her while she rested her head on his chest, feeling him breathe.

"It's the cancer," Angel said. "It's back. In both lungs. I'm going to need more surgery."

"Damn! Damn! Damn!" Steve cried, pounding the mattress with his fist as his wife spilled out the particulars. She tried very hard to sound optimistic; Steve saw right through her.

They were both in tears by the time sticky-faced Steven wandered into the room. He had never seen his parents crying like that before, so he started bawling, too. As Steve and Angel realized how pathetic the three of them appeared, the tears of sorrow were replaced by those of uncontrollable laughter. This made things a lot easier on Steven. Satisfied that all was well, he sauntered back out into the hallway.

Angel leaned back on her pillow and turned onto her side while Steve rubbed her back.

"I don't know how much more of this I can take," she whispered, turning to face him.

"You've got to be strong, honey," Steve said. "Our Heavenly Father has his reasons. We've got to accept it. If anyone can rise out of this nightmare and emerge as a better person, I know my beautiful Angel can."

His words were still echoing in Angel's mind as she drifted off to sleep.

Chapter 26

# A FOND FAREWELL

Frederick Pintye never believed in celebrating holidays. But with a new grandson now in the picture, he exhibited a whole new attitude. In fact, he insisted that Steve and Angel bring Steven to Mahopac so they could celebrate Christmas together. Angel's mind drifted back to those years when the holiday had been a quiet but wondrous event, her mother there to sing her songs and make her children smile. She saw no sign of the callousness with which her father had approached Christmas in the past. He went out of his way to buy a nice tree and let his grandson help decorate it. On Christmas morning, Steven woke up to a pile of presents from Santa Claus, along with a wagon and a wheelbarrow from his grandpa.

The visit to Mahopac was cut short because of Angel's next appointment at Robert Packer Memorial Hospital. Dr. Boselli had little new information to report. He did agree that it would be best if Angel returned to City of Hope for the surgery, because Dr. Grannis was more familiar with her condition and her medical history.

The plan was to perform one operation at a time, beginning in mid-March, trying to preserve as much of her lungs as possible. Steve and Angel were told to plan on being in California for up to three months for the operations and recovery period. Several small newspapers in northcentral Pennsylvania learned that the last family to carry on the famous Wallenda aerial performing tradition was living in the mountains of Tioga County. Steve and Angel granted several interviews, resulting in some complimentary stories. One of these articles caught the attention of American Cancer Society volunteers in Williamsport, Pennsylvania. They invited Angel to address their annual fund-raising banquet and she welcomed the opportunity.

Angel wanted to deliver a message of her own that came from the heart. Hard sleet bounced off the windshield as they traveled down Route 15 through the heart of the northcentral Pennsylvania mountains. Angel closed her eyes and thought about what she could say to a group of cancer patients and their loved ones, as well as the community-minded volunteers who assembled for the dinner.

As soon as she stood before the crowd, the words flowed:

*Hi. I'm Angel Wallenda. Tonight I want to speak about quite a few things*

# HIGH WIRE ANGEL

*having to do with me and about cancer. When I was first diagnosed as having cancer, I really did not know much about the disease and neither did anyone else in my family. In trying to learn more about it, I asked my doctors a lot of questions and I collected all the information I could get my hands on.*

*Much of this literature had been made available by the American Cancer Society for anyone concerned about cancer. We found it very beneficial.*

*Cancer can strike at any time, in anyone. No one in my family had ever had the disease and not long after my nineteenth birthday, just when I thought my life was beginning, it struck me.*

*Right from the start of it, I had hope and decided that I'd fight back. I would not let a physical affliction get the better part of me. The disease itself, I cannot control. I don't have to like it, but I do have to know how to deal with it and live with it—accept it. That's exactly what I do.*

*Life is what you make it; nothing more, nothing less. It's in your own hands. I believe that anyone is able to do anything that he puts his mind to. Sometimes it takes more work and more effort, and sometimes you need a few adjustments to your goals, but with faith in yourself you can win almost any battle.*

*I was able to adjust to what happened only because of the attitude that I kept throughout the whole time. Cancer is a never ending battle, but as long as you don't allow it to get the better part of you, you are fighting and winning.*

*My operations—first my leg amputation; then my lung; then my other lung—taught me that I was not Superman. My family and I went through the same frustrations that anyone facing cancer goes through. But I did my best, whatever the circumstances were, and I never fell into that pit of self-pity. Well, maybe for ten minutes or so. Unfortunately, a lot of patients do fall into that pit and they stay there until they draw their last breath.*

*I looked at walking the wire again as a challenge. In the beginning, usually when I was about halfway across with no way to get down, the thought would occur, "What am I doing? I must be crazy."*

*I couldn't keep that frame of mind very long, especially with a little boy looking up at me, saying, "Mama, that's why you're big, so you can walk the big wire. I'm little, so I walk the little wire." Then there was my husband at his side, saying, "You can't get down, even if you want to, until you get to the other side." They gave me a push when I needed it.*

*Walking the wire was the hardest thing I've ever done, but I still did it. I never gave up because I believe I have a God-given gift. It is inner strength. And I know everyone in this world has it as well, if he or she just reaches to find it.*

*I want people to learn to draw from that inner strength when they see me. With determination and a strong attitude, most anything can be accomplished.*

*We all learn through one another and through our own experiences, as well as those of others. Cancer has taught my family, my friends, and myself many things. In some ways, I've learned and benefitted from it. I'm sometimes tempted to call it a blessing in disguise.*

*That's where the American Cancer Society comes in and my reason for speaking tonight. You're there to help everyone. Your volunteers donate their time and efforts to help cancer victims and their families. You do it as a service, not as a job. I know that your time and efforts have made a big difference in many lives. You reflect the true beauty of the human spirit.*

Angel was greeted with a loud ovation as she made her way back to her table. She also observed that some people were crying. "I hope they're not feeling sorry for me," she whispered to Steve. "If they are, I'm afraid they missed the point. Did I say something wrong?"

"Oh, they got the point all right," he replied. "They're crying because what you had to say struck a chord in their lives."

Steve and Angel sat at a table with Debra, a woman of about 45, who had lost both her husband and her mother to cancer within the past two months. The American Cancer Society was now a driving force in her life.

"I think we're a lot alike," she said as the program concluded. "I only wish my husband would have had the same attitude. I think the day he learned he had cancer was the day he decided to begin dying. I wish he could have met you."

The return trip to City of Hope was going to be a crushing financial burden, even with the medical expenses covered by Social Security. The Wallendas would need thousands of dollars to cover travel costs, living accommodations, and related expenses for a three-month stay in California.

Steve contacted several government agencies and private organizations to see if there was any financial assistance available. Unfortunately, there was none. Steve and Angel bolstered each other's faith that God would provide for them and, within a matter of days, an exciting plan was in place.

It all happened very quickly. They were sitting in the car at an intersection in Mansfield, Pennsylvania. While waiting for the traffic light to change, Angel was struck with an idea. "Hey Steve, let's earn the money ourselves."

He continued to stare out the car window as they spoke. "That's an awful lot of money to earn. What do you figure, five or ten thousand dollars? What kind of work do you have in mind? It couldn't be anything legal."

"The work we do best—the high wire."

"What do you know that I don't know? Where are you gonna make that kind of money on the wire in two months?"

"Right here, in our own town," Angel insisted. A puzzled, skeptical look came over Steve's face. "Listen," she continued. "Dr. Boselli said my performing career would be over after the next operations, didn't he?"

"I guess so. You're the one who talked to him, not me."

"So let's raise our own money with our last wire walk as a family," Angel said, looking up the hill from the intersection to some of the buildings from Mansfield State University. "Let's ask the college to help us. I'll bet they would."

Things took off from there. A handful of people at the university bent some rules and steered the plan through the bureaucracy. Within weeks, a date

# HIGH WIRE ANGEL

had been set to hold the fund-raiser in the athletic fieldhouse on campus. It would be billed as "The Farewell Performance of the Wallenda Family," and it was only appropriate to hold such an event in the community where Steve and Angel intended to spend the rest of their lives. Not only did university officials have a sincere desire to help the Wallendas, they were also mindful of the possible historic implications of the event and the opportunity to gain some widespread publicity for the university itself.

Angel and Steve practiced every day, even in the rain, snow, and bitter cold. On one of those winter afternoons, they had taken a break for some hot chocolate when the phone rang. On the other end was a promoter who had learned of their story from media accounts and was prepared to book them with a circus that was performing in Japan.

This was a glaring reminder of the great limitations that Angel's medical condition now imposed on their career. Because she could not fly, they would have had to travel to California by train and across the Pacific Ocean on a ship. They would not have arrived back in California until April, at the earliest, which would have required Angel to cancel both the "Farewell Performance" and her surgery. She checked with Dr. Boselli and Dr. Grannis. Both were adamant that she should not postpone the operation.

Mansfield University's student body and public relations people did an outstanding job of promoting the Wallendas' performance, helping to make it an unqualified success. More than three thousand people packed the Decker Gymnasium to witness an event that attracted more media coverage than anything else in the university's long history. More than 150 million households were reached via newspapers, magazines, TV newscasts and entertainment shows, and radio broadcasts.

A number of local performers donated their time as warm-up acts, creating a circus-like atmosphere. The show began with a clown routine by Rod-O Wainwright, Ten-Four, and Jimbo Bennett, and continued with bicycle tricks by Charlie and Joyce Van Buskirk, known as the Cyclonians. Hyde & Seek Illusions, starring Steve Hyde and Deanna McNett, then took center stage, followed by rope tricks performed by Phil Hyde and a spectacular act of fire magic by Mike Straka.

During these preliminaries, Angel and Steve nervously paced back and forth behind a curtain in the corner of the fieldhouse, wondering how big a crowd had turned out. The circus performers received an enthusiastic response, but nothing like the ovation that was heard for the featured performers.

Angel and Steve stepped out from behind the curtain into the bright spotlight, walking hand in hand with Steven in front of them. Angel couldn't believe the size of the crowd or the feeling of warmth that was generated from people who had come from miles away to see the show and demonstrate their support.

There were technical problems from the start. Although a rehearsal had gone off without a hitch, when show time arrived a spotlight operator accidentally directed his bright beam directly into Angel's eyes. That put her at risk because, unlike aerialists who have feeling in both legs, she must watch her right foot to know where it is as she steps along the wire.

This high wire Angel was not about to let her supporters down. She began to guess at the location of her leg as she carefully made her way up the inclined wire, the sound system blaring the strains of "Angel of the Morning."

"Get those lights out of her eyes!" Steve shouted. At first, no one responded to him. Still, there was no turning back for Angel. "Clean and smooth," she thought to herself, gritting her teeth and willing herself forward to the platform that anchored one end of the cable. The tension inside Angel began to peel away as she reached the small square of solid footing. Steve hurried up the wire behind her, worried that the spotlight might have shaken her.

Angel assured him she was all right, and they styled while the audience offered a rousing ovation. The spotlight might have been okay for special effects in an otherwise darkened gymnasium, but Angel knew she could not go on until something was done about it. Steve described the dilemma to the technical crew standing under the wire and the house lights were finally turned on.

Angel looked out over the crowd and was met by thousands of eyes, all focused on her. She spotted Steven off in a corner of the gym, playing with a toy truck, oblivious to the scene as he waited for the cue to join his parents.

Once the lighting was restored, Angel began her solo pass across the wire in the direction of the opposite platform. The crowd fell silent as she smoothly moved along the thin wire. Most realized that if Angel fell to the hard floor below, she would be seriously injured. University officials had urged Steve and Angel to allow a life net to be spread beneath the wire, but they would not even consider it.

About halfway across, Angel paused to stand on her left foot and hold the artificial limb high as she smiled to the audience. She then tightened her grip on the balancing pole and continued across to the far platform. Steve hurried along behind her, giving the crowd an extra thrill as he jogged the final few steps before reaching safety.

The music changed to Michael Jackson's "Man In The Mirror" for the next act, which consisted of Steve stepping out on the wire, anchoring his weight and kneeling. Then Angel climbed atop his shoulders and spread her arms wide, parallel to his balancing pole. Near the end of the wire, she smoothly dismounted while Steve held his balance and they walked the rest of the way together.

The grand finale was to be their own version of the "Wallenda Pyramid," with Steve on the wire, Angel balanced on his shoulders, and Steven riding on the back of his mother's neck and shoulders with his ankles locked securely under her chin. Steve had fastened a special harness to the rafters high above and attached it to Steven's waist. In case of an accident, he would dangle unharmed while Steve and Angel tried to catch the wire with their hands.

Steve was clearly nervous as they moved into position for the pyramid. He

# HIGH WIRE ANGEL
167

stepped onto the wire to test its integrity while Angel steadied herself and adjusted her weight to compensate for Steven's movements atop her.

"Lock your legs, buddy, and try not to move," Angel told him.

One step into the walk, Steve stopped in his tracks.

"We can't do it," he said out of the corner of his mouth, a tone of nervousness in his voice. "I don't like the rigging. Nope. We can't."

Their combined weight centralized on one small area where Steve's feet made contact with the wire might cause the rigging to sway, he explained. The results could be disastrous. With the lives of the two most important persons in his life delicately balanced upon his shoulders, Steve Wallenda, for once, said "no" to a stunt.

"It's okay if the weight is spread out," he explained. "The two of us could go, as long as you walk behind me, or I could take Steven across on my shoulders. What do you think?"

"Take Steven," Angel said. "I think the people would like to see him."

A technician climbed the ladder to the platform and helped Angel lift Steven off her shoulders. They then placed him on his father's back so he could wrap his legs around Steve's neck.

"See you in a couple of minutes," Steve said with a polite smile.

"Yea, Mama. We'll see you when we get back. Bye-bye," Steven added, tucking his chin down on top of his father's head and holding on tight.

They passed across the wire and then returned with apparent ease, much to the delight of the crowd. Steven topped it off with his well-rehearsed "Taa-Daa!", arms spread wide and a big grin showing on his face. Camera flashes exploded all over the gymnasium.

After re-checking the rigging and making some minor adjustments, Steve walked on the wire with a couple of celebrity guests following him, holding tightly to Steve's shoulders. The first was John Vogelsang, who won the right to perform on the high wire when his Sigma Tau Gamma fraternity won a fund-raising contest to aid the "Angel Fund." The second guest performer was the Mansfield University men's basketball coach, Tom Ackerman, who accepted the challenge to go across the wire in return for a fifty-dollar pledge to the Wallendas from an anonymous donor.

Angel was unprepared for the outpouring of love and support that filled the gymnasium both during and after the performance. As she and Steve mingled with the crowd, people walked up and handed them money, sometimes telling them of friends or relatives who had cancer or some other disease. Angel and Steve received hugs from dozens of people they had never met. They also signed autographs for over two hours as people stood in line waiting for a chance to meet them.

The morning after the show at Mansfield, Steve and Angel were up before daybreak to meet a limousine that took them to the studios of WETM-TV, the NBC television affiliate in Elmira, New York, for a hastily-arranged live appearance on "The Today Show." This was the start of the flood of publicity that they would receive for several weeks running.

Their telephone started ringing off the hook with friends who had seen them interviewed by co-anchor Katie Couric on "The Today Show," or had seen reports of the "Farewell Performance" on Cable News Network. Angel was particularly touched by a phone call she received from Dick Clark, who had seen the news accounts on TV and said he just wanted to personally convey his best wishes. Letters poured in, offering love, hope, gratitude, sorrow, and money. Angel read them all many times and resolved to answer every one of them, even from her hospital bed in California if she had to.

A couple of weeks after the performance, several of Steve's friends in the Northcentral Veterans Coalition, a close-knit group of Vietnam War veterans, insisted on holding a special send-off party for Angel and Steve at the Tioga County Fairgrounds. The organization had already donated $4,500 to the "Angel Fund."

Hand-drawn posters were placed in the windows of the bank, coffee shop, general store, and on the utility poles in downtown Mansfield, urging citizens to "Come Out and Support Our Friends and Neighbors, The Wallendas." It was rural America at its best, complete with a country music band, a potluck dinner, door prizes, a beer can toast, and other rituals.

The ride back home was a long one. "I hate to have to leave our home," Steve said, taking Angel's hand and squeezing it. "I've been thinking about how much our place means to me, knowing that it's something that we built together. I can't imagine ever being there without you."

Steve fell asleep on Angel's shoulder that night as they lay together on the couch watching the late-night TV shows. Neither of them paid much attention to the programs. Their minds were fixed upon the real-life drama that was unfolding around them.

The day dawned bright and sunny as they loaded the car for the trip to the train depot. Steve stopped to take one last breath of the mountain air and silently stare at their home. It was as if he didn't expect that they would ever return.

Boarding the train, Angel experienced a feeling of excitement, much like the time she and Steve embarked on their cross-country honeymoon. They were prepared to enjoy their time together and let tomorrow take care of itself. All of the adversity they had endured had built a stronger bond. At the same time, their travails allowed them to grow individually and to come to terms with their own faith.

Angel found it relaxing to sit back and watch the scenery pass by the windows of the train, recognizing how beautiful the world is, and how little of it she had actually seen. The ever-changing sky, the colorful sunsets, the open fields and the people—she loved to observe people, imagining who they are and what their lives are like as they till their fields, or wash their cars, or sit on their porch swings, watching the train roll by.

Steve and Angel took turns sleeping and keeping tabs on Steven. He occupied himself by playing with toys, watching the videos that Amtrak offered, making small talk with the other passengers, and looking for the kind of mischief that could be expected from a boy nearing his fourth birthday.

Steven would scurry around the train, imitating the whistle. Angel had a hard time persuading him not to pull the porter's cord every time he felt like having some snacks or soda pop. He ended up with a black eye after he tried to balance on the arm of his seat.

As the train sped across the area of the Santa Fe Trail, Steve and Angel tried to imagine how the first settlers of that area must have felt as they encountered the undisturbed wilderness, or the miles and miles of remote desert. The rocking motion of the train and the rumbling of the wheels against the rails were so soothing they it often lulled her to sleep.

Just before they arrived in California, there was a knock on the door of their room. When Steve answered it, about a half-dozen employees of Amtrak were there to greet them and wish Angel well. They presented a card that was signed by all of them, as well as a souvenir blanket, and a copy of an article which appeared on page two of *USA Today*.

A large close-up photograph of Angel attaching her artificial leg accompanied the story. The text told of her upcoming surgery and the likelihood that she would be further disabled as a result of the lung operations.

Angel had spent so much time relaxing on the train enjoying the scenery that she had blocked the upcoming surgery from her mind. Seeing the *USA Today* feature in black and white was a stark reminder that put the trip back in perspective.

Chapter 27

# CHANGE OF PLANS

All of the publicity that had surrounded Angel's "Farewell Performance" and her medical problems resulted in numerous requests for interviews. For a few weeks in April 1990, the Wallendas were big news across the nation. All three of them reported to the studios of the CBS television affiliate in Los Angeles to be interviewed live for about five minutes on the "CBS This Morning" show. Arriving at the studio at 4:00 a.m., they were whisked into the dressing room for hair styling and make-up by a team of beauticians and cosmetologists. All of the hustle and bustle made sleepy-eyed Steven uneasy and whiny.

Next, they were directed to a small, plain-looking room where they squeezed onto a fashionable lounge chair, Steven sitting on his father's lap. There was no rehearsal, not even a discussion of what they were going to be asked. The questions were piped in through tiny earpieces from "CBS This Morning" anchorman Harry Smith in New York.

A photo feature prepared by The Associated Press was published by newspapers across the nation. *The Los Angeles Times* also featured a full-page story on Angel.

Continuing their media blitz, that night Steve and Angel were the cover story on "Inside Report," a news magazine show that aired on television stations across the nation. Two similar shows, "Inside Edition" and "PM Magazine," also filmed interviews and yet another syndicated television show, "Hard Copy," aired a major story on the Wallendas.

At the end of the show, the producers displayed a telephone number that could be used by viewers to send personal messages. On the next edition of "Hard Copy," tapes from several of the more touching telephone calls were aired, letting Angel know that her efforts were not in vain.

The train ride from Pennsylvania to California had given Angel and Steve time to reflect on all that they had been through over the past three years and to discuss where it all might lead. Depending on the path that Angel's unpredictable form of cancer had taken, there was the possibility that she could

# HIGH WIRE ANGEL

be back on her feet in a matter of weeks, ready to resume a normal lifestyle. She had also been told to prepare for the worst—the prospect that she could be "grounded" for the rest of her life due to the heavy toll that both the cancer and the operation would take on her lungs. Dr. Grannis said it was quite possible that Angel could end up bedridden, or at least confined to a portable oxygen supply.

Before the appointment, they had time to visit Disneyland, fulfilling a promise they had made to Steven. When he wasn't pulling Goofy's tail, Steven was scurrying through Minnie Mouse's legs, lifting up her dress, or trying to sink the boat on the "Pirates of the Carribean" exhibit. Together, they cruised down jungle rivers, shook hands with the life-sized cartoon characters, rode a rocket to the moon, and took a tour through the Old West. The little guy had been through so much turmoil in his short life and his parents realized there would be more to come. At least he could enjoy himself now and perhaps not feel so left out when most of their attention was focused on Angel and her surgery.

After Disneyland, the Wallendas hooked up with Steve's friend Gene, who escorted them on a trip over to Little Mexico, where they dined on ethnic food and were serenaded by a corny Mexican band calling itself "The Sunny Sombreros."

Visits to Steve's relative in the southern California area were also on the itinerary. They stopped off to see Uncle Leon and his 85-year-old mother, Ester Fort (Steve's grandmother). Steve still has a special place in his heart for her, affectionately referring to her as "Mom" because she played such a major role in his early childhood.

They traveled from Leon's to a hospital where Steve's mother was recovering from an emergency heart bypass performed six weeks earlier. She had only recently come out of a coma and was lying helplessly in bed, unable to talk because of a tracheotomy. She was also connected to a respirator, intravenous feeding tubes and various monitors.

La Gay's eyes lit up when she saw her son. She was weak, scared, and disoriented. She could hear what Steve and Angel were saying, but could only respond by rolling her eyes or emitting a faint sigh. Steve found it hard to accept the fact that his mother was in such a condition.

Angel's brother James lived in that same area, as an inmate at Mule Creek State Prison. Visiting him proved to be an ordeal. After a ninety-minute wait, they were frisked, ordered to turn over most of their possessions, and then issued identification cards. Visitors are prohibited from wearing blue jeans, since most of the inmates wear jeans. One of the guards told Angel they had caught people trying to switch clothes with prisoners. Even Steven's clothes had to be changed, causing his parents to wonder how many inmates could fit into a three-year-old boy's jeans.

They were led to a large cafeteria-like room, blocked at the entrance by a table where another guard was seated. "Inmate's name and number," he barked, staring at his clipboard.

"James Pintye, CS-52506," Angel answered.

"Wait over there. Sit at the table and don't leave your seat."

Fifteen minutes passed before the cellblock door swung open and James appeared. He looked thinner than Angel had remembered him. She had never seen him in a crewcut. Instinctively, she hurried over and gave him a hug, drawing a quick reprimand from the guard.

James weakly returned the gesture and broke into a huge smile before looking somewhat uneasily at Steve. Angel introduced them and they shook hands. James said he was doing his best to maintain his sanity under the circumstances, and talked about how anxious he was to resume a normal life after his release. He was more concerned about how Angel was coping with her cancer and the threat of the disease to her life.

Angel explained to him some of the ways her perspective on life and death had changed since she met Steve and began to explore the Bible and other religious teachings. She and James became engaged in a long conversation about these issues. All too soon, it was time to say good-bye.

"You wanna go in the car with us, Uncle James?" Steven asked as they rose to leave. "We have a hotel to live in and you can live there, too. I have a big bed and there's room for you."

"I'd like to," James laughed, "but I don't think that fellow over there would let me get too far."

Steven turned to the guard and said, "I don't like you. You won't let my Uncle James go with us. You're mean!" The guard cracked a smile and, looking at his watch, motioned with his head that it was time to leave.

The next day was Angel's twenty-second birthday. It was also the date that she was to report to City of Hope for a series of tests. Results of the scans were to be reviewed by a panel of specialists the following day and Dr. Grannis would then decide how extensive the lung surgery would be. Out of the hospital in less than an hour, Angel was told to return two days later and be prepared for the surgery and a long recovery period.

When they arrived back at their hotel room, they opened the door to the sweet scent of flowers, so many bouquets that they nearly filled the room. "That should tell you something, Angel," Steve said. "People do care about you. It makes me feel good. I've known all along that you're a special person."

With time to kill, they decided to accept an offer by Steve's friend Bobby Yerkes, a well-established Hollywood stunt man, to join him on his yacht for a cruise out into the bay. Before long, Bobby allowed Angel to take the controls. She guided the vessel up the beautiful, winding coastline while Steve and Bobby talked about old times and Steven roamed the deck, his thick blond hair shimmering in the California sunshine.

There was something manic about the way Angel gunned the boat across the waves. "What are you doing Angel?" Bobby asked. "You're going to get a ticket for reckless driving."

"She just doesn't want to report to the hospital tomorrow," Steve suggested. "She figures if she crashes your yacht, she won't have to show up for her appointment."

Angel pushed the throttle even harder until it rested squarely against the floorboard. Bobby decided he better take over as captain. Angel reluctantly stepped aside, then nestled up against Steve. "Isn't this the life?" he said, wrapping her in his arms. "Maybe I should have ignored Peter Graves and stayed out here to be a stunt man. Maybe we should move back to California." Angel ignored his comment and rested against the man that she loved, soaking up the warm rays of the sun and trying to forget about what was to come the following day.

That night was an agony of sleepless worry. It wasn't so much the prospect of surgery that made Angel toss and turn, but the uncertainty. Steve also had trouble sleeping. He kept adjusting the air conditioner, saying he was too cold, then too hot, then too cold again, and so on. They quietly talked most of the night away while Steven slept.

"It's completely out of our hands," Steve kept stressing. To Angel, that was the problem. She wanted so much to be able to control her own destiny, or be provided with a glimpse of what her life would be like. Based on Dr. Grannis' comments, she had no idea if she would ever be able to function normally again as a wife and mother. Angel also worried about the impact any bad news about her condition would have on her husband and how her son would react if he saw his mother lying helplessly in bed.

Her mind was still racing as they drove over to City of Hope. Walking across the parking lot, Angel reached for Steve's hand. His palm was sweaty and his grip tighter than usual.

"I can't wait until we're back in Pennsylvania," Angel said. "I wish that life was a videotape that we could fast-forward a couple of months to the part where we're pulling into our driveway."

Dr. Grannis was clearly uncomfortable as he greeted the Wallendas and ushered them into his conference room. The scene was all too familiar to Angel. Whenever she was on the verge of being given a medical diagnosis, she would grab the arms of her chair and literally brace herself for the news. The roots of her fear had been firmly planted almost two years earlier.

"It's important that I talk to you both right away," Dr. Grannis said sternly. "Steven, I want you to sit down, too, because this is very important to your Mommy and Daddy. Angel, the results of your scans did not go before our medical panel yesterday. There wasn't any need for the panel to see them. The cancer has progressed so far throughout your lungs that it would be impractical to operate on you. If we did remove the cancer cells we can reach, you would not be left with enough of either lung to function."

A flame of horror erupted inside Angel. She didn't dare look at Steve for fear that she would lose her composure.

"What am I supposed to do now?" she asked in a barely audible voice as her hands began to tremble.

"I have discussed your case with a very qualified oncologist, Dr. Morgan from our staff. I've scheduled you for an appointment with him in a few days and I would urge you to meet with him so you can discuss your options for chemotherapy. There's nothing more I can do for you. I'm sorry to have to break this to you, Angel. Please give very serious consideration to what Dr. Morgan suggests. He wants to prolong your life and make you as comfortable as possible."

Steve put his arm around Angel and pulled her close as they walked down the hall. He had hardly said a word since Dr. Grannis broke the news and the silence continued as they walked toward the car and began the trip back to their hotel room.

Angel felt as though she had just been told that she was going to die within a matter of days. Her mind was racing as she thought about all of the things she would have to do to prepare for the end.

Steve called back to Pennsylvania to share the news with friends and other supporters. Wire service stories and TV newscasts also passed along these latest developments.

"It could be worse," Steve told Angel. "We still have today, and tomorrow, and a lot more tomorrows after that. You're good at finding a silver lining, honey, so I hope you can find one now."

Steve decided that one way to put Angel's current condition in perspective was to pay another visit to his mother's bedside. La Gay looked much better than the last time they saw her. Although she tried to talk, she found it easier to scribble notes. She was very interested in Steve's career plans and the particulars of Angel's medical condition, while barely acknowledging her own problems. Her eyes passed back and forth between her three visitors and she tried hard to smile and appear pleasant. When Steve and Angel were ready to leave, she made them promise to write and send pictures so she could see how Steven was growing.

Dr. Morgan made a favorable impression on Angel the first time she laid eyes on him. An attractive young physician with a southern California tan and a pleasant demeanor, he spent a half-hour asking questions, insisting that Angel describe in great detail what type of pain she had in her lungs and chest area, especially on those occasions when she coughed up blood.

"Angel, I want you to give serious thought to undergoing chemotherapy," he explained. "I know what you're thinking—'I'll lose my hair; I won't be able to eat; I'll feel lousy'—but it's my very firm opinion that the chemotherapy can help you."

"I feel good right now, so why should I do something that I know is going to make me feel bad? Is there any real chance that it will make me better?" Angel asked.

"In the long run, I'd have to say the prospects are not encouraging. But I do think that there is a thirty to forty percent chance that chemotherapy could result in some remission. At the same time, I believe it might decrease some of your discomfort and give you a longer life. There are no guarantees."

"If you're saying the chances are only thirty or forty percent, aren't you really saying that the odds are against it helping her at all?" Steve inquired.

"Let me put it to you this way. With the treatment, you have some odds of being able to slow the progress of the disease; without the treatment, you have no chance at all. That's definitely something to think about—it's the bottom line, Angel."

Dr. Morgan went on to explain that there was no specific timetable for such treatment. He also advised that it would make little difference where she underwent chemotherapy. Angel and Steve returned to their hotel room, drained and discouraged.

"I'm not going to do it," she told Steve as they sat staring out the window. "My instincts are telling me that it's not the right thing to do. I don't think it's going to help me."

"That's something you have to decide," Steve said. "I'm selfish. I want my wife to be with me forever. But I think we both agree that the quality of life is more important than the quantity. I don't want to see you spending the final months of your life suffering and feeling miserable from all of the chemicals they're pumping into you . . ."

Just then, Steve stopped short and pointed to the television, where they recognized Tino Zoppe dropping down off the trapeze. With the Wallenda name back in the news, the hotel chain had resurrected the commercial.

Chapter 28

# COPING

As the Wallendas stopped back at the hospital to complete all of the paperwork before their trip back home, they were presented with a mail sack bulging with hundreds of letters and cards from friends, relatives, and fans from throughout the nation who had heard about Angel's story. Buried within the stack of envelopes and packages were a number of recommendations detailing alternative forms of treatment for cancer. Everything from a special meatless diet to a new chemical compound that could only be obtained in Mexico was presented as a cure for her disease. One elderly woman said she had recovered by praying day and night that God would drive the cancer out of her body.

"I can't do that," Angel told Steve after she read the letter aloud. "I don't think it's right to demand my healing. If God wants me to get better, I'll get better. I can pray that we are strong enough to accept God's will, but I can't be so selfish that I ask God to remove my cancer."

One letter urged her to contact a medical consulting firm in Toronto to get her name on a list of potential lung transplant recipients. That sounded very promising until she read the fine print and learned that the transplants were not available to cancer patients. Another writer listed connections with Dr. Bjorn Nordenstrom from Sweden's Karolinska Clinic, who has been earning recognition for his work with electric currents in the treatment of diseases. However, Angel's problem had already grown too severe for that form of treatment.

As the train rolled through the Midwest and eastward toward Pennsylvania, Steven grew cranky and tired of riding. There was only so much his parents could do to entertain him and neither of them was in the mood to play. Luckily, some of the other passengers took a liking to him and helped to keep him occupied.

Steve remained quiet and introspective. The devastating news about Angel's cancer, the look on his mother's face, the disruption of his life, and the memories of his previous experiences in California were all weighing heavily on his mind.

Angel couldn't wait to reach their country home—her one source of stability and normalcy. They talked about training Steven so that he could perform his first solo wire walk and eventually join Steve in a father-and-son act.

Less than a week after settling back in at home, Angel had a call from Dr. Boselli at Sayre, who had reviewed Dr. Morgan's report and wanted to see her the next morning. She hadn't changed her mind about the chemotherapy and Dr. Boselli made it clear from the start that he was not trying to talk her into it.

"I'm here to provide a service to you only if you want to take advantage of it," he explained. "I'm not here to tell you what to do."

"Do you really think it's going to help me?" Angel inquired.

"I can't answer that. I agree with Dr. Morgan's assessment of your case, if that's what you mean. It's not going to cure your cancer. But, yes, it has the possibility of helping you to some extent."

"But I feel fine. I don't feel any worse than I did before we left for California."

"That's an important factor." Dr. Boselli said. "If you're feeling okay right now, that's something to consider. You're quite right about some of the side effects from chemotherapy being unpleasant, although today's treatment doesn't always have as many uncomfortable side effects as some of the medicine that was used in the past. A lot of it depends on the individual," he continued. "There's no way you can control it or have any idea what it's going to do to you unless you try it. I am recommending chemotherapy, but I can respect your position. You can always change your mind. The option will be open to you."

Angel left his office feeling more comfortable about the decision she had made. But, as they drove back home, she couldn't help wondering, "What if?"

Chemotherapy, special diets, electric currents, laetrile, visualization, and at least a dozen other forms of treatment had been recommended to her. She couldn't try them all. She feared that perhaps she would one day find out, all too late, that she had been presented with the cure long ago, only to choose the wrong one.

After she returned home, Angel told Steve she wanted to be alone for a few minutes. He and Steven went inside while she wandered off into the woods and rested on the wide stump of a tree that Steve had cut for firewood. It was early in the evening, Angel's favorite time of the day. The low, slanting light swept over the surrounding hillsides, highlighting the ever-changing color scheme of the forest. She loved watching the sky through the maze of branches on their maple trees.

"Perhaps I'm going about this all wrong," she thought to herself. Some cancer victims had told her she could combat the disease by demanding that it leave her body. Although she had vowed not to ever do that, she decided it was worth a try.

"Cancer, I command you to leave my body and never return," Angel said with an intensity to her voice. She looked around to see if there was any sign that her message had been received. There was nothing. No boom. No flashes of light. No voices. No shaking of the earth. Nothing. Just the soft breeze that gently rocked the treetops in this pastoral setting.

Angel checked her surroundings to see if anyone had heard her and chuckled at her own foolishness. After a few moments, she walked back to the trailer and found Steve seated at the kitchen table, reading a circus newsletter.

"Hey Angel, it says here that there's going to be some wire jobs opening up next month at some county fairs."

"Oh yeah?" she replied, feigning interest.

Steven was pretending he was a fireman as he played at his father's feet. "Watch where you're walking, Mama, or you'll stomp out the fire," he said, looking up at her with his light blue eyes sparkling like jewels in the overhead light. "You wanna play fireman?"

"Not now, Steven. I'm not in the mood. Everybody please leave me alone." Angel headed for the narrow hallway and down to the bedroom.

"What's your problem?" Steve yelled from the kitchen.

"Just never mind. I said to leave me alone."

A tight pressure squeezed Angel's lungs, making it hard for her to catch her breath. She knew that she was being short-tempered, and that she would become aggravated by the slightest thing, but she felt powerless to control her behavior. She appreciated Steve's tolerance and his willingness to take charge of responsibilities around the house—the cooking, cleaning, playing with Steven, grocery shopping, and other domestic duties.

Angel felt a twinge of jealousy. Steven and his father did everything together. Her son was getting so much love and attention from his dad. But whenever she did anything with Steven, she would soon run out of patience and end up scolding him or telling him to quit pestering her, and to go see what his father was doing.

Cancer was robbing Angel of quality time with the two people who meant more to her than any in the world. She had to force herself to be nice to them. As Angel leaned against the backboard of their bed, she pulled a sock up over her hand and pretended it was a puppet. That was one of her favorite things to do when she was a child. She longed for the days when life was not so complicated. She longed for a life that was free of cancer.

"What has my life really amounted to, anyhow?" she thought. "Big deal—I busted my butt to walk on a high wire, thinking I was doing the world such a big favor. Now, when I might be measuring my time in months instead of years, there's nothing I can do to give my life any sense of meaning."

Angel heard a light tapping on the door. Steve poked his head inside and said, "I have something for you." In his right hand he held a tall, frosty glass. "I made you a strawberry daiquiri." She nodded her approval.

"Looks to me like you could use it. Now what's been bothering you?" Angel felt a surge of love and compassion.

"I just hate to see what this cancer is doing to me, and what it's doing to you and Steven," she said softly, sipping from her drink. "Cancer is trying to take over the time I have left and take away all the good things, and I'm trying just as hard not to let it succeed."

"You still have to face reality, Angel. It's not going to go away, unless you believe in miracles. I would love to grow old with you, but..."

"That's not it," she continued. "I know it's there. I'm only saying that I don't want it to rob me of what's left. I'm not going to surrender to it."

"I'm not going to let you." Steve said. "You have to live life to the fullest every day. Like tomorrow. What would you like to do? Not what do you have to do, but what do you really *want* to do?"

Angel thought for a moment. "I don't know. Take a trip, I guess. See some people. Go see Jeannie and my father."

"Okay, it's settled. Just do it."

The next day, Angel Wallenda was on her way to Mahopac, while her husband and son stayed behind. The week away did wonders for her disposition. She and Jeannie worked together to prepare a huge meal. Angel thought about all of the times in her childhood that she had longed to be able to sit at the same table with her parents and brothers and Jeannie. There were so very few times when they did that, yet she recalled them with great clarity.

When Angel returned to Pennsylvania, she could hardly believe her eyes. The old trailer was gone and in its place was another mobile home and the beginnings of an addition on the side of it.

"Do you like your new house?" Steve said as he greeted her. He and some of his Tioga County friends, mostly members of the Veterans Coalition, had been working all week to get the place in order before she returned.

"It's still going to take some work." he continued, "but when we're done, you won't even know it was a trailer. It will have new siding all around it and you'll have an honest-to-goodness home to call your own."

"There's something else for you to see," Steve continued, walking Angel out to the field behind the house. He and his friends had been working on new rigging for the high wire and low wire.

"They're ready whenever you are," he said, grabbing a roll of tape and wrapping it around the center of a balancing pole. "But you have to promise me that you'll be extra careful and take it slowly. You might not be as strong as you think you are. I don't want you doing anything without me around to guide you. That's an order!"

As much as Angel appreciated Steve's optimism and encouragement, in her own mind she had placed any such plans on "hold." She was more concerned with helping Steven to develop his abilities on the low wire. He had just turned four years old and was already becoming somewhat of a ham. All it took was an audience—one of Steve's friends, a neighbor, or anyone else—for him to spring into action and show off his latest skills.

At first, Angel held his hand as he walked back and forth. Eventually, she let him start taking steps by himself. The biggest problem she had to battle was Steven's short attention span. If he saw deer running through the field or heard squirrels chattering in the tall trees surrounding the training wires, he would stop what he was doing to watch.

Occasionally, Steve took time out from his work on the house to practice his own walking and help his son. He also rigged a safety harness that would prevent Steven from plunging to the ground in the event he lost his footing after he graduated to the high wire.

Steve fashioned a shorter balancing pole for Steven. At fifteen feet long and fifteen pounds, the pole was all he could handle, but very necessary for his training. First, his father had him stand still on the wire with the pole so he could grow accustomed to its weight. Eventually, Steven took his first step and, within a couple of weeks, he felt comfortable enough to walk across the low wire on his own.

One hot July afternoon while Angel was working with Steven, she couldn't resist the urge to step back on the wire herself, though her husband had warned her not to. Steve was working on the other side of the house, unable to see her, so Angel pulled on her slippers, dusted off her balancing pole and began her ascent up the sloping wire to the platform, where the twelve-foot-high practice wire was anchored.

"Mama, I'm gonna tell on you," Steven said, squinting his eyes as he stared up at her.

"Ssshh, Steven! Just keep quiet so I can concentrate." Angel was focusing so intently on her feet that she didn't even see her son walk away. Moments later, she was startled by Steve's booming voice behind her.

"Ladies and gentlemen! It's the great comeback of the most courageous of the Great Wallendas—the amazing Angel Wallenda!"

She didn't dare turn around, for fear that she would lose her footing. "Aren't you mad at me?" Angel shouted, holding her balance as she neared the far platform.

"Actually, I don't know if I'm mad or happy. To tell you the truth, I didn't think you'd pay any attention to what I said. I've learned by now that, once you set your mind to something, it's out of my hands."

Just then, they were interrupted by the ringing of the telephone. Angel continued walking to the platform while Steve rushed inside to answer the phone. He returned a few minutes later with a somber look on his face.

"That was one of my buddies from the Veterans Coalition," he said. "He wondered if we were watching the news. It looks like we're going to war with Saddam Hussein in Iraq. God, I hope this isn't another Vietnam."

Steve also mentioned that the Veterans Coalition wanted to present some type of service in observance of National Prisoners of War/Missing In Action Recognition Day, but no one had come forward with any plans for a program.

"I have an idea," Angel said. "Let's do what we do best. Let's walk on the high wire, both of us."

"Do you really think you're up to it?" Steve asked.

"What's it look like to you?" said Angel. "I'm doing it now, aren't I? I don't see why I can't do it then. It's a cause that we both believe in. Let's do

# HIGH WIRE ANGEL 181

something very dramatic to let people know that there are still American soldiers to be accounted for. I think it's a great idea."

Three weeks later, "The Wallendas: Aerialists Supreme" were back on the wire for Angel's comeback performance. Their walk highlighted a full-scale program held by the Veterans Coalition in Wellsboro, Pennsylvania.

The observance began with a parade, featuring the traditional "riderless horse," and a stirring speech delivered by Harrison Bell, a decorated war veteran whose battlefield experiences were relived in graphic detail. After Steve and Angel each made a solo pass across the high wire, she climbed down so that Steve and a fellow Vietnam veteran, Chuck Follis, could team up for a heart-rending performance that symbolized the hopes and prayers of all who were in attendance.

Chuck, dressed in black to symbolize missing American soldiers, climbed the ladder to the far platform and sat there motionless, depicting a captured soldier, while Steve walked across to "rescue" him. They came back across the wire together, Chuck walking behind and clinging to Steve's shoulders.

"I'm bringing him home," Steve shouted across the football field, prompting a cheer from the crowd. "Let's bring them all home. Tell the Pentagon. We've got people who are still unaccounted for in Southeast Asia. The government thinks they're dead. But we've got picures and eyewitness reports that say otherwise. We need your help!"

A production crew from NBC-TV's "Memories: Then And Now" was on hand, as were local television stations and several newspaper reporters. Angel tried to direct the media's attention to the POW/MIA message, but they were more interested in focusing on her story.

She told the reporters that she felt like a "prisoner" herself. "But no amount of human intervention or political will can release the hold that cancer has on my body," Angel said. "We still have soldiers who are unaccounted for, and that's something we *can* do something about."

Both Angel and Steve were gratified that the event raised a considerable sum of money to assist those organizations that continue the search for U.S. troops who never came home.

Since that performance, Steve and Angel have had occasional speaking engagements, including everything from a program for local elementary school students to an appearance before a professional football team, the Atlanta Falcons. After seeing news accounts of Angel's story, Falcons coach Jerry Glanville arranged for the Wallendas to meet with his team in Pittsburgh. Glanville believed Angel's story of courage and perseverance might provide inspiration for his players as they approached some key National Football League games.

Henry Hurt, roving editor for *Reader's Digest*, interviewed Angel and Steve extensively for a special feature which appeared in the March 1991 edition. As millions more learned of Angel's accomplishments, another flood of cards and letters filled the Wallendas' mailbox. Two months later, Steven was in the news as he made his first-ever solo walk across the high wire. The seventy-foot round trip at the Wallenda training grounds received local media exposure. Steven is apparently the youngest person ever to walk unaccompanied across a high wire.

Most recently, Angel was notified that she was one of three U.S. citizens selected to receive the 1991 Norman Vincent Peale "Award for Positive Thinking." The other recipients were General Colin Powell, chairman of the Joint Chiefs of Staff and a hero of Operation Desert Storm, and Kay Heitsch, an Ohio mother who has responded to her son's tragic death by reaching out to help young people.

Also Steve has begun advertising for volunteers interested in performing as part of a seven-member high wire pyramid. Angel has not ruled out the possibility of being the top-mounter if her health will allow.

Angel has joined a cancer support group that assists patients as they explore ways of coping with the symptoms of the disease through various relaxation methods, visualization, meditation, and other techniques that help the mind adjust to the body's deterioration and help the body fight back.

Angel has also continued to explore the Bible and other material that has come to her attention. She marvels at the wonders and the mysteries of God and the universe.

Although the warmer climate of the South would make it easier for the Wallendas to practice on the wire, they've invested so much of their lives into developing their Pennsylvania homestead that both Angel and Steve consider a move to be out of the question.

Angel loves the changing seasons in the country—the snow of winter; walking along the back roads or forest trails in the spring and fall; the long, lazy summer days.

She would like to go on performing and making public speaking appearances as long as her health will allow. There are causes she would welcome the chance to support.

Steve will continue a regular workout routine and training regimen. Mindful of the family heritage, he realizes that somebody must carry on the Wallenda tradition. While his son is the most likely candidate to follow in his father's footsteps, both Angel and Steve recognize that this decision must be left up to Steven himself.

Chapter 29

# ANGEL WALLENDA SPEAKS

It's tough not knowing how long I have to live—not that any of us really do. Most people my age can say, "Here's what we should do for the next twenty years," or even the next two or three years. We can't. With me, it's always, "We'll see how it goes."

I get a very eerie feeling whenever I speak of the future. The anger and disappointment over the prospect of only living into my twenties, if that is my fate, has faded into acceptance, but by no means resignation. Deep inside, I suppose I am terrified of dying a high-technology death, attached to a breathing machine and so out of touch with my own feelings and the people around me because of the heavy doses of pain killers.

Perhaps I'll make a miraculous recovery and be able to live for 50 years, or maybe God has decided that I've already done enough. We all continue to hope for the best.

It would be easy for me to resent the fact that so many members of the medical community did not take my case seriously.

No, it wasn't all in my head.

No, it wasn't a minor bruise on my leg.

And no, it wasn't some desperate attempt by a troubled teenager to get attention.

My feelings are softened by the realization that even the most accomplished medical specialists are human beings, and nobody is perfect. Maybe my case will change the way they look at other cancer patients in the future. Through that, at least some good has come of it.

Cancer is an unpredictable disease. Miraculous recoveries have occurred in patients who have been diagnosed as terminal. In other cases, patients who have been given a clean bill of health have dropped dead of cancer a short time later.

Author John Gunther called the disease "the greatest and most formidable of all the unknowns of modern science." Things haven't changed much since he wrote those words many years ago.

There are plenty of cancer books, articles, and pamphlets available—by victims, for victims (or their families), about victims. Many of them provide some insight into how people have tried to cope with this terrible disease. I thank God that I have been given the opportunity to share my perspective with others who might otherwise fall victim to the "go home and die" syndrome.

It saddens me that so many victims tend to dwell on their cancer. They focus on it every day, and they grasp at anything. They bemoan their fate. They let the smallest of problems annoy them and they pout, or they let their own circumstances drive them into deep depression. I'm not suggesting that it is wrong to wage a desperate battle for survival, but I don't think that the fight should prevent one from enjoying those months or years that remain.

If I am confined to a bed and hooked up to a respirator, I will have to recognize cancer as a larger part of my life at the time. But why let it torment me today, when I'm up and around?

I can't change the fact that I have cancer, so I have learned to work my life around it. I try hard *not* to think about it. I won't let it become an all-consuming part of my life.

Why did I decide to walk on the high wire and risk my life after my physical setbacks? I wanted people who had suffered any kind of adversities to recognize, through my example, that life *does* go on, no matter what obstacles are in the way.

People have told me that I make wire-walking look effortless. That's not the case at all. It's the hardest thing I've ever done. I must constantly conquer the fear and push myself forward, trusting my own ability to make that vital connection between a narrow wire and an artificial limb.

I don't know why disease strikes. I do know that it can broaden a person's perspective. We can grow through adversity. I have learned so much about facing challenges:

• Life is more about setting goals and working to achieve them than about the accomplishments themselves. Life is not about feeling sorry for yourself or envying others for what they have.

• Life is about understanding God's will for each of us—we all have a purpose on earth—and living by His word as we go about our daily tasks.

• Life is not measured by bank accounts or physical beauty. Too many people become too wrapped up in worldly things, material possessions that bring passing pleasure. The things of this world are temporary, including the human body.

• Life is about living and being loved, about savoring the good moments. I'm so fortunate to have loved and been loved.

• Life is a learning experience. Part of a full life is to never stop learning. Every day I'm alive, I've learned a little more.

Later on, maybe two days from now or maybe in ten years, I hope that people will think about what I did. Why me? Because I have experienced so much adversity in my twenty-three years. All of the hard lessons I had in my life—from not having toys, to being told never to come home, to losing my leg and parts of both lungs to cancer—have made me a stronger person. When adversity comes your way, confront it. Stare it down, and you will beat it if it's beatable. You learn from it. You become stronger.

I could have let it destroy my spirit. I've seen people commit suicide, or gradually destroy their lives with drugs or alcohol, yet I somehow found the strength to rise above all of this.

Yes, I'm going to die, but I'll be ready. I don't look at that as a tragedy, because every one of us is going to die—people don't stop to consider that.

When I face death, I won't feel cheated. I have not just remained alive for over two decades; I have truly *experienced* my life. There are other ways to measure a life besides its duration. I will recognize that I've completed my learning and fulfilled my role in this life. I've crossed the bridge between what I was before and what I will be after I take off this mortal body and advance to a higher form of existence.

After we accept our mortality and the inevitability of death, we are able to live life to the limit. Denial of death is also denial of life. Reconcile yourself to the possibility of death, make peace with it, and you are free.

We all have only so much time left on this earth. I don't want to waste mine by being so depressed about my own physical condition that I forget to get the most out of each day. When I focus on all that is wrong with me, my world looks very bleak. I'll make a very conscious effort to see those things that are positive.

I'll continue to approach my own fate with the kind of inner peace that can only come from *knowing* that there is more.

Appendix

# A GREAT WALLENDA

Many years ago, a columnist in Florida wrote that Steve Wallenda is "consumed by the show business side of his life." Performing *had* become a consuming force very early in his life. It was not until Steve met Angel that he was able to appreciate another dimension of life.

Steve explains: "Angel does have an effect on everyone she meets. But the best example of her special gift can be found in me. Who would have thought that a seventeen-year-old ice cream dipper could change my whole life around? I was drifting aimlessly, feeling unloved and empty, unable to feel human warmth, unable to share love with anyone. I had seen through the shallowness of the show business world and the selfishness of professional sleaze artists whose only interest was to capitalize on my name. The only person I knew I could trust was myself."

Steve has often been asked what he thinks about when he's walking on a wire.

"It's hard to explain, because it's a natural thing," he told a news reporter in the summer of 1982 after he performed before the largest crowd of his career. "Once I'm up on the wire, I feel safe. That's my security. You put the possibility of falling right out of your mind. If I make it, it's a success. If I don't, I'll be in heaven before anyone else out there."

On this occasion, Steve had been booked for a three-night show walking a 400-foot-long wire across the International Fountain as part of a daredevil show at Canada's Wonderland Amusement Park in Toronto. The cable was strung from the base of International Bridge, which runs across the fountains, up to a ledge on the 130-foot-high Victory Falls, a gigantic man-made mountain and waterfall.

His performance was accompanied by a laser light show and fireworks. On the final night, the wire was dangerously wet and slick, but Steve insisted upon going ahead with the walk anyhow. Before he stepped onto the wire, he announced that he was dedicating the performance to his late Aunt Yetty. To

# HIGH WIRE ANGEL 187

add to the grand finale, he did the walk with the balancing pole held far over his head. The crowd of an estimated 36,000 gave Steve a five-minute standing ovation.

"That was the most spectacular and well-performed display of wire-walking I have ever seen," wrote veteran entertainment reporter Chester Mello in *Circus Report.*

Later, back in Florida, Steve gave an impromptu performance at the Colony Beach resort on Longboat Key. He strung a 300-foot steel cable from the resort's swimming pool to the sixth story of the hotel at a slope which reached a top height of about ninety feet. When he was about halfway up, one of the men grounding the cable slipped and the wire jerked back and forth, but Steve managed to stay on it. More than one hundred Colony Beach condominium owners were treated to this private circus act.

He now admits that his attitude has evolved. Although he still oozes a healthy self-confidence, survival, always a very strong instinct, has become even more of a driving force for Steve because he wants to be there to support his family.

Not all of Steve's walks have been staged to gain him fame or fortune. Throughout his career, he has shown heartfelt concern for people who are in need of help. At times, he has responded impulsively, following his instincts with some rather sudden and unconventional demonstrations of support. When the California branch of the Greenpeace Foundation approached Steve with plans for a publicity stunt to help draw attention to its "Save The Whales" campaign, he was happy to oblige. This involved walking on a narrow one-half inch cable on the Bay Bridge between San Francisco and Oakland, about 750 feet above the water. It took two harrowing walks before Steve accomplished his goal—a high-profile arrest that brought publicity to the cause.

Steve's world record came as a result of another charitable effort. Recognizing the possibility that the 1979 Guinness Book high wire record of France's Henri Rochetain could be broken, Steve set his sights on the mark in March 1983, turning his efforts into a fund-raiser for a debt-ridden Little League Baseball program in North Port, Florida. Rochetain had walked the high wire, non-stop, for a distance of 3,790 feet in just under four hours. Steve didn't see any reason he couldn't top 4,000 feet in less time. He had already earned himself a reputation as the world's fastest high wire walker.

It was a warm, breezy Florida morning when Steve stepped onto the 31-foot-high, 250-foot long wire. He was equipped with his familiar white balancing pole, as well as a bright red performing costume.

The baggy silk slacks started to slip from his waist early in the walk after his belt loosened and fell to the ground below. "I guess my costume wasn't made for long distances," he yelled to the crowd gathered below, adjusting the drawstring around his waist with one hand as he held his balancing pole with the other hand.

He had trained hard, walking with ankle weights and expanding his practice routine to several hours each day to prepare for the rigors of such an endurance attempt. Ever the showman, Steve did a headstand on the wire as the wind whipped against his body and bounced the wire. Later, during one of his turns, he caught his foot in the hem of his pantleg, ripping the hem but maintaining his balance.

About halfway through the walk, Steve yelled down to the volunteers holding the nineteen guy wires, telling them that his walking surface was losing its tension. They made the adjustments while he held his footing, despite the many tugs that jarred the wire.

Quite a crowd gathered as word of Steve's performance spread. He joked with the onlookers as he sucked on lemons to quench his thirst. "Come on up here, Joe, I want to talk to you about a little business," he yelled to a local bank executive who had pledged hundreds of dollars for the Little League team if Steve broke the world record.

At times, he would go down on one knee and point to the sky. "I wanted to be sure people knew that when I pointed up, I was pointing to Jesus and thanking him for giving me the ability to keep going," he would later tell a church group that honored him for the walk.

By the time he finally stepped down more than three and one-half hours later, he had covered 4,166 yards and made one hundred turnarounds on the wire.

The people of North Port made Steve an honorary citizen and presented him with a key to the city. "I'm glad to see the Wallenda name back in Guinness, where it belongs," he said in accepting the token of appreciation.

That same week, Steve was recognized by the Sarasota City Council and Mayor Anne Bisphoric for his many aerial feats. Ironically, he was presented with the symbolic "key to the city," right in the backyard of a family that had largely repudiated him.

About two months later, in May 1983, he was back in the headlines for one of the most amazing feats in the history of wire walking. Tempted by a lucrative financial offer, Steve agreed to walk on a cable suspended between two cars speeding around the oval track at the DeSoto Raceway in Bradenton, Florida.

A fall under these circumstances could have been fatal, so Steve spent countless hours plotting his strategy. A special apparatus was built to connect the cars and secure the wire tightly between them. Steve had to calculate the effect of the wind in setting a limit on how fast the cars could travel. He told the drivers that he could remain standing or walking as long as they held their speed under fifty-five miles per hour. With the help of a local welding company, he devised the rigging so that the wire would remain taut, even if the cars got out of sync.

Steve thrilled the sellout crowd by doing a headstand on the wire as the cars slowly began their passes around the racing oval. After he returned to his

# HIGH WIRE ANGEL

feet, he signaled for the drivers to increase their speed. The faster the cars went, the more strength Steve had to summon to battle the fierce wind.

Suddenly, as the cars sped down the track at fifty-seven miles per hour, his balancing pole snapped in half, causing Steve to spin around on one foot for a 180-degree turn as he miraculously held his balance and righted himself. The crowd howled its approval.

As the cars pulled into the pits, Steve stepped down to the ground and knelt in quiet prayer. He realized how close he had come to being killed.

Later in 1983, he was back in action for a difficult wire walk as part of a fund-raiser for the Pop Warner Youth Football League in Englewood, Florida. To add to the challenge and draw more attention to his performance, Steve agreed to do the walk blindfolded, relying only on his instincts and experience. The wire was 270 feet long and stretched from the ground to the top of a seventy-foot-high utility pole.

There were some anxious moments when the anchor pole shifted slightly as Steve approached the steepest part of the incline. He yelled through his blindfold to the men holding the cable, telling them to pull harder on the lines to keep it from sagging.

After Steve made it to the top, he removed the blindfold and waved an American flag before finishing his performance with his patented "slide for life." This involved hanging from a pulley attached to the cable and cascading down the wire at an increasing speed until he smashed into a net being held by a half-dozen men on the ground.

The producers of ABC-TV's "That's Incredible" saw videos of Steve's blindfolded walk and were so impressed that they signed him to perform a similar act for their national television audience. The show, which aired in 1984, proved to be one of the most challenging walks of Steve's career.

As soon as he mounted the 160-foot-long cable strung at a forty-degree angle outside the ABC studio in Hollywood, he was confronted with gusting winds that grew stronger as he moved higher. At about the midway point of his walk, Steve stopped to sit down, straddling the wire with his legs and allowing the balancing pole to teeter back and forth on its own while he reached into a bag that was hanging from the wire. He pulled out his black blindfold, draped it over his head and tugged at the drawstring to secure it around his neck.

Leaning forward on his arms, Steve extended his legs backwards, as if he were doing a push-up on the wire, and got back on his feet to continue his ascent. A fierce wind whipped at his body and vibrated the cable, causing Steve's feet to slip with almost every step. There was no turning back, and no net below. His very life depended on covering the final thirty feet, with little traction and no way of seeing where he was.

A few steps later, he handed his balancing pole to one of the helpers and climbed safely aboard the platform. Steve topped off the performance with the "slide for life," hanging by one arm as he whirred down the wire on his pulley and crashed into a net at ground level.

"That blindfold was no magic trick," Steve told John Davidson after the walk. "I couldn't see a thing and when that wind hit me, I was scared. I probably shouldn't have even gone up until the wind died down."

Within a matter of weeks after the television performance, a newspaper story detailing the plight of a Scottsdale, Arizona man in desperate need of a heart transplant caught Steve's attention. Joel Aronson, a 47-year-old self-described workaholic whose life in the fast lane had caught up with him, was now near death in his Arizona home, unable to be placed on a list of potential heart recipients because he could not raise the necessary $45,000 to match his insurance coverage.

When Steve read this, he dropped what he was doing and went straight to Aronson's home.

"He knocked on the door and said, 'I'm here to save your life'," Aronson told a newspaper reporter in recalling the encounter. "I didn't know what to think." The two became very close friends in the span of just two days.

"There was something special about Joel," Steve explained. "One of the TV newscasters suggested that he and I hit it off because we were both involved in something that brought us close to death. I think it runs deeper than that. There was something that drew my attention to Joel's situation to begin with. I felt as if I had known him all my life. It was like we were brothers."

The plan was for Steve to make a four-day marathon wire walk, soliciting donations for the Joel Aronson Heart Transplant Fund. However, in the days leading up to the performance, Aronson was notified that his health insurance company had re-evaluated his request and agreed to pay the bulk of the costs. Nevertheless, Steve decided to go on with the show, designating the money to help pay Aronson's uninsured expenses and establish a heart transplant fund at the University of Arizona.

For more than three days, without the benefit of any sleep, Steve walked back and forth upon a forty-foot-high wire at the Rawhide Old West Theme Park in Scottsdale, attracting the attention of the national news media. Donations poured into the Aronson Fund from across the country. Aside from an occasional break to rest and sign autographs, Steve remained on the wire, crossing back and forth hundreds of times.

"Sure, it's hard to do," Steve told one reporter on the final day, when the signs of fatigue had set in. "But I'll be able to rest and be good as new in a couple of days. Joel's fighting for his life."

The fund swelled to thousands of dollars, but Aronson never could use it. He died in his sleep a few hours after he and Steve celebrated the successful fund-raiser by dining and enjoying live music at a restaurant on the grounds of the theme park.

After that, Steve was selected to take part in "Americafest," a traveling patriotic extravaganza that toured California, Arizona, Utah, Nevada, and Okla-

# HIGH WIRE ANGEL

homa. His wire-walks took place across the tops of stadiums, over a sea of red, white, and blue as a prelude to a music and fireworks pageant that starred the Osmond Family, Sylvia, and Vanessa Williams.

Steve also performed as a warm-up act to several other performances by The Osmond Family during a national tour that year while he and Richard were making arrangements for the Wallenda Museum itinerary that would bring them to the Westchester Mall.

# ABOUT THE AUTHOR

It has been said that Paul W. Heimel cut his teeth on a pica stick. A third generation newspaperman who serves as managing editor of two northcentral Pennsylvania weeklies, he is the author of two other books, *No Longer Any Danger: The Fitzsimmons Story*, focusing on a murder trial involving famed criminal lawyer F. Lee Bailey; and *Shattered Dreams: The Ole Bull Colony In Pennsylvania*, chronicling the experiences of the nineteenth century violin virtuoso. For over 16 years Heimel has been affiliated with United Press International, having assisted with UPI's coverage of the Patricia Hearst case and other events of national significance. He has provided editorial guidance for the publication of over a dozen books. In addition, his work has appeared in *Outside, Women's World,* and numerous other magazines and newspapers.